Weavers and War

By the same author:

The Blanket Makers (with Dr Alfred Plummer)
Apprentice: An Historical Novel
Master Weaver: An Historical Novel

Weavers and War

A True Story by
Richard Early

Routledge & Kegan Paul
London, Boston, Melbourne and Henley

First published in 1984
by Routledge & Kegan Paul plc

14 Leicester Square, London WC2H 7PH

9 Park Street, Boston, Mass. 02108, USA

464 St Kilda Road, Melbourne,
Victoria 3004, Australia and

Broadway House, Newtown Road,
Henley-on-Thames, Oxon RG9 1EN, England

Set in Baskerville, 10 on 12pt
by Taylor, Young (Printers) Ltd, Cheltenham, Glos.
and printed in Great Britain
by St. Edmundsbury Press, Suffolk

Library of Congress Cataloging in Publication Data

Early, Richard E., 1908-
Weavers and War
Completes a trilogy with the author's novels, Apprentice and Master weaver
Includes index.
1. Early, Richard E., 1908-   Biography.
2. Novelists, English — 20th century — Biography.   3. World War,
1939-1945 — Biography.   I. Title.
PR6055.A735Z475   1984   823'.914 [B]   84-6823

ISBN 0-7102-0186-9

Contents

Preface   The setting

'Subtlety may deceive you:
integrity never will.'
— Oliver Cromwell

The two novels which I have written about Thomas Early, who lived three centuries ago, have caused readers to query which of the events described are written history, which have been passed down by word of mouth, and which are imagined.

In the novels about Thomas, I have taken great trouble to adhere to known and incontrovertible historical facts; but these have led me to imagine still more — to imagine the thoughts and motives which history does not record.

In the case of the following story I can say that I was living and observing while the events recalled took place and, instead of being three hundred years away during most of the time described, I was usually no more than three hundred miles from Witney, the home both of Thomas, my five-times great grandfather, and of myself.

Whether three hundred years or three hundred miles away from the town where he was born and has played and worked most of his life, a writer has more to guide him than bare historical facts. Indeed there is more to truth than such facts alone. There are aspects of life which can only be appreciated by those who have had a share in them and whose ancestors have done the same. In those cases imagination becomes intuition.

During the period 1938 to 1945, in whatever part of the world I found myself, the centre of my world was Witney, England. There was a war going on and at times my view was limited and news was distorted. However, I believe I knew the essentials of what was happening at home. This was largely due to letters from family and other friends all over the world. Time and distance give an added perspective; but there is more to knowledge gained and feelings experienced than this. There is the unexplainable, which pene-trates barbed wire, distance and all other manmade barriers.

This book is dedicated to my daughter, Inger — nurse, weaver, wife and mother — and to a dear close relative who lost his life in Denmark during the occupation.

Richard E. Early 1983

1 1938, Southern Africa

'They that go down to the sea in ships,
that do business in great waters;
these see the works of the Lord.'
— Psalm 107

This is a story about the Second World War, which, although most people did not realise it, started on 15 September 1938, when Mr Neville Chamberlain, British Prime Minister, flew to Munich and was assured by Herr Adolf Hitler that Germany did not intend to subjugate Czechoslovakia or any other country not already occupied. The Prime Minister returned with the impression that 'here was a man who could be relied upon when he had given his word.'

Mr Chamberlain came back to London waving a slip of paper signed by the German Dictator and promised 'Peace in our time.' In war the first casualty is truth. After all Hitler had defied the League of Nations and France by occupying the Rhineland and unchecked had gone on to subjugate Austria. 'A scrap of paper' had not deterred a German ruler once before. Mr Chamberlain was mistaken in his opinion; but Hitler was to fail to understand the character of the British Prime Minister. Before that, however, the British Government, instead of leading the League of Nations in total opposition to Italy occupying Abyssinia, had finally come to a compromise agreement with France, which had led to the comparatively well-armed Mussolini, with his Fascist Italian Government, annexing the whole of unfortunate Abyssinia. Mussolini, or a member of his Air Force, commented in the World's press upon the wonderful effect that could be produced by dropping a bomb upon a primitive round Abyssinian hut. 'It blossoms like a lovely opening flower' was the wording.

Having worked and played cricket for our three-centuries-old blanket firm at Witney for eight years since I left Oxford University, I had suggested to the Senior Directors that I might take my turn at overseas selling. After consultation they had agreed that trade with the Union of South Africa and Rhodesia would be helped by a visit. I had taken great trouble in preparation and in packing clothes and samples suitable for a prolonged journey in a Southern African early summer, with a view to finding out what blankets were needed and selling as many as possible myself.

Then had come the threat of an almost immediate Second World War. All my careful preparations for what in those days was considered an exceptional and extremely exciting business tour by a young man had seemed to hang in the balance. A week before I was due to leave Mr Chamberlain came back to England with his promise of peace. I was one of the many who heaved a deep sigh of relief because of the success which the Prime Minister believed he had achieved at Munich. I can still remember personal relief. On 7 October 1938 off I went from Southampton towards Cape Town, Second Class, aboard the Union Castle's beautiful vessel *Warwick Castle*.

It was a wonderful voyage and a new experience for me. The journey can, perhaps, be best described by excerpts from some of the letters I wrote home to family and friends. On the first evening abroad I wrote to my sister.

The Boat Train drew alongside R.M.N.V. *Warwick Castle* at Southampton and we all trooped into her up covered gangways. At exactly four o'clock, after cranes had removed all gangways and we were towed away from the quay, the thrill of this journey really came home to me. We stood to attention as the Band played 'God save the King'. The friends on the quay shouted good-bye and we were soon moving down Southampton Water past two other Union Castle boats and one huge Cunarder.

My cabin companion is a South African — a pleasant little man about my own age. Places in the saloon for those who are alone are arranged for us. I find myself next to a decorative lady who was once a teacher of dancing in Cape Town and is now married to a doctor in England. He is sending her back to South Africa because of the danger of War in Europe. She is terribly fussy about her food but fun to talk with. Perhaps my geographical position at meals will earn me one or two dances later on!

2

Just past The Needles we dropped the Pilot. The sea has become rougher: one can just feel the diesel engines as the vessel rolls slightly. However I made a fairly good supper and the feeding is lavish! Somehow I have an idea I am going to eat rather a lot during this journey!

The next day at 10.45 p.m. I wrote to my parents.

We are now about eight hours into the Bay of Biscay. It will be another twelve hours before we are across the Bay. There is a heavy ground swell. The fussy lady next to me at breakfast complained bitterly about sea sickness; but she still ate delicately! There was an outburst when the steward failed to bring her milk and soda immediately and she recounted with obvious delight that when she lost her balance on deck she had been carried to safety in a swooning condition by some gallant man!

The young South African who shares my cabin has been speaking to me about the various races to be found in the Union of South Africa and the necessity for not mixing them up if one wishes to avoid being stabbed in the back! He and other South Africans are kind — at any rate to me — and prepared to talk about their country. I did, however, hear one passenger complain to the steward that she had been asked to sit at the same table 'with a damned nigger'. Perhaps the South African native to which she referred was the same young black gentleman with whom I talked later. He is returning from the Youth Congress, which has been discussing peace, just finished in New York. Nearly every nation was represented at that Youth Congress. Germans were not there; because Herr Hitler had stipulated that his countrymen could only attend if Jews were excluded.

On Sunday I wrote to my brother.

This morning the Captain conducted service in the 1st Class Saloon. We from the 2nd Class and from the Tourist Class were invited to join in. This gave us a chance to see more of this wonderful vessel. After the service I took the opportunity for more talk with an African native delegate to the New York Youth Peace Congress. I said that there was a feeling in England that we enjoyed a special talent for governing and

3

could not justify giving away the British Empire. He said that this view was merely the English patting themselves on the back. Naturally we discussed South Africa most. He said that for a nation that believed in justice and fair play in games, there was a contradiction in the Union where there was no semblance of justice. In Rhodesia, which is more British, he said there was less justice still. In Portuguese Africa, punishments were severe; but an intelligent native had as much chance of advancement as anyone else. He added that in many ways Cecil Rhodes had helped Africa; but Rhodes's trustees had forgotten the people who helped him and them. Of all the money Rhodes had amassed not a scrap was spent on the natives. He said that South Africa was a wonderful country with plenty of wealth for everyone, if properly used. We went on to speak of The Boys' Brigade and The Scouts. Later, when I met my South African cabin-mate, he said, 'I suppose you know there is such a thing as a colour bar in South Africa?'

Well there is the problem for 1938! I look forward to hearing news from Witney and wonder what the Firm's figures were like last month?

Writing on 11th October after the *Warwick Castle* had cast anchor off the Island of Madeira, I wrote,

The sea was deep indigo blue. Madeira itself is mountainous with little white houses sprinkled over the steep slopes.

Many small rowing boats with an occasional larger motor boat surrounded us. The Portuguese spread out their wares in the boats below, as we looked down on them from the deck, and started bargaining with us passengers at the top of their voices. Some boats contained boys anxious to dive for silver three-penny bits – known as 'tickies' in South Africa. These boys looked marvellous stripped to the skin except for slips. They swam and dived beautifully and if we threw a 'ticky' from above into the sea, retrieved it before it had sunk three yards below the surface.

The Portuguese Marine Police also turned up looking very smart in a large motor boat and came aboard. It was a noisy and picturesque scene — the lovely Island sheltering more than one liner and a Portuguese destroyer as well as the small craft surrounding the *Warwick Castle*.

Some of us passengers crowded into a large motor boat and were taken ashore. A newly found lady friend and I opted for a most exciting trip to the summit of Madeira and down again. We ascended in an ancient motor car driven upwards round precipitous hair-pin bends at what might well have been breakneck speed! The Portuguese driver knew enough English to tell us about the sugar cane, bamboo and banana trees with fruit pointing upwards. My South African lady companion already knew something about these and we both wished he would concentrate more on his driving! At the summit the view was somewhat obscured by fog. However, we visited the parish church at Monte, where lies Charles I, Emperor of Austria. The Emperor was buried in the lower part of the altar of the Immaculate Heart of Mary Church.

I will break off from my letter home to say more about the Emperor Charles which I have learnt since 1938. Perhaps it is relevant to our story. He was born in 1887 and, as well as being Emperor of Austria, was King Charles IV of Hungary and King of Bohemia. He reigned only from 1916 to 1918. He was a devoted Catholic and his life was an example of faith, piety and abnegation. As Europe was in the throes of the First World War there was not enough food in Austria and large towns were beginning to suffer from other shortages. The Emperor helped his distressed subjects with his private fortune and set an example by frugality at his own table.

On the dismemberment of his Empire he was expelled in 1919 by the Austrian National Assembly. In order to avoid bloodshed he submitted to exile, and later, when urged to return as a Regent for Hungary, risked his life by giving himself up as a prisoner for the same reason. Exiled again, the Emperor arrived in Madeira in 1920 on board a British ship. With him travelled his wife, the Empress Gita, of Portuguese origin. Living on a very few resources, the imperial couple took up residence at Monte.

Although he was a sick man and an exile, the Emperor was a person of radiant character and kindness. He used to walk in the park and from time to time would ride around Monte, nearly always entering the parish church to pray. It was here that he died with a smile on his lips, without having feared death. He accepted it rather as a passage, a transition, a flight to eternal life.

The foregoing is the story of the Emperor; but I will return to quoting from my letter to Witney written from the *Warwick Castle* just after she had left Madeira in September 1938.

Just before entering the church, we stopped to buy my lady companion a necklace and bangles offered by a wayside vendor. 'It's worth three shillings,' said the lady. The man offered it to us at five shillings. He would be ruined if he sold it at a lesser price! I showed no signs of advancing my price; so he looked at my extremely attractive companion and said that, as the lady was so lovely, he would be willing to ruin himself for her sake: I could buy the jewelry for her at four and six. I looked anxiously into the fair one's face. She was a South African Scot and pressed her lips together while shaking her head and trying not to laugh. Therefore I said to the man, 'Three shillings!' Then he laughed and we walked into the church. With considerable delicacy he refrained from following us into the church; but he was waiting for us when we came out. The necklace and bangles were still in his hand and imploringly he pleaded, 'Three and sixpence!' I said, 'We have no wish to buy if it pains you to sell; but it would be worth three shillings to us!' By now, we were on the point of getting into a sledge for two — the standard means of conveyance down to the harbour. The man almost fell on his knees before us and said that he would clinch the sale at three shillings for his firm; but would I give him sixpence for himself because of his trouble. I said, 'No', and gave him the three shillings at the same time taking the bangles and necklace from the woebegone salesman. He looked so sad that I offered to cancel the sale and take my three shillings back. However he laughed heartily and said, 'O no! I stand by my sale!' He waved us good-bye obviously as pleased with the transaction as I was — and, of course, as was the South African lady companion. I hoped that it would not be as difficult to sell blankets in Southern Africa as it was to buy trinkets in Madeira!

The return journey down the hill was a thrill! Two young Portuguese men pushed the sledge down the steep cobbled track. Sometimes they pushed us running at top speed and we wondered how large a tip they would be able to extract from us by threatening to let go!

When, later in the day, the *Warwick Castle* drew out with us safely on board, Portuguese were desperately rowing alongside us concluding sales – doubtless at ruinously low prices! — of goods that were hauled up onto the deck in baskets. There had to be a good deal of mutual trust in such arrangements!

It was not only local methods of trading and the hazardous excursion that my South African lady friend and I had discussed. It amused her that I treated, and spoke with, African natives on the *Warwick* in the same way as when addressing others; but she did not seem to disapprove. We were remote from world politics; but I remember her volunteering about Mussolini, 'I don't trust him one little bit!' I fancy her opinion of Hitler was the same.

With the voyage from Southampton to Cape Town half over, I wrote to my sister on 15 October.

Things are warming up now. The sea is calm and the Officers and Stewards have changed into white uniforms. There are tournaments and dances on deck. We have passed our most westerly point and the ship's clocks were advanced half an hour last night. The sun goes perpendicularly down into the sea at six p.m. Lightning plays round the horizon at night. The dancing on the open deck is real good — but 'my' isn't it hot!?

The Lambeth Walk and the Palais Glide are the favourite dances. Earlier in the day we played 'deck cricket' against the 1st Class passengers and in the tournaments my lady partner and I succeeded in winning the wheelbarrow race together after qualifying through two strenuous preliminary heats during which most of the less serious opposition collapsed owing to poor co-operation between wheeler (lady) and barrow (man)!

I have joined a Physical Training class, meeting on deck at 7.30 a.m. and conducted by a pupil from a Physical Education School in Johannesburg. He was educated by a past President of Cambridge University Athletics, who has set-up the P.E. School in the Capital. Thereby I have learnt some fresh exercises to teach The Boys' Brigade.

We are getting to know our ship. Some of us joined in a conducted tour and, amongst other items of interest, inspected the Captain's Bridge and the engines. Yesterday there was boat-drill for the crew. As you know the vessel has only just left dry dock after a refit. One or two minor adjustments have not been perfectly carried out. Some alterations were needed in apparatus for lowering the boats. After the recent crisis, the *Warwick* came back to the passenger service somewhat abruptly; because the *Windsor* on which we were originally booked was commissioned by the Government to be used for other purposes. The newly appointed crew of this ship may not as yet have settled down as a team and some critical passengers thought the drill went rather slowly. Perhaps it is as well that it took place before a possible ship-wreck rather than after a disaster!

Three days later I wrote from just south of the Tropic of Capricorn.

Sunday evening we had a concert in the 2nd Class. I was asked to sing 'Ho Jolly Jenkin' and 'The Gentle Maiden' to open proceedings. It was the first time I had sung into an amplifier, which was necessary on the open deck. There were among the passengers one or two pianists — and, of course, a funny man! Finally, four of us dressed-up as chorus girls with paper skirts, cardboard hats and fairy wands and danced with plenty of high kicking. The dance and, indeed, the entertainment ended by my breaking away from the other three to execute a hand-spring. In the excitement of the moment the momentum of the hand-spring was such that it had to be followed by a fly-spring, which brought me first bounce into the ample midrift of an elderly gentleman, who fortunately was the first to join in the merriment! Quite a dramatic ending to our little show!

Before the voyage was completed, of course, we had crossed the equator and Father Neptune and his Queen had supervised a shaving ceremony: there was a fancy dress ball in which the ladies displayed much charm and ingenuity in adorning themselves. There was also the 'Warwick Derby', each lady, or filly, being required to cut along the centre of three and a half yards of narrow tape with curved nail scissors. Of course, I had to put a shilling on my filly and she won her heat and six shillings for me. I lost one of my shillings again in the final in which, amid great excitement, she 'ran' well but was defeated.

Today it is cooler and, as we approached Cape Town, we encountered the Cape Rollers head-on in our South Easterly course. It has been an enjoyable voyage with friendly people — mostly South Africans. Some have been holidaying in Europe and, as is the way with visitors, have seen European Countries where I have never been. Some who were recently in Germany, assure me that Hitler would have faced a revolution had he gone to war recently. He got what he wanted without! We get brief news sheets on board. They can be read quickly and are not mixed-up with editorial opinion.

So the 'Diary' of this voyage ends. Many years later I retain the memories of standing near the gangway and being approached by several black and coloured passengers who took the trouble to come up and shake hands before they left. I did not see them approach any other travellers in the same way; but some of the white South Africans, including the attractive young lady who had befriended me at Madeira, smiled quizzically but, I thought, in no unfriendly way as they also said goodbye. 'The attractive young lady' had an understanding with a South African Store Manager in Durban, whom she subsequently married; but she left me a poem written out in her own hand.

A Prayer

I want, dear Lord a heart that's true and clean;
A Sunlit heart with not a cloud between,
A heart like Thine, a heart divine,
A heart as white as snow;
On me, dear Lord, a heart like this bestow.

I want, dear Lord, a love that feels for all;
A deep strong love that answers every call,
A love like thine, a love divine,
A love for high and low;
On me, dear Lord, a love like this bestow.

I want, dear Lord, a soul on fire for Thee;
A soul baptised with heavenly energy,
A willing mind, a ready hand
To do what e'er I know,
To spread Thy light wherever I may go.

Once ashore at Cape Town, I was in the hands of our agents and anxious to justify the faith my firm had displayed, when the Seniors agreed to my going upon this mission. For the most part I could not worry professional tradesmen directly about Witney

Blankets at weekends and at other times outside office hours. However, it is well to remember that, when one is representing a good firm with a reputation for high quality and fair dealing built up for nearly three hundred years, one is never off duty.

Bearing this last thought in mind, I felt no qualms in spending the first weekend visiting a fruit farmer near Cape Town and describing the visit in a letter I wrote to Bessie Marchant, a remarkable elderly Oxfordshire lady, who during the course of an extremely busy life had found time to write a number of novels. (She would have smiled to think that when I became her age, I would follow her example!) I told her,

> As there is no business to be transacted at the weekend, I took a train at 4 o'clock on Saturday from Adderley Street Station, Cape Town, to a small village in the Hex River Mountains called Orchard. I was commissioned to deliver a note from his fiancée in England to a fruit farmer in Orchard, whom she expects to marry in England early next year. He will then bring his new wife out to his home here.

> Orchard is about a hundred and twenty miles north east of Cape Town. The great steam locomotive with cow catcher drew our train up through increasingly beautiful and mountainous scenery that spring evening. The sandstone Hex River Mountain scene changed from blue to red and eventually to dark blue again as night fell and the stars came out. In one place the line rose a thousand feet in six miles. We pulled into Orchard Station at 9.53 p.m.

> My new friend, Chris Dicey, was at the station to meet me with his car. There are six brothers in his family and they jointly own a company consisting of several fruit farms. The one at Orchard is managed by Chris and his brother Arthur. We drove up to the one-storeyed Dutch type house. It was lovely to be in someone's home after sixteen days of boat and hotel!

> We talked over coffee and sandwiches. In the afternoon Chris and his brother had been playing polo. They ride a lot in the course of their work and it is not much trouble to send five horses down the line to the polo ground and then follow by car themselves. During the return journey they had found and killed a puff-adder. Most wild beasts have been driven from these parts; but there are still snakes and, in the wilder districts,

leopards roam at night and attack the cattle.

The Diceys usually start work at 6 a.m.; but it was Sunday and I was allowed to sleep until 6.45 a.m.! After breakfast I really saw the outside of the house and its surrounds for the first time. The garden was wild and beautiful with tropical flowers. There were palms and cactus plants. I had heard the call of peacocks during the night and now I could see one sitting on the roof. There is a large mixed dog population on the farm.

Chris and I mounted two horses, which he had recently broken-in himself and started round the farm. The Diceys supervise from horseback and are in the saddle most of the day. The chief fruits grown are pears, peaches and grapes. Pear and peach are in blossom now and look lovely. The trees are in lines so long that one can not often see the full length. The vines are trained along wires and the farm is so large that it needs one hundred and fifty 'native' and 'coloured' to look after it. There is little rain here and not much grass between the trees where there is mostly dusty sand. Outside the area of the farm is veld and beyond that mountains rise to seven thousand feet — twice the height of Table Mountain.

At eleven thirty we came in for tea and then went to look at the mechanical part of the farm late morning. Most of the fruit is exported either after being tinned or in its natural state in the cold-storage room of a ship. In both cases it needs to be sorted, washed and packed into boxes here. A lot of the necessary work is done by machinery; but, in the season, about two hundred native girls are employed in picking the fruit. Power for the machines is supplied by a 120 H.P. Diesel Engine with an older Gas Engine as a stand-by. Some electricity is supplied by a water turbine on a mountain stream in the hills. There are large store rooms kept at 34° fahrenheit.

After lunch Chris kindly drove me back to Cape Town. It was a wonderful run! I was staggered by the beauty of the scenery as we travelled through the mountains by a more direct route than the railway could take. Sometimes we found ourselves on a ledge 450 feet above the River with great crags towering above us. As it is still Spring here, snow is to be seen on some of the higher mountains. Yet, such was the penetration of the sun's rays, that when I put my hand on the roof of the car the heat prevented my keeping it there more than a few seconds.

However, the heat is dry and pleasant, not sticky as it is sometimes during an English summer and as it certainly will be at Durban.

I continued to meet friends to whom I carried introductions from England; but our very efficient local agents, Haes Gledhill & Co., made sure that I started visiting customers and prospective customers at 8.30 a.m. each working day. My companion in Cape Town during these visits was a cheerful and athletic young man named Clifford Johnson. He was over six foot four and a high jump champion. I thought the two of us made a very good team!

It was not difficult to sell Witney Blankets. We were able to say that it was unlikely that prices would fall. There were too many wars, or rumours of wars, about! Also, as Clifford and the rest of the Haes Gledhill staff more than once assured me, 'Customers do like to see a principal from a British firm out here; so that they can speak directly to the manufacturer.'

Clifford and I used to travel around Cape Town in a car complete with a Zulu chauffeur, who had a great sense of humour — and considerable driving ability! When we went into a hotel for a meal we were looked after by Indian servants who were amazingly attentive and obliging. We went into some very fine shops including a multiple store establishment, of which there were other branches in Port Elizabeth, East London, Durban and Johannesburg. Mr Donald Garlick, Director, told us that he was apprenticed at Elliston and Cavell, an excellent departmental store in Oxford, eleven miles from Witney. This store in Cape Town was somewhat like it. When it came to high-class blankets we were told that our Witney products could not be bettered. As for 'Kaffir Truck', restrictions on foreign imports were more effective in keeping us out. When I questioned the propriety of describing anything as 'Kaffir Truck' the reply was, 'Well that's the trade name for the stuff; you can put it down in your notes!'

There were other blankets which at the time were outside Witney's scope. Among these were the multi-coloured lower-quality bed coverings and robes, important to the Cape coloured and native populations.

We visited a number of beautiful shops in and around Cape Town as well as those catering for lower-class trade. Clifford Johnson and I visited all to which we thought we could sell blankets. When it comes to trade one just tries to offer whatever the customer wants, whether the customer has European, African or Indian blood in his veins — or a mixture of all three. A Jew, too, who was a blanket manufacturer like myself, most kindly and broad-mindedly showed me carefully and thoroughly round his mill. I could only offer to do the same for him if he ever visited Witney. So Clifford and I made a good start in adding to the firm's order book and in learning what was required for the future. I was also grateful for the help given by the rival manufacturer. We all seemed to be on the same side.

On the Sunday before leaving Cape Town to voyage north east up the Indian Ocean, I attended service as usual. This time the service was easy to attend as it was at Cape Town Cathedral. The singing was beautifully led by boys from St George's Grammar School and it happened to be the headmaster of that school who preached. I stopped to admire the Cathedral afterwards and, when I eventually left, I fell in with the headmaster as he was walking home. We talked about the problems arising in a mixed population and he said that really the natives, unless exceptionally brilliant, did not get a fair chance. It was fear that impelled some Europeans to keep them down. He had lived in Swaziland for a time and had found the uncivilised natives to be very good chaps. 'Of course, they go in for rather a lot of murder; but then that is part of their religion', he added.

Undeterred by what might be regarded as a warning, I continued to spend some of my evenings and the occasional Sunday morning in visiting Boys' Brigade Companies in action. Most of these were 'Coloured' (men and boys, whose veins contained African as well as European blood) and commanded by 'Coloured' Officers. However, they did not seem to mind being visited by a 'White' Officer from Witney and they sent good wishes to our 1st Witney Company.

Soon after, I was off on R.M.S. *Edinburgh Castle* to call at Port Elizabeth and East London before reaching Durban. It was well worth looking aft as we left Cape Town Harbour. There was Table Mountain with a light mist extending part way up and its flat summit clear of cloud. I think I had never seen anything that gave a greater impression of might and solidarity. Beyond Table Bay and quite dwarfed by the great mountain were other hills — the Lion's Head and the Twelve Apostles. They all passed us by until finally we steamed out beyond Cape Point itself.

The *Edinburgh Castle* was smaller that the *Warwick Castle*, her displacement being 13,000 tons. The First and Second Classes were combined. On the *Warwick* a well-known businessman had, one afternoon, invited me to join him for tea in the First Class and had said that, although he appreciated that Second Class passengers were probably more charming and neighbourly than their shipmates in the First Class, he had to travel First otherwise uninformed people would believe that his famous Company could only afford Second! Well, we didn't need to disagree about that with First and Second combined on the *Edinburgh*!

The local Methodist Conference had taken place in Cape Town whilst I had been working there. Some of the representatives were travelling home on our boat. A few of these were Ministers of Religion. One was a great uncle of mine and he told me that he and his friends did not understand why we in Europe, now that we had settled matters at Munich by discussion, which he believed was the right way to settle world problems, continued to speed up re-armament more than ever — and the countries that considered themselves most progressive were in the greatest hurry. Most people, however, believed that the mailed fist was all that dictator countries understood: the more one gave the more they wanted. I met a good many Jews in the course of business and was at that time surprised how apprehensive they were. Anyway, this journey was made for the sake of Witney Blankets; so we must return to business!

At Port Elizabeth and East London I did not have the support of a helpful agent visiting with me. Possibly this was an advantage. Not many buyers are grumpy when a young inexperienced salesman has come six thousand miles on his own to see them! In one case, at Port Elizabeth, the head of a store visited not only gave me a substantial order but invited me to meet his family and attend a gymnastic competition at Grey High School. His son, Denis Parker, won the Senior Championship. Nothing could have pleased me more!

Another advantage of being alone and coming straight from the mill is that the customer knows that, uninfluenced by outside considerations, the manufacturer is saying exactly what it is practicable to make and supply. If he says, 'All right, we will do that for you', that is it!

One more experience during this part of the journey remains with me more than forty years on. Although in general the passengers during this comparatively short voyage were not such a merry lot as those travelling from England to Cape Town, we did have fun, including an occasional dance. So I found myself talking with an attractive young lady in her late teens, who turned out to be a shop assistant in one of the Durban stores, which I was to visit. She was a kind girl and wanted to help me get an order at the shop where she worked. Perhaps she did! When eventually I had met the buyer at this important Durban firm, she met me as I was leaving. She must be an elderly lady now — but, if she reads this perhaps she would like to know that I still remember the concerned expression on her lovely face as she anxiously asked, 'Did he give you an order?' Ah well, I was almost as young as she was!

Business in Durban and, after that, in Pietermaritzburg and Johannesburg, followed much the same pattern as in the earlier part of the tour. Fowlie and Whytock were our agents in Natal and their representative who accompanied me visiting customers was a most pleasant middle-aged bachelor named Alec Ross. He was a man of wide interests with a quiet sense of humour. He spoke, like most European inhabitants, to natives in their own language. He told me that they called him 'old four eyes', because he regularly wore spectacles. After meeting customers in Pietermaritzburg, Alec and I took a trip on a char-a-banc to the near-by Zulu Reserve. Afterwards I wrote about this experience to The Boys' Brigade 1st Witney Company as follows.

Dear Fellow Members,
... The Reserve is a stretch of land 70 miles long and 45 miles wide in a district which includes 'The Valley of a Thousand Hills'. The native huts are built on the tops of the hills. It is said that this arrangement is to allow the inmates a view of approaching friends and enemies and prepare for them. The huts are well spread — not more than one family living on each hummock. I suppose that conditions in this particular place have not changed much since Dr Livingstone visited Southern Africa seventy years ago. However, one difference is that now some of the round huts, instead of having thatched roofs, are covered by corrugated iron, which is even more of a protection against sudden violent hail. The Zulus come down to a stream

at the foot of the hills to fetch water and bathe. I imagine these excursions give rise to some quite sociable gathering. They are beautiful people. Most of the men and women wear only brightly coloured cotton loin cloths. The small children wear beads and sometimes not even as much as that! They all have short black curly hair and wonderful dark brown shining skins. When they smile, as they frequently do, they display a wide expanse of brilliant white teeth.

The laws and customs of marriage amongst these people differ from ours. Their Zulu king, Soloman, rules through four Zulu chiefs. We were introduced to one of these, Chief Piwa (pronounced Peeway). He was a fine old boy set over 10,000 Zulus: he has seven wives and twenty-one living children. We were shown round the Chief's home, or kraal. There is a circle of trees about twenty-five yards in diameter round the kraal. Under the trees are buried the ancestors of the present Chief. Each past Chief, when he died, was buried with great ceremony in a sitting position facing inwards towards the large hut or kraal, where his successor now lives. Inside the ring of trees is an enclosure for cattle; so you see that the Chief's quarters are somewhat confined! The kraal itself is in fact circular and about twelve feet in diameter and six feet up to where the thatch begins. The floor is hard mud; so is the circular side wall.

We had met one of Piwa's grown-up daughters outside and now she led us into the kraal where there were a few children. They ground some 'mealies' for us by rolling one stone on a much bigger one underneath. We saw their beds, which consisted of mats laid on the hard floor with pillows made of wooden blocks. They put skins of animals over themselves or, if very up-to-date, blankets! This comparatively big hut is the Chief's reception house. Each wife has a hut of her own to prevent quarrelling!

Outside again, we found some great Zulu men with spears which they were anxious to sell for two shillings each. Now, when a fierce looking Zulu comes up to you waving his spear and asking you to buy it and you do not want it, what is the tactful thing to do!?

Forty-two years after these incidents I cannot exactly remember how we got out of the foregoing impasse. Certainly the Zulus with their threatening spears had an advantage over us, who could not bring the same kind of pressure to bear when selling blankets! My memory is that our kindly agent, Alec Ross, came to the rescue with a bag of sweets, which melted the hearts of the fierce-looking Zulus! I remember we were not so successful in escaping the Zulu women, who succeeded in selling us necklaces!

Well, I met African natives in far different circumstances down and around the gold mines of Johannesburg, separated from their families in order to earn money. I also called upon the African native, Richard Ratheby, whom I had met on the *Warwick Castle*, at his Bantu Men's Social Service Centre. He was Secretary. The Centre was in a fine building and he had about seven hundred members. They usually spoke English in the Centre, as there were, of course, many native tribes represented in the membership and, if he had used one of their languages, he might have been accused of favouring one tribe, or group of tribes, at the expense of the rest. I met the Centre's Scout Master and was able to tell him that I had supported The Boys' Brigade since an early age!

There was plenty of business to be found in 'The City of Gold'. It is a centre for trade and South Africans, I was told, say that, if they wait there long enough 'everyone' turns up in Johannesburg. Anyway, I was made welcome, as before, by helpful agents and customers and took the opportunity of visiting Lourenço Marques in Portuguese East Africa, where I appointed an Indian Agent. He spoke perfect Portuguese: I did not and, when I made an enquiry at the railway booking office using my own native language, was obliged to submit to a severe reprimand for assuming that I would be understood when speaking to the clerk in outlandish English!

Southern Africa is a wonderful territory and 'the works of the Lord' were evident on every side. Others have described these and I will only touch upon the two that particularly moved me. It was during a weekend that I returned from Lourenço Marques by train that I broke my journey at Nelspruit, so as to spend Saturday and Sunday, with the night between, in the Kruger National Park.

Through a travel agency I had booked a car and driver, who proved, during this two-day excursion, to be much more than just a chauffeur. The Park is unfenced and extends two hundred miles from north to south and forty miles from east to west. There is a gate across the rough narrow road; but that is only to prevent unlicensed humans in cars from entering. The animals stay within the area of the park; because they know that they are safe there and will not be shot. They are not afraid of humans in cars; nor do they want to attack them. These particular men, women and children in cars have never done these animals harm and, in fact, are always friendly and interested. Perhaps we humans in our relationship with each other can learn something from this?

We were fortunate in seeing lions and lionesses very near to the car, hippopotami in, and on, the banks of Crocodile River, zebra, giraffe, kudu and wildebeest. At night we slept in an encampment of rest-houses, or huts, and could hear the sound of divers animals on night patrol. The roar of lions awoke us in the small hours. However, the greatest thrill of all came to the two of us in the car on our second day: we came suddenly upon a herd of elephant in front of the vehicle and a little to the right. We drove gently on until we were level with the herd on the right. Only then did we notice a huge solitary bull elephant immediately on our left. He was evidently upset because our car with inmates was now right between him and his lady friends in the rest of the herd. He raised his trunk in a magnificent gesture, trumpeted and then charged. My driver brought the car to a halt as the great creature hurtled towards us. I waited for the splintering crash. However, to the elephant we were only of secondary importance. It was his relationship with his friends in the herd that mattered. His prime object was to get back to them with no interruption to his progress. But what a sight and sound as he hurtled across the track a yard or two in front of us raising clouds of dust trumpeting and devastating the undergrowth as he went. Nothing could compare with this until we reached the Victoria Falls.

I had travelled from Johannesburg to Bulawayo by train and again arranged business transactions, this time through our Rhodesian agents, W. C. MacDonald and Company. Indeed we had together worked out an idea for a special light weight — and therefore lightly priced — all wool camel coloured blanket to suit this particular market. After that it was train again to the Victoria Falls Hotel still just inside Southern Rhodesia.

With the best will in the world there was but little hope of selling a great many blankets in the nearby town of Livingstone over the River Zambezi in Northern Rhodesia. (The River is spanned by a fine single arched bridge built by a Darlington firm in 1905.) I therefore felt justified in spending the night at the hotel and looking at the Victoria Falls the next day.

Two young South African men asked me to join them in viewing the Falls. We walked on to the bridge and looked up stream along the four-hundred-foot-deep ravine with the river, there deep and comparatively narrow, rushing towards us and under us far below. Beyond that was the vast roaring descent of water dropping into the tumultuous gorge four hundred feet below.

Then we went down to the depths of the ravine and this time looked up at the tremendous down-pouring. Next some natives paddled us in a canoe just above the Falls to Livingstone Island on the very brink of the precipice with thousands of tons of water falling past us and into space. Lastly we were flown in a 130 H.P. Fox aeroplane with a wing span of thirty feet through the spray rising three hundred feet towards the sky.

Eighty-three years before we were there, Dr David Livingstone was the first European to see the tremendous wonders which we had seen that day. He heard the mighty roar and watched the towering cloud of spray, which he learned the local inhabitants called 'the smoke that thunders'. The thunder was with us as we walked, climbed and flew and when we just stood by Livingstone's statue gazing, as he had, across the one and a quarter mile width of the Zambezi crashing into the ravine. I could not help comparing his lot with ours. We had come to this spot in a comfortable train with dining saloon and sleeping berths and were staying in a luxurious hotel. He had come down the river in a canoe propelled by African friends close to crocodile and hippo with danger on the banks and the unknown ahead before he stepped on to Livingstone Island.

However, David Livingstone was not the only great personality who found work in this fantastic place. I discovered that H. G. Owen Smith was filling a medical post near at hand. I will describe how it was that I already knew him. The first time I saw him was when he made fifty playing cricket for South Africa against England. After that he came up to Magdalen College, Oxford, and then completed his medical training at St Mary's Hospital, London. During this time he captained the English Rugby Football XV and, of course, gained a triple blue at Oxford University.

Our Witney Mills had an enthusiastic cricket club. The secretary of the club was Maurice Fyfield, Assistant Mill Manager and devotee of cricket. He amazed me one day by saying that he had written to the secretary of Oxford University C.C. for a fixture. I was still more amazed when during next Saturday's game which was against a scratch XI, called Magdalen College Ramblers, our leading batsman, Stanley Bridgeman of the Blanket Room, came back into the Pavilion somewhat bewildered saying that he had been bowled out by a Test Match player. He had indeed fallen to Owen Smith, who must have come to spy out the land. The University cricket secretary must have been favourably impressed and two days later a card came for Maurice Fyfield saying that the University Cricket XI would be coming to play us upon the day suggested.

The University came and we re-inforced our Witney Mills Team with some most obliging professionals. My memory is that more than four hundred runs were scored during the afternoon. As Owen Smith made a good many of those runs himself and I, as wicket keeper, was the Mills player closest at hand, we began to become acquainted. All the same it was exceedingly good of him, his brother and sister-in-law to invite me out to a meal at their home in Livingstone when I diffidently let him know that I was in the neighbourhood.

I suppose we must have talked mostly about rugger and cricket; but he was a very modest star! There were several cricket teams in the Livingstone League when Owen Smith took up his job as doctor there. He joined the team at the bottom of the League and by the time I arrived it had risen to the top. It was the measure of the man, although most certainly not of me, that, as we talked about his visits to Witney, he remembered that I had 'stumped' him. For his ending an exemplary and extremely lively innings in this way I give full marks to the bowler concerned, Sam Staples of Nottinghamshire. Perhaps, having been beaten by Sam's wiley ball, Owen Smith did not try to regain his ground with all the speed of which he was capable? I don't know; but the moment was mine to cherish to this day!

After seeing the Falls and meeting a triple Blue and double International who, with all that, was so kind a man, I tend to remember the rest of this business journey as somewhat common-place. Of course, it was not. After Northern Rhodesia it was a case of voyaging from Beira south to Durban by a Dutch cargo vessel. Then, after tying-up loose ends in Durban and travelling by a splendid train to Cape Town for Christmas — most generously

20

entertained to Christmas dinner and a visit from a lightly clothed Father Christmas in blazing sunshire on the lawn of a friendly family — I was off on the *Pretoria Castle* for home.

Before ending this chapter there is one special day which I must recall. It had been during my short stay in Johannesburg that I decided to give direct 'business' a rest for a few hours. Mr Arthur Gillett, who lived and worked in Oxford and was then Vice-Chairman of Barclays Bank, had invited me out. His three sons had overlapped with me at Leighton Park School.

I wrote to my brother,

> Arthur Gillett is a most delightful man. Just now he is out here for the benefit of his health and is staying with General Jan Smuts, a very great friend of his. Mr Gillett is a Quaker; so I asked him how he got on with a General. He owned up that he, Arthur, was a 'bad' Quaker. He said that he tried to enlist three times during the 1914-18 war and offered to resign his membership of The Society of Friends. The Army turned him down on medical grounds and the Society would not allow him to resign!

> Arthur Gillett met me with his car at Pretoria and first we looked at the Houses of Parliament there. They are just magnificent, made of yellow stone and built in 1910. They look wonderful on the hillside with great spaces all round. The architect was Herbert Baker, who also designed the Government buildings at Delhi and the newer parts of the Bank of England. I think he had a genius for making the most of pillars. At Pretoria, when one moves close up to these pillars and looks away from the building, one gets a wonderful view of the Town and the surrounding country. Most of the houses there are one-storeyed with white walls and corrugated iron roofs. These roofs are preferred, because the summer hail there would crack the strongest tiles.

> We drove out to Hartebeeste Pool Dam, constructed to hold back water during the rains and then release it to irrigate this part of the Transvaal during the dry season.

> After bathing in the Lake and enjoying a picnic lunch we went to the General's home at Irene for tea. He and his wife live on a large farm consisting mostly of cattle and deer. Their house is another one-storeyed building — rather untidy to look at, but

homely. Mr Gillett told me that when Mrs Smuts is here she avoids anything dressy and all ceremonial. Accordingly neither of us visitors put our stockings on after bathing and we drove in with bare legs. The General, in his shirt sleeves, was walking along the road towards his home with two other guests, when we arrived. I got out and walked with the trio to the house while Mr Gillett put the car away.

You will know that General Smuts was the skilled soldier who, with the Boer troops immediately under his command, was undefeated by the British when the Boer War ended in May 1902. Since then, Boer and statesman as he is, he has co-operated to bring about the Union of South Africa. No one could have been more interested in what we had been doing that day than this very great man: we were put through a cross examination! I thought it had rained rather hard at times; but when, after my assertion, he asked Arthur Gillett about this, I discovered that, by South African standards, it had only spotted!

One can tell that the General is not English. He speaks English more distinctly than most Englishmen. He must be six feet tall and is well built. He has grey hair and a pointed little beard. His face is calm as if he were looking into the far distance.

Ouma Smuts came in while we were having tea and, when I was introduced, said, 'Well, I am glad you are not Mr Late anyway!' She is a pleasant plump lady who wears glasses — at least she was wearing them then: perhaps she leaves them off during great receptions at Cape Town! Unfortunately she did not have very long to view the legs, as both she and her husband were called away to deal with some other and doubtless much more important guests.

The foregoing is what I wrote at the time; but I remember that before Arthur Gillett and I parted that day I asked him how General Jan Christian Smuts regarded African natives. The reply was something like this, 'Well, I believe he thinks of them, and to some extent treats them, as children. Most of them have not as yet reached the stage of being able to fill the same roles in Society as "Whites".'

Saying farewell, Arthur Gillett and I must once again have discussed the question of peace and war. Perhaps I had said, 'It seems mad to try and stop wars by threatening to kill people'. Forty-two years later I remember his reply, 'That may be so; but this is a mad world!'

2 Europe on the brink

'Whom (Satan) would destroy he first sends mad'
— James Dewport, 1706-1771

On my return to Witney it became evident that the world was probably approaching the greatest catastrophe that had ever befallen mankind.

It was brought home to me that wickedness was abroad as never before, when I received a letter from a Danish girl with whom I had become acquainted while on holiday some time previously. She wrote to say that her sister was extremely friendly with a young Jewish man. He had escaped from Germany, because he was certain that had he remained in his native land it would have meant for him imprisonment and worse. Even after reaching Denmark he still felt insecure and now wanted to make his home in England. Could I help?

Although I was a director in an old and well-established blanket-making firm in Witney, I was still, at the age of twenty-nine, a bachelor living in the family home. At first, even at this stage, I could hardly believe that the young Jew was in physical danger. After all, Denmark was an independent kingdom, which had not been involved in war for a lot longer than our own country — and was the oldest dynasty in the world. Surely he was safe there. My father and mother were more politically minded than I was and they took the matter seriously. They said that the young man was welcome in our house until able to obtain work in this country.

Assisted by the promise of accommodation and a probable job, the Jew obtained permission to come to England and then arrived in Witney. I was glad to help by buying a bicycle for him and eventually getting him employment on a farm at Didcot near at hand. It was not long before his Danish girlfriend also turned up

24

for a holiday and stayed with us at Witney. Our family looked after her also and, as far as I was concerned, she paid her way by teaching Danish Folk Dancing to a mixed Boys' Brigade and Girl Guide dancing class for which I was responsible at that time. Of course, I was delighted to escort this attractive young Dane to the farm where her young man was getting on very well. She stayed a few days on that farm before returning to her somewhat decorous family in Denmark.

During my next visit to an annual holiday gymnastic course, which I had twice before attended in Denmark, I was summoned to the home of the girl we had done our best to befriend. When I presented myself, her father and mother accused me of helping in the seduction of their daughter. I stoutly defended the young couple to her worried father and mother and upon returning to Witney drove over to the farm at Didcot to see the young man. He told me that should anything occur to prevent his eventually marrying the lady it would finish him. He wanted me to help him financially to journey to Israel, where the two could make a home.

Well, the war started in September 1939 before these hopes of his could be realised. I learnt later that he joined the British Army, married an English girl who, according to a photograph he sent to Witney, was another remarkably smart young woman. His Danish girlfriend married a Dane in Denmark. But, that is looking ahead and I do not know whether Benjamin, shall we call him, ever got to Israel with his wife or, indeed, whether he survived the war. I hope the arrangements have worked out well for both couples.

The foregoing experience began to open my eyes to what was going on in Germany. In that country Jews could expect only extermination. Hitler, having occupied the Ruhr, Austria and Czechoslovakia, would soon grab as much of Poland as Russia would allow him and then Denmark and Norway. After he had got that far would anything prevent his spreading his German Aryan Empire to the remainder of Europe and indeed to the rest of the world unless armed force was used to stop the madman? Winston Churchill thought he could have been stopped without war had Britain and the League of Nations taken a firm stand earlier. Anyway I had made up my mind what I would have to do when war came: the question was — how?·

Our family knew a good deal about war. I could remember 1914, although I was less than six years old when Britain declared war against Germany on 4 August. It was Belgium that was being over-run by Germany that time. During the first few weeks of that First World War, father had told us three children that he was going to join the army. I could remember my own words at this news, 'Isn't Mummy very sad?'

In fact Father had done more than volunteer himself. He had facilitated the recruitment of about forty other young Witney men in August 1914. They had felt, as he did, that Germany had to be stopped. Most were Old Boys of The Boys' Brigade 1st Witney Company, of which he was Captain. The party formed-fours and marched together to Witney Railway Station. They enlisted as a party in Oxford. Eventually they were to form the nucleus of F Company, 1/4th Oxfordshire and Buckinghamshire Light Infantry, of which an Oxfordshire man, E. G. Dashwood, was Captain.

Father volunteered as a private and before the Company went to the trenches in France at the end of March 1915 had risen to the rank of sergeant. He declined a commission, because that would have meant leaving his Witney Boys to become an officer in another battalion. Only after most of the Witney men had been dispersed by transfer or death did he agree that it was his duty to become a lieutenant. Twenty-seven Old Boys from his Boys' Brigade Company in Witney were killed on active service in the terrible First World War — and for the front-line soldier it can still be described with dreadful truth as the most terrible and depressing war in history. Father served in France until wounded — almost fatally — leading an attack near the River Somme in 1917. Some of his companions were not killed by explosives or gas, but met their death drowned or otherwise suffocated by mud and slime in foul trenches.

I regard my father as the finest Christian man it has been my good fortune to know. He set the family a magnificent example and never failed to give good advice when asked for it or when he thought it would help. However, it was his way of life that counted most. Perhaps it was one of the stretcher-bearers that carried Lieutenant Early in from 'no-man's land' who told me years after the event that he was the bravest man he had ever met. I have often thought of that remark since and do not believe that the first-aid man spoke only of courage in battle. What distinguished father was his unfailing loyalty to his faith and his friends. He made no secret about either. Amid the mud and filth, immorality, pain and death, his Oxfordshire companions, to whom he was devoted, knew where he stood. When the stretcher bearer offered him brandy hoping thereby to ease his suffering, he refused the bottle, because he was a teetotaller. A fellow Boys' Brigade man from Witney told me that, when practicable, before turning in at night father knelt to say his prayers. In a letter from 'the Front' to my mother, he said,

As regards our fighting at all, it seems to me sufficient to try and picture Europe as it would be now, if we hadn't declared war (which don't forget we did). Germany's intuition is sound that we (the British) are the fatal factor in the case. I don't at present distinguish between the Hohenzollerns and the German people. Perhaps we shall later on. Meanwhile, although it *is* a painful fact that we are fighting for England and against Germany, isn't there something else behind it that makes the reckoning of human lives in the question mere idolatry? For both the 'pro' and the 'con' cover a lot more than lies on the surface. 'Germany' stands for expediency as against *right* and her expediency is handmaid to the settled belief that wealth and force and success are the things that count and that love is all very well in its way — and England (I cling to the belief that this is true) stands not for the sordid disappointing place we know too well, but for the dream which our children may live to see.

When starting training in England father had also written to mother, 'I have been thinking that (with reservations) I have never been so happy in my life.'

A quarter of a century later, when training in Birmingham in the Friends Ambulance Unit during the first months of the Second World War, I was conscious of a similar elation.

Later, during the worst of the fighting in France, father wrote asking mother not to worry unduly and asked her to remember that during his working life in Witney he was used to moving among machinery. This was standing him in good stead at 'the Front': since instinctively he avoided exposing himself unwittingly and unnecessarily to destructive forces. He went on to say that he had left Witney and come out to 'the Front' not in spite of his love for her and us children but because of it.

In 1917 my mother, escorted by my grandfather, was permitted to visit father in France: he was near to death, wounded and in hospital there. However, he recovered and was invalided to England. After a spell in.two hospitals in England he became near enough to normal to be stationed with the rank of Captain in Camps, first at Seaton Sluice in Northumberland and then at Reading. At both camps he supervised the training of other soldiers. This instruction of others lasted until the end of the war; but, although he rarely spoke of it, the horrific impact of slaughter and misery during those dreadful years at 'the Front' affected his spirit to the end of his life. He never became what is understood to be a pacifist; but it is noteworthy that before the war ended and he returned to blanket-making my brother and I were sent to an excellent Quaker Preparatory Boarding School, The Downs School, Colwall.

The fact that father, as well as being a blanket maker all his life, had shared wartime danger and hardship with others at the Mill, stood him in good stead as an employer; but he served the community in many other positions of responsibility. Only the fact that his wife was as unselfish and self-sacrificing as he was himself made these extra public duties possible.

Mother's interests outside the home, as well as inside, were as wide as father's. Someone once quoted in her presence,

> I wish I liked the human race:
> I wish I liked its silly face.
> When I am introduced to one,
> I wish I thought 'what jolly fun'.

Mother's surprised and quite serious response was: 'But that is what I do think!'

It was probably her idea that at the Mill a number of high-quality pictures should be hung on the walls of various departments and periodically moved on, so that we could all get a view of them as we worked. She was very artistic and a classical scholar, widely read and helpful to as many people as possible, but particularly to her family. Both parents felt the strain which so many public demands imposed on family life and she more than once advised me with such words as, 'Remember that a good many people could help run The Boys' Brigade; but only one can take up tea to your wife in the morning as you can, help her with the house and family and take her out as you should.'

28

She also told me that Sir William Smith, the Founder of The Boys' Brigade, when he stayed with us at home, told her she should give similar advice to her husband!

It was mother who, when we were children, used to conduct afternoon Sunday School for us in the drawing room while father was engaged in teaching other people's children at Witney Methodist Church. Later on in term time I was away at school; but, in the holidays, she helped me at home with Latin, an essential language for gaining admittance to Oxford University in those days. Perhaps rather than worrying about nursery schools, it would be better to make sure that every mother could teach her own children up to a certain age at home. At any rate, it was my mother who got me to Oxford University; but maybe my parents were special!

There is one other remark which I particularly remember my mother making when the strain of facing the near certainty of a Second World War was becoming almost intolerable to her. Remembering that her husband had spent over three years away from her in almost unbearable conditions when she needed him most and had nearly lost his life, because of mistaken leadership in Germany — and evil men — and that now once again a far more wicked man, supported by others in Germany and elsewhere, was about to take away her children (all five were finally to be called away to dangerous places), she said with obviously genuine distress, 'I find it so difficult not to feel hate!'

It was to be expected that my brother Patrick would be needed in the Air Force if and when a war broke out. He was already a keen and skilled amateur pilot, and most people thought that war, when it came, would largely be fought in and from the air. He and some of his friends were more politically minded than I was. He was a good public speaker and intended to stand for Parliament as an 'Independent Progressive'. Had war not come he might well have deviated from the career upon which he had embarked in the blanket industry, to continue principally as a politician. Like the vast majority in the country, he hated the very idea of war; but he thought war would be forced upon us and that he would have to play his part in overcoming aggression by force of arms. He would feel it his duty to join the RAF when required.

It will be well understood that my brother and I — still living in the same home and very good friends indeed — often argued about

29

and discussed international affairs and our personal responsibility for them. Of course, our conclusions as to which way our duty lay were different. I am sure that he often out-argued me. Finally I was driven to declaring that, no matter what anybody else thought, or said, or did, I believed it wrong for me to kill and maim other people and would never do it. Whereupon he answered, 'When you say that is your belief, no one can justifiably say you are not speaking the truth. You know your own feelings better than anyone else!'

Ruth, the eldest of my three sisters, had recently completed a course at the Royal College of Music. Devoted to music, she became a great all rounder and a concert pianist. In one way her profession was in line with that of doctors and surgeons, nurses and ministers of religion. Like those she could, during war, continue to comfort and encourage as she did in peace. Indeed, her services of cheer would be in even greater demand and of still greater value in war.

Rosemary, my second sister, was born almost exactly halfway through the 1914-18 War. From her earliest years she had loved animals — nearly all animals — and birds as well. She could keep them in order and there is a story of how she more than held her own, at the age of five, against an enraged turkey cock. As she grew up she specialised in dogs and horses; but she also took trouble to go through a course in house-keeping. On occasion she tried out her skill on the remainder of the family, so that Mother could give more time to other interests and go away on a world tour with father. Rosemary became engaged to a Wing Commander in the RAF who immediately became involved in hostilities when this country declared war. In fact it could well be argued, even before that event, that he was employed in the defence of the kingdom.

Hostilities had broken out in Spain during 1936 and were to continue there until 1939. There the Communist element had taken advantage of weak government to murder and rebel. Whereupon the army, including military cadets, under General Franco had sought to take charge. The result was more bloodshed and Civil War. Britain and other European countries officially kept completely neutral and refused to supply arms to any of the warring parties. This appeared to be an advance on the way our government had behaved during the 1861-1865 Civil War in North America, when this country had recognised the belligerency of

both sides and presumably felt free to supply arms to both sides —
as Witney doubtless did blankets! However, whatever the government thought, some of our friends volunteered to fight in Spain and
others undertook ambulance work. A few of these volunteers sadly
enough were killed. Civil strife to gain political ends is the anti-
thesis of statesmanship. Most of us could only be ashamed.

Patrick, Ruth and Rosemary took care of Basque refugee
children by helping to organise a hostel at Aston, near Witney.
Some of these Basque children remained in our district for life, and
at the time I am writing, I am occasionally stopped by a kindly
Basque lady in Witney, who enquires after Anastasia, the affec-
tionate name she and her compatriots gave to Rosemary, forty-five
years before!

Hazel, the youngest of my three sisters, had been born in the
early 1920s, when father was standing as a Liberal Candidate for
Parliament. His defeat in the General Election and her arrival in
the World were announced on the same day. When father con-
gratulated the Conservative victor in North Oxfordshire upon his
success, the triumphant and friendly Major Edmondson
responded, 'Ah well, Early, you can't expect to get everything all in
one day!'

In 1939 Hazel was still a teenager at school and was loved by the
whole family. During the first eight months of 1939 the world slid
nearer to war. Most people realised that this was happening and
felt powerless to prevent it. In these circumstances it was difficult
to settle down to worthwhile endeavours. I, at any rate, just did not
know then what I should do when war was declared. However, our
London Agent, Ronald Thackrah, whose father had also sold
Witney Blankets in London, a man of the highest character,
mentioned to me that, during the 1914-18 War, the Quakers had
organised a voluntary ambulance unit, which had done good work
in France. Having attended two Quaker schools, in my time, I
knew something of The Friends Ambulance Unit, which was
founded and at first led by no less a man than the Olympic middle
distance runner Philip Noel Baker, and Old Boy of a Quaker
school, Bootham, at York. Soon after this word from Ronald, I
decided that, when the worst happened, I would join The Friends
Ambulance Unit.

At last Britain had discovered that Hitler made agreements only
to break them and gain time. The Munich agreement was broken

31

when Czechoslovakia was subjugated. Hitler also denounced the German-Polish non-aggression pact. In addition to Poland, Finland, the three Baltic States (Estonia, Latvia and Lithuania) and Romania felt threatened and may have been anxious that Britain and France should guarantee their borders against German aggression. However, it was difficult to understand how remote France and Britain could help them in case of emergency. Of course, Russia could have helped; but in the event of Germany invading any of these from the West, Russian resistance could only come by Communist forces from the East passing over the countries concerned to engage the Germans. Perhaps these forces would not withdraw, but would remain to impose the Communist system. On the other hand, the British government did not want Russia making an agreement with Germany.

There were thoughtful and apprehensive people in England who feared aggression from Russia. I can remember a cultured Doctor of Music saying at this time, 'Germany is dangerous; but Russia is far, far, more dangerous!' Neville Chamberlain and the Foreign Office were baffled by this 'riddle of the Sphinx'. Their indecision suited Hitler well! It seemed that Molotoff, the new Soviet Foreign Commissar, would prefer to divide Poland with Germany rather than defend that country.

Looking back on 1939, it appears that Germany could only have been stopped in Poland (by arms or threat of arms at any rate) through understanding and combination between Russia, France and Britain. By now no one could trust Hitler's word. He and the rest of us were soon to learn that we could trust that of Neville Chamberlain and, after him, that of Winston Churchill.

Bearing the foregoing in mind, the spring and summer of 1939 assume in retrospect a certain unreality. For those of us at Witney and at the Mill at the time it was much the same as previous years. On Shrove Tuesday we held Tuckers Feast — this time in the Mill Canteen. Tuckers Feast requires explanation.

Tuckers are the crafts people who finish blankets after weaving. In the old days the tuckers had operated separately in water-powered mills — the only kind of blanket mills in those times. They washed, shrunk, tentered and raised woven blankets for the Master Weavers to whom the blankets belonged. For the last one and a half centuries or so, during which time the tuckers had been incorporated in our family firm, the partners, or directors, had continued an old custom, whereby they, as Master Weavers, entertained the tuckers to a satisfying meal each Shrove Tuesday.

Tuckers Feast had been held in various locations including 'The Coffee Tavern' and Witney YMCA Hall; but in 1939 Tuckers Feast was in our own Mill Canteen and described by the chairman as 'the best dinner we ever had'. The chairman for the get-together that year was Master Harold, as father was known at the Mill. Grace was said before the meal, and a collection held afterwards. The proceeds from the collection, according to tradition, were allocated by general vote to those of our number who had come on bad times and been away from work. In the days before state aid this must have been very welcome.

After the collection was disposed of, Master Harold extended a welcome to the tuckers on behalf of the Master Weavers and made one or two other remarks appropriate to the occasion. He was a good and sincere speaker and particularly enjoyed Tuckers Feast. He then called on Fred Middleton from the Gig Shop to sing *Wonderfully Curious*, the ancient tuckers song, 'hatched up' it was said by a hand-loom weaver, Joseph Fowler, born about the time of the Battle of Waterloo. Since Joseph Fowler's time the song had been passed down from mouth to ear and Fred had already sung it for several years. We all joined lustily in the chorus and at the finish Fred exercised his right to call on the next singer. The next singer was an elderly man from the stockhouse, William Lewis, who sang a plaintive ditty including the words, 'Give the Soldier more pay; that is all I desire. These were my thoughts as I sat by the fire'.

So the evening wore on in leisurely fashion amid smoke from clay pipes: songs were rendered by successive singers. *Good Old Yorkshire Pudding* from Bert Collis of the dye house and *The Farmer's Boy* had their place. Chris Hicks, a new man to the firm, ex-Boys' Brigade and member of near-by Cogges church choir, sang *There is a Lady Sweet and Kind* most beautifully. He was a big cheerful fellow with a lovely bass voice: some may have thought that he had been recruited by the stockhouse especially to sing at Tuckers Feast!

We ended Tuckers Feast, 1939, by taking hands for *Auld Lang Syne* and standing to attention for *God Save the King*. How long would it be before we could join together again in a similar carefree way?

Like other factories our own became busier with the approach of war. We made blankets, of course. But some of us, who were keen on cricket, took the trouble to teach that game to boys at the Mill and a cricket match was played between them and the Boys' Brigade 1st Witney Company. I was determined to behave as long as possible as if the world was to continue in so-called peace and arranged to attend a gymnastic course in Denmark during an early fortnight in August; but I made one variation from my timetable of previous years. On two occasions previously I had spent my summer holiday in the same way and passed on some of the knowledge and skills acquired in Scandinavia to the youth of Oxfordshire. These former visits to Denmark had for me lasted three weeks. This time it was to be a fortnight and I was glad afterwards that I had thus chosen to shorten my course abroad. Some of the members who stayed the full three weeks experienced anxiety as to whether they could get back at all. We suspected that one of our friends, who had obviously fallen in love with a charming and athletic Danish girl, actually cherished the prospect of being detained against his will. However, he finally had to come home like the rest of us!

Returning to Witney apart from the others, I bought a paper and read that Russia and Germany had entered together into a pact of non-aggression and mutual support. The question now was whether Great Britain faced, in all probability, by Germany allied with Russia, would or, indeed, could fulfil our Prime Minister's promise to come to the aid of Poland should that country's borders be crossed by German troops. The world was soon to have the answer to that question.

Back in Witney, while we started to become busier in making and selling blankets, there were other activities to be enjoyed before the outbreak of the Second World War.

The Annual Cricket Match between Witney Mills Cricket Club and the Drapers' Chamber of Trade Summer School had first been arranged in 1929, by my Uncle Edward Early and another splendid man and devotee of the great Game, Stanley Baker. Stanley Baker was the owner of his own store in Birmingham, appropriately called 'Stanley's'. Of course, he sold Early's Witney Blankets. Blankets and cricket were the ties between his firm and our own. Perhaps he knew that Doctor W. G. Grace, Jack Hobbs, Owen Smith and many another famous cricketer had delighted the inhabitants of Witney on what was now known as Witney Mills

Cricket Ground, and did not see why his own cricket friends in the drapery trade should not be granted a similar opportunity. Anyhow, the first match in a fine series of games had been played in 1929 with Stanley Baker himself captain of the Drapers' side.

In 1939, another Stanley — blanket finisher Stanley Bridgeman — was Captain of the Mills team, which for this important fixture included Dave Edwards, then sports master at Witney Grammar School, and an Oxfordshire County player. After all, to suit the Summer School programme this particular fixture had to be fitted in on a working weekday; the firm was beginning to get busy again after a bad patch and not all our regular players could be spared from blanket making. The extra help was, therefore, most welcome.

Witney Mills were put in to bat by Stanley Baker. Dave Edwards opened the innings and was promptly dismissed by the enthusiastic visitors. Whereupon, my father, who was watching, said to the Drapers' scorer, 'Well done! He is our best batsman!' I was near enough to hear this remark and can remember internally deprecating it, as giving comfort to the enemy. I believe I was the next man in and, determined not to fail my side, made what I have to admit was one of my comparatively rare half-centuries. Witney Mills won a very good game, 198 runs to 190.

The Drapers' were just beginning to realise that they could call on some very fine first class cricketers connected with the drapery trade. Such a one was to be Arthur Marment from Marments of Cardiff — a Glamorgan County player, who later knocked up more than one prodigious score against the Mills. His kindness, however, extended beyond that, as the inscription on a fine clock on the front of our pavilion indicates to this day: 'Presented by Arthur V. Marment, M.C., Chairman and Managing Director of Marments, Ltd., Cardiff, 1959'.

Stanley Baker's own son, Ted, was a wicket-keeper — as was Arthur Marment — and Ted played for Worcestershire. Of course, he also played for his father's team against the Mills and it was Stanley Baker himself who was to 'open the door' of a reconstructed Mills Pavilion after the war. He also gave a fine up-to-date score board, which we inscribed: 'This score board was presented by our dear friend Stanley Baker of Birmingham, 21st June, 1966.'

After the war, the Mills team was to be captained by Len Hemming, the firm's deservedly successful Sales Manager. As well

35

as being a fine salesman, he was a splendid cricketer, playing for Oxfordshire and the combined Minor Counties Team. He was awarded the Queen's Jubilee Medal on 6 February 1977, for leadership in selling Witney blankets, in voluntary work for the mentally handicapped and — surely — in playing cricket!

But let us return to the dreadful AD 1939. At the close of the game against the Drapers some of the Mills Team were invited to Balliol College, Oxford, where the Drapers' Summer School was meeting. There was the usual jollity to be expected when rivals meet after a good game of cricket. The match was played again with talk and merry laughter in the College Junior Common Room.

Then the Chairman of the School came in looking so distressed that joking subsided into silence. He quietly told us that the international situation had deteriorated to such an extent that he thought it advisable for us all to return to our own firms. Some delegates had come a considerable distance and he was sure we would agree to his closing the 1939 Drapers' Summer School at once. We went home to our radio sets. It was the end of a chapter.

The reason for the Chairman closing down the School must have been that he, like the rest of us, was realising how uncompromising were the terms of the two-days-old Russo-German pact. My father sent a telegram to Lord Halifax at the Foreign Office, 'Respectfully suggest Anthony Eden be sent without any delay to Moscow where he is persona grata stop Cabinet status and wider discretion obviously desirable.'

We soon learnt that the above advice was too late to be useful. Father wrote in his diary, 'It is hard to see how this time the smash is to be avoided except that all the common people of the World loathe the idea of war'. I remember as I left the office the next night our thoughtful, kind and very efficient Company Secretary saying to me, 'Good night', and adding, 'It looks as if the lights are going out over Europe once again'. I replied, 'Well, I suppose life will go on afterwards'. Sadly enough his own life was not going to last that long.

There was plenty to do in Witney. There were other games of cricket on Witney Mills Ground. It takes a lot to interfere with the Englishman's love for that game! However, the game I was to remember most clearly for the next six years or so elsewhere was that close-fought and sociable match against our old friends and rivals the Drapers' Summer School.

Blankets continued to be in demand for air raid precautions and other government undertakings: the Mill and dispatch department were at last at full stretch. We started 'blacking-out' the whole plant. At first this was accomplished by using the dark waterproof paper in which we baled blankets for export. It now had to be stretched over the windows.

Apart from business, Witney had to be prepared for evacuees — mostly from London. Father was chairman of Witney Grammar School Governors. The headmaster of the school was preparing to receive 3,200 children during the first four days of war. These would be under eleven years of age and need feeding and caring for before being passed on to live among families in the district. In the event far fewer evacuees than were expected arrived. Very naturally a good many London parents did not relish their children being separated from them.

A Warden's Post was established, near to our house and to the Company's Warehouse and Offices in Newland, at Tom Smith's Garage. Tom Smith throughout the war and, indeed, afterwards showed great public spirit in allowing his premises to be used in this way.

Simple gas masks were distributed and I supervised the building of elementary air-raid shelters in the firm's wool warehouse, where we piled up bales of wool leaving a space between and using other bales for a roof. I wonder how much falling masonry and high explosive these makeshift retreats would have withstood?

Soon came that never-to-be-forgotten Sunday when we went to church as usual for 10.30 a.m. service and found a radio receiving set on the Communion Table. I cannot remember much of the service; but I can still hear Mr Neville Chamberlain's tired and disappointed voice reminding us that German troops had entered Poland and that Britain's demand that they should withdraw had been ignored. Therefore this country was at war. The Prime Minister had kept his word.

Later the same day I drove to Birmingham to visit Paul Cadbury at his home. He was a leading Quaker, Managing Director of Cadburys Chocolate and Cocoa firm and Old Boy and Governor of my own Quaker School, Leighton Park, Reading. Moreover he had undertaken to restart The Friends Ambulance Unit, which had done good work during the 1914-18 War. The

Unit was to consist of young men who had attended Quaker Schools and other pacifists who wanted to help the victims of war by philanthropic means, which involved sharing the dangers and hardships of battle. I had for long regarded Paul Cadbury with some awe. I had been to Old Leightonian gatherings where he was President. He was considerably older than I was — a big difference when one is hardly more than a schoolboy! He had been a Member of the FAU himself during the First World War.

I believe I had an idea that he would say to me something like this, 'Yes, of course: you were a Prefect at L.P.S.: we can do with you. You'd better report at Northfield Quaker Meeting House at eleven o'clock tomorrow'. However, it was not so easy as that!

First, as we talked together, I began to get to know Paul Cadbury and the better I knew him the more I admired him. He explained that the FAU was a war-time organisation and had still to be restarted during this war, which had begun only a few hours previously. His elderly and much loved relative, Dame Elizabeth Cadbury, was willing to allow a unit of men to use her Manor Farm — near at hand — for accommodation and training. I was the first actual volunteer. We then began to discuss together — and quite frankly — whether I would be the right man to take immediate command. Eventually he said, 'Well, I shall write down that you are somewhat diffident!' He, himself, was not in a position to give full-time service or go to any part of the world when and where required. Sixty men could be housed in the buildings at Manor Farm, Northfield. They would need training as ambulance workers prepared to operate in conjunction with the armed forces of any nation willing and able to employ us.

First, however, sixty young men, suitable and anxious to join this first camp, would need to be recruited. Some people with authority would need to interview volunteers and accept the most suitable. The unit was not to be officially organised by The Society of Friends, but could depend upon support from a few individual Quakers formed into a council. Some of these had served during the previous World War. Although no one else had so far actually volunteered to join the ranks, half-a-dozen likely young men were willing to do so when told how — and would help prepare camp. Accordingly, Paul Cadbury asked me to present myself at Manor Farm on Monday, 11 September. I got there punctually at 1.50 p.m. that day, complete with kit bag, bicycle and a roll of water-

38

proof paper and sent home a postcard announcing, 'So far our Camp consists of one man plus luggage.'

However, this is primarily a story about Witney and blankets. Even before I left, the 'blacking-out' at the Mills was complete. Soon air-raid wardens, of course, including my father and brother, had to spend watchful nights on the premises in case incendiary bombs were dropped. With added responsibility falling on directors and staff, it could not have been easy for the firm to facilitate my departure. However, when my wishes were known, Charles Early and Company Limited not only let me go but undertook to continue my salary whilst I was doing an unpaid job. I diverted a proportion of this salary to pay the FAU for my living expenses while serving firstly at home and then overseas. I was part of the firm's war effort!

The absence of a good many of us meant extra work and responsibility for those who remained blanket-making in Witney. In September 1939, there were five full-time directors in our firm of about five hundred men, women and young people. My great-uncle Charles William Early had been Chairman of the Board since 1910, the year the firm changed from a partnership to a private limited company. He had succeeded his father (my great-grandfather), Charles Early, who had been Senior Partner before 1910. Charles William was nearly ninety and, although still a good judge of wool and an excellent mathematician — when it came to working out salaries — was obviously past much active management. Responsibility in leadership, like a good many other responsibilities, therefore fell mostly upon my father, his nephew.

Father's brother, my uncle Edward, had for some years shared the leadership with father, especially in buying and selling. However, he had recently been very ill: Doctors advised him to take things as easily as possible. He was a most able businessman; but I realised afterwards that when I eventually shook hands with him at his front door before leaving to go overseas, he somehow knew that we should not be meeting again.

The other two directors were my brother Patrick, and myself. Patrick expected to be called-up by the RAF at any time. However, we had a most excellent senior staff and the very serious recession of the 1930s, although still with us until the outbreak of war, was about to disappear largely owing to an influx of government orders. I felt I was not leaving the company in the lurch, in spite of the very poor results of the year ending January 1939. In February 1939 father described those results as 'thoroughly bad' and he had followed up, in the words of his diary, by having 'a short talk to all Witney Mill people together in the Weaving shed at 12.20 p.m.' He had told them there was no profit, explained some reasons, commended and thanked and added one or two obvious reflections. He wrote, 'They took it very well', and, indeed we were soon to get down to work on sixty thousand 'Seamen's' and twelve thousand 'Officers' blankets. These made my little effort in Southern Africa appear quite a trivial contribution! When war actually came we found we had to ration our regular customers. There would have been no need — and hardly any possibility — for my going out to seek fresh orders had I continued to make Witney my headquarters.

Apart from considerations of war and peace, I had during the summer offered my services to Witney Fire Brigade. It had seemed to me that fire fighting at any hour of night or day was a service which an active young man should be willing to give to his town and community. Quite rightly, the Fire Brigade had told me that I could not join until I had taken a course in First Aid with St John Ambulance Brigade. I was attending such a course instructed by a Witney doctor when war was declared. After that grim Sunday it was certain that the knowledge acquired would prove useful in some way. It also became obvious that —like it, or not — I would find myself in charge of the first camp consisting of sixty young men, largely Quaker, at Northfield Farm. The prospect of this would have alarmed me more, had I not during the preceding eight years been helping, as a lieutenant, to train the Boys' Brigade 1st Witney Company in various activities including drill.

An officer in the BB would be unlikely to go far in attaining the object of the movement — 'The advancement of Christ's Kingdom among Boys and the promotion of habits of Obedience, Reverence, Discipline, Self-respect and all that tends towards a true Christian Manliness' — if he had not taken the trouble to train himself. I had taken pains to learn how to teach drill and gymnastics. This knowledge was now going to be of advantage in forming a disciplined ambulance unit, able to work in conjunction with armed services.

BB drill was very like military drill. There were minor differences. The BB had no need to carry firearms as the army did —

and certainly the Friends Ambulance Unit was not going to do that! The army had simplified drill by recently abolishing for general use the formation of 'fours' and 'two-deep'. Marching in threes had been introduced instead, but the BB had not at that time 'come into line' so to speak! Accordingly, I obtained permission from a fellow blanket-maker — now known as Major J. H. Lawton-Smith, because of his rank in the Territorials — to attend a drill parade in Witney's drill hall and learn how drill was ordered in threes.

Before leaving Witney perhaps I may comment on my father's way of leading and managing. Mention has been made of one occasion when he addressed the whole workforce. We were a profit-sharing company and, as there was no profit at the end of the year, he spoke of how he had felt he had no alternative but to explain and encourage personally. When possible, however, he asked our foremen and managers to give instructions and the directors attended a weekly foremen's meeting. He also told me that he welcomed the advent of the trade union movement as substituting negotiation for fighting. Sometimes he left the trade union to do the talking. I remember once some of the boys walked out — quite unjustifiably — upon 'unofficial strike'. We summoned them together and asked Mr Bert Collis of dye house and Tuckers' Feast fame, and a union shop steward, to come and speak to them. Father and I stood and listened. I cannot remember any set of boys ever receiving a more measured and uncompromising reprimand. They went back to work without another word.

The day before war was declared, my sister Rosemary married her RAF love at short notice. Doubtless the two of them thought that, if they did not marry at once, they might never get another opportunity. Sister Ruth was able to get to the church near to Donald's place of duty. Ruth formed the whole congregation except for a heartily responding clerk at the back. Rosemary was in everyday white and Donald Lee, who became her husband, discarded his RAF uniform for the ceremony and donned 'civvies'. On the next day, father again talked to all the mill about arrangements to come. In those days we all worked from 8 to 11 a.m. on Saturdays. He did not interrupt the week's work until a quarter to eleven on the last day of the week: then he told his people about how we were to continue. Everyone knew it was to be war the next day.

A week later I left for the war-time job I had chosen. Father drove me to Oxford railway station: my bike was tied on the roof of the car and I took a big roll of waterproof paper from the warehouse to 'black-out' the buildings at Manor Farm, Northfield, Birmingham, as well as my camp kit. Father says in his diary, 'It was as much as I could stand, but R. shook hands and went off with the happiest brave look'. Thinking back more than forty years later, I so very much hope that, whatever I looked like, I had similar feelings to my father's.

3 War in Scandinavia

'Go out into the darkness and put your hand into the hand of God. That shall be to you better than a light and safer than a known way.'
— Quoted by King George VI of England in Christmas Broadcast, 1939

A new full-time occupation started for me and for the other young men who shortly joined me at Manor Farm on 12 September 1939. My whole attention was needed for the new job — and so it was with all of us.

Amongst the advance party were Peter Hume, who became Camp Quartermaster, Alan Dickinson, an accountant, and Michael Rowntree, lately Head Boy of Bootham School, York. Just down the road at Bournville was Paul Cadbury, who from the start of the reformed Friends Ambulance Unit gave unbelievable support. He was always ready to come and advise us and to negotiate with authority on our behalf.

The Manor Farm was ideal for housing sixty young men bent on training for active service. There was a barn large enough for drill and gymnastics — and also for communal meals. Surprisingly enough there was a kitchen and toilet facilities. In the small stables and cowsheds round the farmyard could be erected enough bunks to accommodate the whole party at night. I have no idea for what Dame Elizabeth used the farm in peacetime; but we became more and more grateful to her for allowing us its use in war.

I had had experience in blacking-out windows and doors at Witney Mill. The other five pioneers were also adept in making the most of the roll of waterproof paper I brought from home. Other constructional changes were made with the powerful assistance of the maintenance staff and other kind helpers from Cadbury's. I was amongst a small interviewing panel who went up to London to meet applicants for the first of the twenty-two six-week camps which were to take place at the farm.

As Commandant I organised the camp of sixty men in the only way I knew how — like a Boys' Brigade Camp. Indeed it turned out rather like a BB Camp. We had a lot of fun submitting to necessary training and discipline.

We drilled and undertook route-marches — sometimes to hospitable Quaker homes in the neighbourhood, where most generous teas were provided by the kind owners for us hungry sixty. One exhausting outing was to Paul Cadbury's country lodge, where after a very long route-march on the way out, with another equally arduous return march to come, we spent the night on the floor in restricted quarters.

It is not to be thought that there were no complaints from some campers because of what was for most a sudden increase in activity from usual peace-time occupations. However, our energetic training, which included free-standing gymnastics in our large barn and jogging before breakfast each morning, prepared us physically for any eventuality.

The personnel were divided into six squads, mainly because this made for orderly sleeping and feeding arrangements. It also made orderly classes in first aid, air-raid precautions, nursing and finally, when we knew what our job was to be, in driving ambulances and other large vehicles.

I feel sure that beside myself other members of the first two camps look back with unmixed gratitude upon the devoted help and instruction given by the local medical practitioners, Dr Rutter and his son, and by dear Sister Gibbs of Bournville to whom we all lost our hearts. However, there were also the professional local ARP workers and the newly formed Citizens' Advice Bureau and countless other skilled well-wishers to be thanked.

The amount of time which I had to give to arranging the timetable, myself instructing, preparing and making announcements and generally encouraging this party of very free thinkers made me wonder whether I was giving enough time to learning the job for which we had all volunteered — caring for the sick and wounded. However, I managed to pass the various necessary tests with the rest.

Among these first sixty were a considerable number of Quakers. Others, like myself, were Methodists. Some further denominations were represented and I should think a few members were

44

agnostics. We started off by meeting together for evening prayers. Sometimes a member of the 1914-19 FAU would come and talk with us. More than once Paul Cadbury was the visitor and I remember his telling us that sometimes during war there might not be time for formal religious meetings. 'In that case', he added, 'your Worship may well be in your Service'.

Donald Grey, Headmaster of Bootham School, came one evening and I still remember the scripture reading he chose, Micah 4, 1-5. He also discussed with the CO the good qualities of those of his past pupils who happened to be in the unit!

We listened to the radio, although the time thus spent was far less than that spent viewing and listening-in by the average family forty years later. We heard an archbishop express sympathy with out-and-out pacifists and then add, 'but what would happen if everyone thought as they do?' One answer to that question comes later in this story.

Most of us attended a local service, or Meeting, on Sunday mornings — sometimes in the hope that we should be invited out to a good Sunday dinner afterwards! I remember that at Northfield Quaker Meeting I said that I had never seen a dead human being until I joined the FAU and that when I did actually see a dead man for the first time my thought was that I was not examining a real person at all. That real person was somewhere else. I went on to add that it was not surprising we were at war: we had been calling each other 'fools' long enough to ensure the 'hell fire'!

After sixty of us had been training for a fortnight, my grandmother died and I went back for a day in Witney to attend her funeral. She had been a widow for a good many years, but was much loved by us all and particularly by my father who was her eldest son. The health of her second son, Edward, a mainstay of our blanket firm, was deteriorating: he had undergone surgery. He remained game and steadfast as ever; but the family at home must have known that time left for him to help in industry was running out. My brother Patrick contemplated putting off his 'call-up' to the Royal Air Force and I was asked whether I would consider returning to Witney to help. I had to say that I was committed to the FAU for the duration of the war in spite of the fact that no one at this juncture saw exactly how the FAU could help.

As far as England and France were concerned this was the period known as the 'phoney war'. Neither we, nor the Germans, seemed anxious to precipitate matters by full-scale invasion and bombing of cities. Perhaps Hitler still thought he could get what he wanted without undue violence outside the area which for the time being concerned him most. His attack on Poland on 1 September had led to Britain declaring war. Since then Hitler had continued with the systematic destruction of that country. Fifty-six divisions were unleashed against the weaker state in a three-pronged attack upon Warsaw. More than fifteen hundred modern aircraft were also used against the meagre and out-dated forces of Poland. By 20 September the Germans could announce that 'one of the greatest battles of extermination of all time had taken place' — and no other country was in a position to interfere except Russia. The Russians, towards the end of the German onslaught, moved in on the other side of Poland and advanced to a line pre-arranged with Hitler.

It was difficult to see how anyone from outside could have helped — or could help. I had nebulous and entirely impracticable visions of the FAU dropping in by parachute to clear up the mess. Anyway at this time not even the first camp at Northfield had completed preliminary training. We wanted to do something useful and after negotiation the first sixty members were accepted for work in various London hospitals and in some young people's clubs in London as well. At the same time a second contingent of sixty men arrived for another period of training at Northfield Farm.

I was asked to keep an eye on both the London and Northfield contingents. In direct command at Manor Farm was John Bailey, who had the great advantage of being married to Edna Bailey, personal assistant to Paul Cadbury at Bournville. Needless to say Edna helped both Paul and John in every possible way she could. Whether we were stationed in Birmingham or London during this time of 'phoney war', we had the opportunity to gain experience in hospital operating theatres, on the wards and, indeed, in mortuaries. The second camp also spent time and muscle power in digging a deep trench to prepare for air-raids, which were expected at any time. Another way in which I hope I gave help was by witnessing in favour of young men due to be called up for service in the Armed Forces, but who were already members of the FAU or who wished to join us. I believe that it was thought my smart Red Cross uniform would have a good effect upon the presiding judge

46

or magistrate! I do not suppose it did; but I was impressed by the fairness and helpfulness of all concerned.

At the beginning of December we were told that the Russians had invaded Finland. At that time it seemed to us — and to most of the world — that this invasion was just another heartless political act — a large country with overwhelming manpower and armaments attempting to subjugate a small one. Obviously there was more to it than that. Russia was afraid that some other large power — almost certainly Germany — would use Finland's strategic proximity to Leningrad to mount an attack on the Russian homeland. Of course, we in the FAU wanted to go to Finland to relieve suffering.

The plight of the Finns aroused the sympathy of the whole British people. However, we understood that the government hesitated to send official armed assistance to Finland, because our country was already engaged in a life-or-death struggle with Germany and did not wish to bring Russia in full strength on the German side. Such were the politics of war. Another difficulty was that the remainder of Scandinavia, anxious to stay neutral, was between ourselves and Finland. In fact, Sweden was already exporting vital iron to Germany through Narvik or the Gulf of Bothnia.

The FAU Council — and in particular Paul Cadbury — negotiated through the now joint organisation of British Red Cross and St John Ambulance Brigade with Finnish authorities. Just as Paul's first letter to the press had resulted in three hundred volunteers so a letter he now sent to *The Times* appealing for money to help us yielded £10,000 and more financial support came from a general Finland Fund organised by Lord Phillimore. Through Madam Gripenberg, wife of the Finnish Minister in London, our offer of help was accepted by the Finns.

I remained Commandant; but, for the most part, my command was limited to the sixty-odd men chosen to go to Finland. Dressed in khaki Red Cross uniform we sixty assembled at Buckhurst Hill Youth Hostel near Epping Forest. Looking back afterwards, I think it would probably have been better had Dr John Gillespie, a splendid Irish medical volunteer, been Commandant with one of us wartime ambulancemen as a good strong second-in-command. After all we were a medical unit. Perhaps with this in mind, I consulted Alan Dickinson, who was designated Adjutant of the

47

Finland contingent, and Peter Hume. They told me that, although I had been appointed Commandant by the Council, they believed it to be the wish of every individual in the Finnish party that I should continue as such. So the job became my life. The three of us sat at a restaurant table in London as we talked. Only one of us three was to survive the war.

I had been home more than once during our work at Manor Farm and in London. It was at home on Christmas Day 1939, that I heard our King George VI speak the words at the head of this Chapter. I remember my last sight of our house in Witney and how I thought I would prefer not to see that home again until our job and the war were over. There was also that wonderful afternoon when the family came up to London and we all went to a magnificent pantomime performance of *Cinderella*. Afterwards as their train drew out from Paddington towards Witney, I can remember holding my youngest sister's hand through the carriage window until I was left alone standing on the platform.

Well, on 18 January 1940 the first half of our Buckhurst Hill party left by road for Newcastle. There were twenty-seven of us driving ten ambulances, two store lorries and two other cars. The smaller of these last two was a Ford owned jointly by my sister, Rosemary, and myself. The kind and generous Rosemary was never to see her half of the little vehicle again!

Owing to the generosity of many Quakers, of the Red Cross and of individual families, we were excellently equipped for work in dark and sub-zero conditions. The winter of 1939-40 was one of the coldest Europe had ever experienced. For us it started in England. The counties on the way to Newcastle-upon-Tyne were snow covered and the highway frozen and treacherous. We spent a night in the Meeting House at Doncaster and were met by Arnold Rowntree, who was said to have commissioned Paul Cadbury to restart the FAU in 1939. When we parted from Arnold Rowntree, I still remember, he said to me, 'Thank you for doing this for us'. Forty years later I do not forget how grateful we felt towards him and to all others who had used their influence and worked hard to set us on our way. I also remember receiving a letter of good wishes from my father at this time. It said, 'I expect you have considered the possibility of your party falling into Russian hands. Should that occur you can remain sure that we will all be making determined and continuous efforts through every channel to get you back'. I did not forget that either: Russia had not accepted the terms of the Geneva Convention relevant to such a situation.

We crossed the North Sea on SS *Iris,* taking a northerly route, so as to keep out of trouble. I asked the captain whether we should take off our clothes in our bunks at night. He said, 'You can do as you wish; but I advise you to sleep in full uniform'. However, it was not to be the *Iris* that was sunk this time. At 09.30 on the second day at sea, a Sunday, we came to a raft with nine dispirited Danes huddled on it. They were the survivors from a Danish coaler with a crew of twenty, which had been torpedoed without warning. The captain and ten members of the crew had gone down with the ship.

It was a silent sad meeting as we hove-to. The Danish ship had been carrying coal from Newcastle to Denmark. All that was left of the vessel was a black patch of coal-dust on the surface. A destroyer in our convoy and SS *Iris* rescued the nine from the raft. When they came aboard our doctor, John Gillespie, and the rest of us did what we could for them. We gave away some of our ample warm clothing. At a service at sea we remembered those lost and their friends and repeated the King's words quoted in his Christmas message. We arrived at Bergen in Norway early afternoon 22 January.

We had time to become acclimatised and to learn to ski at a pension near Oslo. After nearly three weeks two of our ambulances and two lorries also completed the slow round-about voyage across the North Sea and an advance party consisting of Dr John Gillespie, Alan R. Dickinson, Tom Burnes, Pitt Corder, Ralph Davis, John Heywood, Ian Kyd and myself drove to the north of the Gulf of Bothnia. At 16.00 hours on 18 February we entered Finland by crossing the bridge which links Haparanda with Tornea — the first FAU party in the Second World War to go into action in an overseas country! The remainder of the Finland contingent complete with cars was soon to follow us. The journey of well over a thousand miles from Oslo to Stockholm and then north to Haparanda taught us more of how to control and look after our vehicles on rutted hard snow-covered roads and on frozen rivers with the temperature falling to minus 30° centigrade. It was clear where the sympathies of Sweden lay. Sweden had already given considerable medical aid to Finland and, when we were obliged to stop for minor mechanical repairs, the Swedish police insisted upon finding the advance party accommodation for a night and stood us an excellent and sociable meal. At Tornea we loaded our ambulance and lorries on to a train which took us to south east Finland where was the main Russian invasion. On the train we needed to start-up our engines regularly night and day to prevent freezing-up. Both on road and rail we had at intervals to leave our seats smartly and plunge into the nearest snow drift, camouflaged in our white overalls, to take cover from Russian aircraft.

So we arrived at Leppasyrja a few miles north of Sortavala on the great Lake Lodoga. This was to be our headquarters. Various Finnish colonels and majors told us what to do, but our best and most helpful Finnish friend was Nils Hahl who besides being a good soldier spoke Finnish, Swedish, French and English. Some Finns considered Swedish their mother tongue, others Finnish. As interpreter he was essential, but Nils was a great deal more. He had ideas of his own and sympathised with ours. We regarded him with great affection and respect. It must have been grievous to every member of our party to learn, about a year later, that he had perished in a second unnecessary Finnish war.

Fourteen men were stationed with me at Leppasyrja HQ with vehicles. We were ready to operate to and from the hospital at Sortavala, where we had left our doctor; we could also support our own outposts nearer the battle area and — even 'in reserve' — had our fair share of excitement in this freezing snowclad country. However, certainly the outposts were in a still more dangerous situation.

Determined not to shirk, one night I went out to Soanlahti, where Old Leightonian Ralph Smith was stationed with his ambulance. He had taken part in several errands of mercy to and from casualty-clearing stations at the Front and, as necessary, from Soanlahti to a base hospital. After a good deal of driving without lights along undistinguishable snowclad tracks he must have been glad enough to make way for me as driver and I have a note in my diary that during the night of 10 and 11 March 1940 I was 'twelve hours — on and off — at the wheel'.

Our ambulance was staffed on this occasion by Ralph Smith, a Finnish soldier and interpreter named Linsted and myself. While Ralph looked after the patients, and I drove, the interpreter was ready to enquire about the route and negotiate with any inquisitive Russians we might meet. This was important — just previously another FAU ambulance had been stopped by a Finnish sentry and been warned 'Had you driven another two hundred metres, you would have been in the Russian lines!'

In fact the 'Loimola front' just here did not appear to be a line at all. We were sent to what appeared — covered with snow as it was — to be a dugout. From it we carried, or otherwise helped, eleven wounded men into our ambulance and drove them to Umalati Hospital. It was easy to write this into my diary afterwards but the journey was hazardous. We needed more than once to take cover from shell fire and aeroplanes. Russian shells could be heard passing over us and exploding in Finnish territory, but we had to be ready to take evasive action should the odd one fall short.

That journey was only one among many undertaken by FAU ambulances during just a few days. Ralph Smith had borne the brunt of driving. Conditions for the fighting men were terrible. Many Russians inadequately equipped died of cold, but they vastly outnumbered the better-trained, better-equipped Finns, who were fighting to preserve their country. Very soon numbers told and the Finns tended to fall asleep at their posts for lack of relief. At first the Russian government had greatly under-rated the determination and patriotism of the opposition. Finally, however, according to my diary the end came like this.

12th March. Quiet day. Eric Rydman arrived as interpreter. Interview with Major Jokola in the evening. 13th March. Telephone call from John Gillespie at 1.30 a.m. Up at 5 a.m. Started with Eric Rydman and two Members to supplement Soanlahti forces at 6.30 a.m. Took cover from aeroplanes once and arrived at 8 a.m. At noon heard that peace had been signed. Distressing scenes as house-holders learnt that they were now in Russia (like all of us) and would have to leave their homes. Came back at once to H.Q. with Eric Rydman. John Gillespie soon met us there. Saw Major Jokola. He told us to stay where we were and await orders.

As I recall these events, my wife has produced a letter to her dated 15 March 1940. The address at the head of the Red Cross writing paper is:

Friends Ambulance Unit
Militarypost
Finland

It starts,

'Dear Gerda', and continues . . .

It was good to get news of old Fredensborg and 'Cope'. You might give Ebba a dig in the ribs for not writing to me for about half a year! Please remember me to the Holtzes when you next meet them.

I have also skied a little for the first time in my life during our journey through Norway. It is a great winter sport isn't it? I envy you being able to enjoy it every winter, and am not surprised that you spend a lot of time at it.

It is a very tragic situation here. When peace was declared the day before yesterday I was at the house of a lady whose husband was killed in the war two months ago. She now learns that she is to lose her home as well; for all this part of the country from which I write is now Russia and all inhabitants will have to leave. Anyway it is better than war and although Finland has lost part of her land she has saved many of her people by making peace now and not allowing the war to go on until a great proportion of her best manhood is wiped out.

The other night some of us enjoyed a Finnish bath (or sauna) being thoroughly steamed and ending by a roll in the snow. That is one thing you have never done, isn't it?!

With all good wishes,

I still remember some Finns saying sadly that peace was better than war. Some who said this were women, who must have lost husbands, brothers or sons. I also remember that some Finnish soldiers who, with the Finnish army as a whole, had not been allowed alcohol during hostilities, took undue advantage of the ban being lifted. The deeper thinkers wondered whether German pressure had not hastened Finnish capitulation. After all both Russian and German governments had connived over dividing Poland.

The plight of cattle seemed almost worse than that of humans. In Finland cattle are kept inside during the winter. Now, numbers of these had to be turned out of doors to die frozen in the snow while their owners fled.

After five months' preparation, we had found ourselves in a place where we could render three weeks' concentrated service.

Wars are often like that. However, here we were in Russia and I remembered my father's letter. I must have mentioned what could be our predicament to interpreter and friend Nils Hahl. He replied somewhat sharply, 'You needn't worry about that: you and your men are absolutely safe serving with the Finnish Army'.

He was perfectly right: the Finnish army made an orderly retreat to the new borders of their country and our last sad service for Finland was helping the civil population to do the same. As far as I know no Finns remained in the ceded territory.

One can understand how invaluable in helping with the evacuation were our ambulances and lorries, especially when augmented by the second party of our contingent which arrived and made numbers of vehicles up to twenty ambulances, two lorries, a kitchen car and two staff cars. When lined up together, which was not very often, manned by a contingent of nearly sixty, it was an impressive sight!

Briefly we encamped at Liperi inside the new Finnish borders. Douglas Lister and I paid a visit to Red Cross Headquarters and other authorities in Helsingfors, where we arrived on Easter Day. We were told how as FAU members we could employ ourselves most usefully in Finland. For the time being lack of transport was the great difficulty and that was where we could help. We met George and Peggy Grippenberg, who had commissioned us in London, Baron Wrede, who had met us on arrival in Scandinavia and had been Finland's propagandist in America, when the war first broke out, with his wife — and the British Minister and Military Attaché. Others who were kind to us were the Salvation Army and Mary Runciman, who was in charge of a party of FANY: they wished to help Finland in her extremity. We ended up by broadcasting to England from the Finnish Broadcasting House.

Evidently there was at least a month's work in redistributing the population for the combined FAU party. We established what could be termed a temporary office in Joensuu. I walked there at a pre-arranged time each morning. One morning I was overtaken by a horse-drawn sledge. The driver on the front seat looked rather like an English Edwardian coachman. On the rear seat sat a beautiful Finnish girl, who to me looked in her white furs like the Snow Queen. She asked the driver to stop and offered me a place on the seat beside her. I felt my reputation had risen considerably when eventually I got down from the sledge, proffered my thanks and walked into the 'office'!

Then the situation and our whole outlook was changed by momentous news on 9 April when Dr John Gillespie came into our encampment at supper-time and told us that German troops had occupied Denmark and certain ports in Norway.

Immediately we continued with the job in hand — the fortnight's work in moving people from Joensuu to Kuopio, well inside the new Finnish borders, had taught us to work as a team and show consideration for both passengers and cars, but available employment was obviously running out and what there was could soon be accomplished by the efficient Finns themselves. On 13 April we saw Colonel Salminen of the Finnish army and told him that we felt bound to offer our undivided assistance to the Norwegian government in their need. This time it was John Gillespie and I who went by train to Helsingfors and made our offer to Major Hansteen, Military Attaché, at the Norwegian Legation. It was accepted early in the morning of 16 April, but we nevertheless waited and obtained permission from the Finnish Red Cross and army to end work with them before sending the following cable from the British Legation to England.

> Every member of the Unit wishes to go to Norway stop Nevertheless Gillespie and self visited Helsingfors carefully investigated possibility further work Finland stop Finnish authorities grateful but say continuation of work here not necessary and liable to cease stop Services of complete convoy accepted by Norwegian Government stop Expect to leave Joensuu for Norway via Tornea Sunday.

On Saturday 20 April 1940 Colonel Salminen, Head Doctor of the Finnish 4th Army Corps, expressed his gratitude to our men who had served in Finland and promised that special Red Cross Medals would be sent for us to the Finnish Legation in London when circumstances allowed. Needless to say, this promise has been kept.

On Saturday 21 April, the whole convoy consisting of twenty-six vehicles and sixty men set out through Haparanda and Lulia in Sweden towards the port of Namsos in Norway. In marked contrast to the Swedish attitude towards us on our way to Finland, we found now that certain Swedish Authorities were anxious to get rid of this body of men in British uniform as quickly as possible.

The crew of a British naval vessel, after a shipwreck, had recently escaped across Norway in rags only to find themselves interned in Sweden. We supposed that now the Germans had occupied Denmark and part of Norway, the Swedes did not wish to give Hitler an excuse for occupying Sweden as well. They were also nervous about any interference with the export of iron ore from north Sweden through Narvik, or down the Gulf of Bothnia, to Germany.

The convoy reached Gäddede on the Swedish-Norwegian border and proceeded into Norway during the night of 29 and 30 April. Progress was very slow and by 11.30 a.m. we had been virtually brought to a standstill in the melting snow. We decided to wait until the snow froze again the following night. The twenty-six vehicles with large bold red crosses painted on the roofs were drawn up tandem on the mountain road. Then two German aircraft flew along the road from East to West and sprayed the convoy with machine-gun bullets on the way. Fortunately no great damage resulted. Most of us had been wise and quick enough to take cover in snow at the side of the road by the time the attack materialised. However, Harold Cadoux and Edward Backhouse were lying on stretchers in their ambulance. Its fabric was penetrated by bullets, which passed between them and Harold was slightly scratched by a flying piece of equipment. After that we managed to move on and await the nightly freeze-up under cover of some trees.

On the way, at a small hamlet, we met an English newspaper reporter making what speed he could towards Sweden. He urged us to do the same, which we thought impracticable. However, I rang Namsos, where we got the same advice. Neither would give a reason; but finally Namsos said, 'Oh, very well, come on!' We did and the English national daily concerned reported news of us — and the Heinkels — in England the next day.

It took ten hours for us to cover the almost impossible fifteen miles immediately before reaching Godejord. From there four of us went on ahead to find out how we were to deploy our forces in the Namsos area.

The Colonel in charge of the British ambulance services in Namsos told us that the Norwegians were at present adequately provided with medical help but would be glad of support from five cars and twelve men, who were to remain at Godejord. Five more ambulances with personnel were to go to a place called Raanem. The rest were to be posted round Namsos itself. I was to remain with a staff car, to keep in touch because of 'important moves that were pending'. I cannot remember whether at the time I realised the significance of the words in inverted commas. Immediately there was another German air-raid; but I was actually receiving further instructions from the Colonel when a messenger came to him and said that the British Forces were evacuating.

I remember wishing there was someone in authority who would tell me what to do. The Colonel said that we had a chance of being shipped to England with the British troops — leaving our ambulances behind. I did not like the idea of losing our vehicles. However, Oswald Dick as transport officer was in touch with the men at Godejord telling them to get together and be ready to move. He would help them. I went to see General Carton de Wiart V.C. who was in charge of all British operations.

I was impressed when I found that the General already knew about us volunteers who had turned up from Finland. He must have had a lot of other things on his mind. He said, 'You don't want to be captured, do you? Come to England with us!' When I said that we should lose our ambulances that way and might have the alternative of driving them to Sweden he said, 'Yes, you are Red Cross, you could well do that'.

It is more than forty years after the event now; but in his history of the FAU during the Second World War published in 1947, A. Tegla Davies says, 'Richard decided on evacuation'.

We told all those members in and close around Namsos to abandon their ambulances and avail themselves of a sea passage to Great Britain with the evacuating troops. Oswald Dick and I, with a couple more who would otherwise have got away, made it our job to get together the remaining scattered members and make a dash for the departing ships. By telephone we told those to whom we could speak to meet us at Formofoss on the direct route from the Norwegian-Swedish border. The roads were difficult, getting to Formofoss took longer than we expected. When all were present we piled into two ambulances and made for the port again. Both Oswald Dick and Maurice Woodhead drove like furies and heroes. We left Formofoss at 3 a.m. on 3 May and arrive at the dismal deserted Namsos Harbour at 4.10 a.m. Officially the evacuation had been completed just over two hours previously. There were three of our ambulances, some bombed lorries, discarded stores and a mobile anti-aircraft gun on the quay. I cannot remember seeing any human beings beside ourselves. We knew we had got to get ourselves and — out of self-respect — as many vehicles as possible to neutral Sweden as quickly as we could.

We began our almost desperate journey in the immediately available ambulances, stopping at two temporary depots at Raanem and Godejord long enough to fill up from, and load into our vehicles, several barrels of petrol, which the retreating British and Norwegian soldiers had left. We increased the number of vehicles we drove to fifteen: then we put into them what stores we needed and set out for the pass over the mountains.

We expected to find a party of hostile belligerants round every corner. Upon coming to a spot where a snow-drift had blocked the way we thought we had been taken in a German ambush. However, a little spade work soon cleared the blockage and our journey out of Norway continued. In fact there were fewer delays than during the journey in the other direction two days previously. Perhaps winter was having a last fling and the snow, diminishing during the daytime, was also freezing rather harder at night.

All thirty-one of our party were determined to get those fifteen cars and ourselves to safety. I remember that some of us had to drive thirteen hours without a break. When we arrived once again at Gädede, just inside Sweden, it was during the small hours of 4 May, and some of us had been on the road since we left Namsos for the first time during early afternoon on 2 May. Even today I can see again the bewildered disappointed faces of the Norwegian country folk in and around Namsos as they watched the sudden departure of those who had come, as they thought, to help them. I have a note in my diary that on arrival in Sweden I slept until eleven in the morning and then cabled England giving the names of the thirty-one who had escaped to a neutral country. We could only hope that the rest of our party would safely reach the British Isles by sea. We were soon to get word that they had — but not without incident. We also learnt that the Germans crossed the tracks we left as we headed towards Sweden through Norway six hours after we made them.

On 5 May we left our vehicles in charge of two of our members to be handed over to the Swedish Red Cross. The Swedes later paid for our vehicles — just one example of help given by neutrals to the

International Red Cross during war-time. The rest of us left by night train for Stockholm, where we arrived at 7.30 a.m. on the following day. Upon instructions from the British Embassy we packed our uniform away and donned civilian clothes, bought at Swedish shops. Then we set about trying to persuade some authority to take us either to England or to another war-affected area. The Russian government at that time were not prepared to help. We had been serving the Finns and on the wrong side. When our spokesman said, 'We helped wounded Russians as well as Finns', the Russian official replied, 'Yes, we know what you in the Red Cross do to Russian prisoners! You gouge out their eyes and torture them' — and he genuinely believed that we did. We therefore could not get out to the east and the Germans were occupying Denmark and Norway to our west.

Of course, we might have flown out; but this mode of travel by civilians was neither easy nor usual in war-time and the British Embassy told us with a smile that when it existed at all, it was reserved for even more important travellers than ourselves! Bearing the foregoing in mind, the party, now stranded in Sweden, passed what in one way was a most frustrating five months enjoying a beautiful Scandinavian summer, while our families and friends were suffering the effects of the most terrible war in history. However, we made the most of the situation and nearly all of us found paid or unpaid work as schoolmasters, agricultural labourers or students — or a mixture of all three. It was an opportunity to learn Swedish. Two members I know about married Scandinavians after the war.

Our doctor, John Gillespie, was the first to get home. We all had great respect and admiration for him. He was sacrificing more than the rest of us. In war-time there is unfortunately plenty of extra paid work for qualified doctors such as he. He preferred to come with us although his pacifist views were different from those held by most other members. He would have been willing to carry a revolver for self-defence. He said he had been anxious to join us, because he believed strongly that whether or not a man in war should have any part in carrying or using modern weapons was something which that man alone should decide. However, he was not going to spend longer than he could help in Sweden and, being a neutral Irishman, he applied to Berlin for the necessary papers to enable him to return to Dublin. Then he could travel to any part of the world where he could help mankind. Permission was granted and, at the second attempt, he succeeded in making another hazardous journey by boat across the North Sea.

Another five members who had sought work in Finland also managed to get home from a northern port. This was largely due to the efforts of our Finnish friend and interpreter, Nils Hahl. I believe that Oswald Dick, also in Finland during the latter part of our enforced stay in Scandinavia, could have got away too. However, he chose to come back and join us again in Sweden when we were able to move to another war zone as a party.

After many abortive efforts in Sweden on our own behalf it was at length members of the FAU in England who persuaded the Russians, as represented by their ambassador in London, to allow us to travel through their country — and it was to be some journey! It was a case of 'air' to Moscow, train to Odessa, ship through the Dardanelles and 'land' travel again from Istanbul via Mount Carmel, across the Suez Canal to Cairo and then on to Alexandria. The British Red Cross Commissioner in Cairo had accepted the offer of twenty-six 'trained voluntary ambulance drivers' from Sweden.

Before we left Stockholm we changed leaders. Oswald Dick with my best wishes and the support of the whole party became Commandant and I changed my smart officer's uniform for a much rougher outfit as I joined the ranks. I was not surprised that the remainder of the contingent wanted this change. After all I had learnt the trade of an apprenticed Master Weaver in Witney and had only taken charge of this unusual, indeed unique, party because I had been invited to do so. In Oswald we found a splendid dynamic leader. It was a privilege to serve under his command.

For me it had been a difficult job. It was a good thing to have a change.

4 Witney and war

'Keep the home fires burning'
— old song

Now to talk about what was going on at home since I had ceased to be a regular Witney inhabitant.

I learnt a great deal from my family's letters to Scandinavia at the time and now have the advantage of looking at my father's 1940 personal diary.

Witney has always been a friendly town — not too large to prevent us knowing our neighbours; although I did once hear the following conversation at a Witney party. 'It's good to see so many Witney folks together, isn't it? Why there's old Harry Jones!' 'Don't be so daft, young man!' came the scornful reply, 'Harry bain't no Witney man: he only come to the the Town fifty year agone!'

Well, there were plenty of extra people who came to Witney during the first year of the Second World War. Largely these were evacuees from London. In the case of our own Newland House, where our family had been brought-up since I (the eldest of five children) was four years old, the first evacuees were a father and mother with two infant children. When the parents had both to be back in London for the sake of their work, my mother looked after the juniors.

Then a major, on duty in our neighbourhood, was billeted at our home and, accompanied by his wife and young son, Nicholas, occupied my room as a bed-sitter. One week-end there were sixteen people in the house and — knowing my parents — I am sure they were very well looked after. More evacuees and service men received similar kind treatment in our own and other households. Newland House, though full to overflowing, afforded but a minute proportion of the hospitality shown by Witney to those away from home. The Clerk of Witney Urban District Council of the time, Mr John Welch, tells me that even before hostilities officially started on 3 September, he was advised that four hundred children from London would be arriving at Witney railway station by a special train the next day. The gallant clerk made all arrangements for the reception and accommodation of the Londoners. At the stipulated time local householders were ready near the station to take the expected newcomers to their homes.

The special trains did not arrive and eventually there was a radio announcement indicating that the evacuation had been completed elsewhere. The clerk, therefore, apologised to the prospective hosts and hostesses and sent them home with many thanks for being willing to put themselves out in order to help. A few hours later the special trains filled with hungry and excited children arrived! Of course, Witney coped. By the end of August 1940, father estimated that there must have been two thousand added to the town's pre-war population of about five thousand.

As well as showing a new kind of sympathy and fellow feeling to newcomers, Witney became more understanding of those who lived elsewhere — especially of those who were serving overseas. Some boys whose families had moved to Witney joined the Boys' Brigade 1st Witney Company. Other young people — and older people too for that matter — came and joined other local organisations. The BB recruits from other areas received hospitality in the Skipper's home and doubtless teas, and such luxuries as hot baths were made available for other visitors as well. A good many of those who were shown hospitality themselves undertook voluntary service in the town as well as earning their living here. Some stayed for the rest of their lives.

My father's diary at that time often gave the names of visiting members of the armed forces, some from overseas, who looked in for a meal and a bath. Closer friends, as the war proceeded and bombing became worse, would come down unexpectedly from devastated London, where they worked, to enjoy a few days' rest and safety. How this continued to be possible during a period of strict rationing I cannot imagine. However, continue it did, particularly in our house where the family had a good many outside connections.

It is a sad reflection that, during what became called 'the phoney war' in 1939, some parents insisted on their children returning to

London. Not all of those children survived the war.

A refugee organisation of an interesting kind was the London School of Dramatic Art. Plays were rehearsed and performed before extremely cosmopolitan audiences of about seventy at a time in a large room behind Tite's Outfitters Shop in High Street. A well-known visiting actress, Miss Beryl Cook, was kind enough to invite a Boys' Brigade Dramatic Class to the 'Repertoire', as it became called, for drama lessons. 'First Class!' was the Skipper's comment. My mother used sometimes to accept an invitation to act in the productions of the London School of Dramatic Art. During the war there were far more men and women working away from home than in peace-time: they liked to be entertained and, indeed, educated. There were, therefore, openings here for artists of various skills. My sister, Ruth, when not teaching at Benenden School, enjoyed playing the piano to visitors at Newland House and, of course, to larger audiences in Oxford Playhouse and further afield.

In Witney full employment and overtime returned to the blanket industry. At the request of the weavers at Witney Mill it was decided to switch on the power in the weaving shed at 7.30 a.m. instead of at 8.00 a.m. and to keep it on until 6.30 p.m. instead of 6.00 p.m. This made it possible for operatives who so wished to work their loom for an extra hour a day. At the same time the management recommended that, to lessen monotony and increase alertness, regular breaks of a few minutes — long enough for a cup of tea — should be taken by the weavers and others at the Mill. Some men agreed regularly to work overtime.

Master Harold, as my father liked to be called, would on occasion call the whole workforce together and explain how trade was going and what was happening to the blankets we were making: he encouraged and expressed gratitude. We were a profit-sharing firm and on 15 March 1940 he announced that 5 per cent of the company's profits was to be allotted as an extra, over and above regular remunerations.

At Early's up to this time it had been customary for one girl, or woman, to be in charge of a single loom. Now thirty-six weavers volunteered to operate two looms each. This increase in responsibility was agreed with the management and, also, encouraged. Output did not fall; it increased to 516 stockfuls a week (every stockful consisting of about a hundred pounds of blanketing). That was an all-time record for our Mill, soon and often to be bettered during the next five years.

The trade union played a part in increasing productivity and fully supported the management. The management also supported the union. 'There was a Union Meeting in the Woolhouse by arrangement to try and whip up our very low Union membership', wrote father. The advent of trade unions had been welcomed by him 'on the grounds', as he put it, 'that they stood for negotiation rather than fighting'. Not that we had ever had much fighting in Witney. There had been a bit of trouble between the Master Weavers and Journeymen Weavers back in the eighteenth century, when an anonymous note had been pushed under the door of the Blanket Hall as the Witney Blanketers were meeting there for Common Hall. It read:

> This is to infarm you, Sirs, that there is an agreement made between some Men that whoever will not give the journeymen weavers their two pance a nowhor, i say, take care of yourselves or you will die and wot a thing to die for oppressing the Poor, i tell you in a word you shall Die two or three in pertickler of the masters without a spedi Refarmation
>
> 19th September, 1794.

However, we in Witney seem somehow to have reached a compromise and managed to co-operate in continuing to make the most famous blankets in the world: we are proud to say that this still applies nearly two centuries, or so, after the above 1794 letter was penned. Anyway Master Harold did his best to help by co-operating with the Transport and General Workers Union, in the Witney blanket industry.

A sad aspect of long absence from the town of my birth and upbringing was the number of lifelong friends who died while I was away. One especially sad loss of a close relative was that of my father's brother, Edward Cole Early. He had been particularly kind to my brother and me when we were learning the craft and trade of blanket-making. As war approached his health had declined. Soon after the outbreak of hostilities he was sent to hospital — not for the first time. However, he continued to give invaluable advice upon business matters to those who were left to control the fortunes of our blanket firm. Father visited him almost every day. On 11 April 1940 Uncle Edward was told that there could be no recovery. He took the news calmly and continued the helpful counsellor until he could no longer recognise his visitors. He passed away on 13 May 1940.

Edward Early's death revived a good many memories for his nephew in Sweden. Since boyhood he had advised and helped many and particularly his friends in Oxfordshire. He had become a Methodist local preacher and continued so until he decided he was even more needed as superintendent of the Sunday school at Witney Methodist Church founded by John Wesley. However, his main life's work had been blanket-making. He was as good a judge of wool as was his nonagenarian uncle, Charles William Early. He was also a lively and practical mathematician in that, using slide rule or ready reckoner, he could calculate the economic price for finished articles in various qualities and quantitites and — incidentally — what we could afford to pay employees (including directors). We were then a private limited company and, over the years, just had to make a profit to keep going. Needless to say he was a good salesman, whom customers could trust.

With all this Uncle Edward had humour and a love of artistic skill and achievement — very much as displayed in sport — particularly cricket. I remember he took me to my first wool sale of East Indies wool in Liverpool. Doubtless the visit to Liverpool was well worthwhile from a business point of view. However, in the evening he decreed that we should go and enjoy the great Furtwaengler conducting the Berlin Philharmonic Orchestra in Liverpool Town Hall. One of the works presented was the Overture to *Die Meistersinger*. I can still remember — fifty years later — his wistful remark when the Overture finished, 'Ah, how I wish we could go on to the rest of Wagner's wonderful Opera now!'

Uncle Edward would also take us young ones to see the visiting Australians play against Gloucestershire at Cheltenham College and it was he who paid the fee for Jack Hobbs's first visit to Witney. Hobbs made a century. I remember my uncle exclaiming happily during that game, 'I am really getting my money's worth!' My memory is that it was not Hobbs's century that accounted for this outburst of pleasure: but a particularly fine piece of fielding and return to the wicket-keeper by the master from cover point.

Incidentally, when it came to payment, I have it in my mind that Jack Hobbs hesitated to take any fee at all, saying that he had just come down to Witney as an outing for his wife. However, finally he was prevailed upon to accept; because one of us said that the fee was given by Master Edward who would feel much put out should it be refused!

Edward Early had been one of the first people in Witney to own a private motor car and it was he who had given us our first driving lessons when we became seventeen. He had also been a member of Witney's Volunteer Fire Brigade at about the period when Witney saw its first motor car. I can well believe that he would have helped again in this direction during the War, had his last illness allowed.

Uncle Edward brought a light sensitive touch to everything he said or did — and he did a great deal outside regular business. From early manhood he had taken a keen interest in local government and had soon become chosen as Chairman of Witney Urban District Council, the position held later during the war by another blanket-maker, Mr Ernest Taphouse. As chairman of the Council he also served as Justice of the Peace. For a number of years Edward Early had helped the forward-looking Radcliffe Infirmary which was concerned just about this time with the discovery of penicillin. As an Oxfordshire County Councillor he was chairman of the Public Health Committee and he became chairman of the Management Committee of the Infirmary. He was an excellent chairman and always started meetings exactly on time. When he got home after, perhaps, a stormy meeting which he had chaired, he might report to his family jocularly, 'Well, there was a good deal of hot air forthcoming: so I just listened. At the end I summed-up with a résumé of the sensible remarks made and I suppose the others gave me the credit for them'.

Master Edward always tried, usually with success, to get to the root of other people's problems. I remember once he had the job of interviewing a really awkward employee, who had got to the stage when he could not get on with anybody. Dismissal seemed the only remedy and was what the whole Mill expected — together with a first-class row. I fancy no one was more surprised than the employee himself when the boss began, 'Now then, Reg, what is the matter?'

After he died a remarkable tribute was paid to him by Father Lopez during a sermon at Witney Roman Catholic Church. I can believe that similar kind and true words were spoken at St Mary's Church of England, the Congregational Church, and I am sure by the Quakers, as well as by his own Methodist Church.

Edward Early had a humorous almost mocking way of expressing himself, when he disagreed with someone or something, and an encouraging and equally cheerful manner when he agreed. He was a wonderful leg-pulling family man. There was, however, nothing weak, unstable, or unkind about his character. Witney, his firm, and most of all, his family owed him more than can be said. When my mother wrote to me giving the sad, but expected, news of his death, she described his life as 'founded upon a rock'.

The absence of my kindly and public-spirited uncle from the Witney scene cast an additional burden upon men and women left to work and guide the destiny of others in and around the town. When it came to blankets, extra responsibility fell mostly upon my father and brother in our firm. As previously indicated, Master Harold did his best to help the Transport and General Workers Union along in the Witney Blanket Industry. His diary for Saturday 1 June 1940 records, 'At stopping time in the [Weaving] Shed I introduced Harry Beale [Local Union Secretary] and the election of representatives [followed].'

Of course, everyone knew Harry Beale already, but not in the capacity of Union Secretary. Anyway, whether they were members of a union or not, all Witney people seemed to have been on the same side. I like to believe that in basics we still are forty-three years later. There was an obvious reason for us being so in 1940, when an almost desperate situation arose in the rest of Europe and united the whole country. Immediately it seemed that nothing could stop the German military machine. The occupation of Denmark and Norway beginning on 9 April was not much more than the start.

On 10 May Hitler invaded Holland and Belgium. On the 16 the Dutch army capitulated and another immense German onset was in full swing. So far Witney was peaceful enough in the sun; as was Sweden during that summer of beautiful weather.

The massive German attack burst through into France. Father's comment was, 'At any rate Hitler has at last committed himself.' I remember that he wrote to me, saying 'Hitler is hitting someone his own size now!' On 21 May the Germans had reached Arras and Amiens. On the 28 Witney and the rest of the world learnt that the King of the Belgians had capitulated.

Owing to so many being away and consequently there being a

larger proportion of sick and elderly than heretofore in and around Witney, my brother Patrick was working overtime. He joined the Home Guard and during May 1940 took his first term at regular guard duty (8 p.m. to 1 a.m.). This later included digging trenches at the local aerodrome. Similar extra jobs by countless others, who were already in full-time work, was to continue indefinitely. When Patrick was eventually allowed to join the RAF, much later in the war, life for him was to become a great deal simpler.

The British troops in Belgium and northern France became almost encircled: worse was expected. As for the blanket trade — a telegram from the Ministry of Supply was received in Witney asking us to hasten delivery of a huge order for hospital blankets. The telegram urged an increase in overtime. Father passed on this request at a meeting of those concerned at our Mill. Needless to say, the extra work and consequent delivery of the hospital blankets well before the original delivery date resulted.

Next, father's diary records, 'Some hundreds of British soldiers — and perhaps some French — evacuated from Dunkirk [appeared] sauntering around the Town, enjoying quiet and sunshine. The Red Cross [set to] collecting socks for them'. Mr Welch, Clerk to the Council, whose office adjoined the Church Green, noticed that many of those saunterers were so exhausted that they could do no more than flop down on the Green and go to sleep either inside or outside temporary accommodation there.

In a letter to me father mentioned that one of the returned warriors from Dunkirk was asked wonderingly, '— and did you really see a Jerry?' 'Oh, ah, I seed him alright and Jerry seed I!' was the reply.

A cable came from the firm's Agents in New York saying, 'Our deepest sympathy and prayers are with you during these anxious days, John and Edith Workman'. We replied, 'Deeply value your encouraging message. Early'. Roosevelt and Churchill were exchanging similar communications.

As the war proceeded, father found more occasions when he thought it wise to speak at Witney Mill meetings and, of course, he was in consultation with individuals on the shop floor nearly every day. He was a good speaker with a good voice. Of greater importance, he always spoke with complete sincerity and with humour. More important still, he knew the people with whom he was talking at the Mill — and most other people in Witney as well. A meeting at which he did not get on particularly well was that of an 'Information Committee' in Oxford where he did not feel at home and from which he eventually resigned. However, he did warn our own people in Witney against 'careless talk'.

To understand the help Master Harold was able to give to employees we should look back to his 21st birthday on 23 June 1902. He was by then established in the family firm and Charles Early, his grandfather and the Senior Partner (with the other two Partners) had arranged a day's excursion to Weymouth for all to celebrate. Charles Haley, the oldest employee present with nearly sixty years of service to his credit, made a kind speech and presented young Master Harold with a beautiful mahogany writing cabinet on behalf of all present. In replying Master Harold referred to the feelings of 'good will, comradeship and confidence', which must have prompted the greatly valued gift he had received. He warmly reciprocated these sentiments and made known his own gratitude to the old hands for sharing with him, a newcomer, their knowledge of blanket-making. He regarded all employees, he told them, as 'members of the firm' and as such he would always consider their happiness to be his happiness and their welfare and prosperity his first concern.

These words may appear to some now to be merely conventional and somewhat presumptuous. If any hearing those words in 1902 thought like that they soon found their mistake; for when father said something he meant it and what he said in 1902 he stood by for the rest of his life. He often felt anxious about the responsibilities borne by an employer during the earlier part of the twentieth century. He was apprehensive about the fairness of one man, or even the board of a company, being able drastically to affect the course of other people's lives. Sometimes he himself was responsible for employees' work, homes (some lived in houses belonging to the firm), morals (a good many were in the Boys' Brigade or other church organisations, such as ninety-year-old Charles William Early's Men's Bible Class) and education (most blanket directors were also managers or governors of local schools). I believe that for him, as well as for others closely concerned, one of the worst days was when he had to sack an old friend, whose son was also an employee. The son had been arriving at the Mill each morning at the correct time and stamping both his own card and his father's in the 'clocking in' machine. The father himself would come in later with the records, showing that he had been present from the correct time onwards. Master Harold had absolutely no choice but to dismiss both men. It was a sad duty, which he would not delegate. I doubt whether I have ever known him more distressed than he was after this incident.

When, during the war, I was some distance from Witney and was asked how the blanket trade was going, I seem to remember replying, 'In a way it is more straight-forward than in peace time. Some branch of the Government tells us what raw materials to buy, what we are to make and sell and fixes the prices.' Well, that was most certainly an over-simplification. We used, for example, to run out of wool on occasion and there were government meetings to be attended. However, all essential trade and manufacture was severely controlled and regulated, which did not always lead to less work for management. It did bring about what was intended — enabling mills like ours to produce and sell more. Someone had to make decisions at the highest level and my brother Patrick attended Wool Control Meetings at Ilkley, about the supply of wool, and Joint Industrial Council Meetings, about wages, in the West of England. He was sometimes so tired at these meetings that he would momentarily nod off to sleep! His attendance might well follow a night of sentry duty and trench digging at Witney Aerodrome or a weekend driving an ambulance in London, in addition to his usual working days at the Mill. However, I am sure he was always fully awake when Witney's needs were being considered. At the Mill the Directors had to be ready for drastic action should a shortage of raw material, lack of fuel or indeed an air attack occur.

In war-time as in peace both my father and brother, like others whose professional job concerned the well-being of their friends, were concerned in a number of voluntary self-imposed duties. Father was a Justice of the Peace. He attended an Agricultural Wages Committee and also found himself at this time upon a Good Neighbours Committee designed to relieve distress in those anxious times. Mr Jack Thomas, MBE, and Hon. MA, of the Transport and General Workers Union has told me about this last committee. He expressed the opinion that father was very fair minded, the two men had great respect for each other and often served together.

Father and Patrick were both Governors of Witney Grammar School, indeed father was Chairman of Governors for twenty-nine years. He was also Chairman of a fund to help learning in the town called Witney Educational Foundation. However, none of his out-of-business interests demanded more of his care and attention than the Boys' Brigade. Stanley G. Smith, son of the Founder of the BB, and Brigade Secretary, once told me after the war that he believed that the Brigade owed more to father than to any other living man. Perhaps he forgot himself! Anyway it was the BB Company in Witney which meant most to Skipper Early. Witney Boys grow up into Witney men. He had much to do with the founding of the 1st Witney in 1902 as part of Witney High Street Methodist Church. Boys entered industry then at a much lower age than now. There were then many boys aged twelve and up-wards making blankets in the family firm. Those in the BB knew better than to expect any different treatment at the Mill from the Skipper than any of their mates could expect. Nor did the Skipper allow the BB to interfere in any way with his loyalty to the firm.

Whatever were his other interests, father spent a great deal of time walking round the Mill wearing cloth cap and overall, watching and listening. I didn't understand why at the time, but I do now. Then I thought that 'the boss' should be spending his time better doing sums, writing letters, interviewing prospective customers and working out new inventions. However, other people could have done those other jobs. Only the owners of the firm could do what father was doing.

Back to the Boys' Brigade and the Church! The BB sometimes involved him in journeys to the north of England, a central meeting ground for the Executive Council of the Brigade, which was founded in Glasgow by Sir William Smith in 1883. The Executive on occasion met near York Minster, and father, writing to me, said he enjoyed the view of the magnificent West Front. It stood for something, he wrote, that would long outlive the antics of Hitler.

Father's visits to London often included attendance at meetings of the Worshipful Company of Weavers. Our family had been represented on Livery or Court for generations and he was elected Upper Bailiff for the second time on St James' Day 1940. Hitler failed to hold up the work the weavers had been doing for eight hundred years supporting the craft and trade of weaving in and around the City of London and in aiding charitable endeavours.

Some of father's work for the Weavers Company could be accomplished in Witney as could his work as Editor of the *Boys'*

70

Brigade Gazette and as Captain of the 1st Witney Company. Perhaps he regarded that sort of work as recreation — even when he was finishing BB galley-proofs for press after midnight or when, after BB Bible Class and two church services of a Sunday, he could not help calculating that he had sung seventeen hymns, excluding the National Anthem during the day!

I have dwelt on the doings of my own family: but many other Witney men and women were involving themselves in similar or more specialised ways. One foreman at the Mill, Mr Ernest Taphouse, JP, was Chairman of Witney Urban District Council. He was also Secretary of Witney Mills Housing Society of which Master Harold was the Founder and Chairman: most of the Society's houses were occupied by Mill employees and their families; but Ernest Taphouse and other blanket-makers were engaged in other necessary and worthwhile pursuits beside 'just earning a living' at blankets. Cyril Nunn, that stalwart of the stockhouse, singer and sportsman, tells me that his department was 'just earning a living' by fulling blankets regularly for fourteen hours a day. After that, most likely, the siren would summon them to their 'Post'. As German aircraft seldom strayed over Witney, they would probably find time then to fry-up an evening meal.

In war, the Palace Cinema, Witney, proved even more essential than in peace. There was no television; so it gave relaxation, instruction and news. However busy people were, most found time to relax and keep in touch by frequent visits to the cinema.

By the end of June 1940 Witney, like other towns in the British Isles, was expecting invasion. One responsible member of the forces during a brief visit warned our family that 'a mass attack [was] expected this week — perhaps Wednesday'. Whether this contravened the warning against 'careless talk', I do not know. However, people were encouraged to donate blood in readiness and to do, or say, nothing that would give comfort to the enemy.

Witney was taking no chances. Father wrote to me saying, 'The sight of Witney Mill would make you blink!' I interpreted this as meaning that we were adequately camouflaged. Air-raid shelters had been constructed at strategic points and a particularly solid brick one (as I write it has become changing rooms) appeared on the Cricket Field opposite our house. An RASC Guard was posted there and the household sent him across hot water, for shaving and making drinks, when he wanted. Small forts, 'pill-boxes' and walls

71

were built with slits through which rifles could be aimed and fired by the Home Guard, if necessary. Some of these are still to be seen more than forty years after. They were to resist invading ground troops in our inland town; but to make landing from the air difficult, stakes were driven into most wide open spaces such as golf courses. At least one influential householder arranged a party at which the guests were to come protected by gas masks. I suppose social games if not eating and drinking had to be performed with the gas masks still in position — 'Very good fun!' as one commentator said. Some householders were surprised to find that the army had made holes in the walls of their gardens or business premises for protective reasons.

During late summer there occurred terrible bombing raids on London. Patrick used to come back after weekend ambulance work in the capital amongst destructive fires caused by these attacks round St Paul's Cathedral. Oxfordshire did not entirely escape. A landmine fell at the small village of Swinbrook seven miles away causing considerable damage to property — and making a shattering report. On 16 August Stanton Harcourt and Brize Norton Aerodrome caught it. That was still closer and Witney was very much concerned. Indignant complaints to our North Oxfordshire Member of Parliament were contemplated. Perhaps we thought that a stiff letter should be sent to Hitler!

The country had been told that if and when the German invasion started the Church bells would sound forth the warning. Bristling with 'pill-boxes' and determined in spirit, the town was ready. Then came the anticipated crashing peel from the 152-foot medieval steeple of St Mary's Church, Witney.

This was it — a false alarm!

I am not sure whether it was on this occasion or on another when the Witney authorities were advised that an invasion was imminent. Witney did not believe it and consulted Father as to what to do. 'Well,' said he, 'how about telling the ringers to sound a peel of bells as quietly as possible?'

As the days shortened and the weather deteriorated, the possibility of a German invasion from the sea became more remote: had Hitler tried it, most Englishmen like Mr Churchill thought that it would fail; but there would have been terrible bloodshed on both sides. Father wrote to me in more light-hearted vein,

72

We have been preparing in this country for the reception of a somewhat publicised and over-rated European figurehead. His welcome in the British Isles would have been warm, indeed — one might even say — extremely hot. There has been general disappointment that we have been denied the opportunity of receiving him as he deserves.

Witney folks were, of course, prepared to assist in the effort the whole country was making by voluntary gifts of money. A committee was formed in town to recommend how a sum of money could be raised and used; Mr Ernest Taphouse acted as a very efficient Chairman of this Committee. I still have a photograph of my mother standing among a number of Town Council dignitaries and addressing a meeting in the Market Square about what became known as the 'Spitfire' Fund. This puzzled me as, more recently, it has puzzled my son, who is just old enough to remember my kindly mother in her old age. He could not believe that his gracious grandmother (and she looks most gracious and beautiful in the photograph) would encourage voluntary gifts for a death-dealing Spitfire aeroplane. I have since found out that very likely she did not. My parents at one stage sent a letter to the Chairman of the Committee asking that these voluntary gifts should be used for supporting the Red Cross. Perhaps she made her speech before the Committee decided on the Spitfire!

On the whole, however, the authorities went out of their way to assist organisations which did useful work for the community both during peace and war. Like many other Old Boys of the Boys' Brigade, Ted Winfield of the 1st Witney had joined the British army and, doubtless partly owing to his BB training, almost at once was given a 'stripe' and the responsibility of serving as a Physical Training Instructor. He was stationed near Oxford and given permission to visit Witney and conduct a BB gymnastic class. He started to do this on 2 October 1940. Father's diary for that evening says, 'Ted Winfield took P.T., both Junior and Senior. A first-rate show! I wish Richard could have been here to see it'. Well, Richard was to be 'there to see it' when Mr E. J. F. Winfield, Old Boy instructor of the company and one time army teacher of gymnastics, took charge of 1st Witney Company giving a free-standing display to thousands of other BB members and their lady friends in the Royal Albert Hall, London, on 20 and 21

May 1960. A lot of other things were to happen before that!

My sister Ruth who gave great pleasure and comfort with piano-playing during the war — at home, at Benenden School, at public concerts and eventually in ENSA overseas — brushed up her knowledge of first-aid, and when in Witney during an alarm used to report to the Swan Laundry for duty. The training given her for this service must, like Ted Winfield's extra gymnastic training, have often stood her, her family and friends in good stead since.

Amongst other people who took lessons that concerned home defence in Witney were boys in the Boys' Brigade. A course of six talks was arranged for 1st Witney Company. At the first of these talks forty-one BB members were present and, as the class was open to others, twenty-five other boys were there as well. Although by the end of October 1940 Hitler seemed temporarily to have given up the idea of invasion, he had not finished with Witney. BB activities, as with blanket-making, were frequently interrupted by the siren announcing an alert. On such occasions a decision needed taking as to whether those present should go to the air-raid shelters and places of readiness for duty or not. In the case of blanket-making, at any rate, the tendency was to take a chance and carry on working.

On the evening of 20 October father gave the second lecture in the home defence course to 1st Witney. It was about high explosive bombs. Hitler allowed it to continue uninterrupted to its conclusion; but, as if to illustrate the talk, the Luftwaffe dropped two high-explosive bombs on the town early the following morning. One bomb fell close to the brewery on the west side of Church Green at the south end of Witney. The second bomb fell on the opposite side of the Green in front of a house called St Mary's Close, the home of Mr Fred Marriott, Chairman of Marriott and Sons Limited, blanket-makers. His mill was close at hand and as busy as was Early's.

The two earsplitting explosions resulted in non-fatal wounds to a sentry stationed on the Green and very minor injuries to a few other townsfolk. Considerable damage occurred to windows, ceilings and roofs of buildings surrounding the Green on which were parked some army lorries. The attack came without warning. At the brewery the nearby explosion, as well as breaking windows, scattered glass into a stock of freshly brewed beer, which was then

74

adjudged unfit for human consumption. It was strained as carefully as possible to be used as pigswill, but the pigs refused it.

The shattering detonations brought Mr William R. Dominey from his home at the other end of the town. He was Managing Director of Marriott's and wanted to know what had happened to his Chairman and the mill itself. The mill was all right, but the Chairman was nowhere to be seen. Bill Dominey therefore hurried into St Mary's Close and up to the bedroom where he knew Mr Marriott had been sleeping. He found the Chairman considerably shocked but still calmly lying in bed covered by pieces of plaster from the collapsed ceiling.

It is worth pausing to say more of the two Witney men mentioned in the last few lines. The Marriott family had lived in Witney longer than the Earlys and had been involved in blanket-making and agriculture for at least three hundred years. Fred Marriott had been a farmer all his long working life; but early in the war, when his brother Harry died, he had agreed to become Chairman of the Marriott family blanket firm. He made a point of living close to the factory and was conscientious in visiting the mill daily and often during night shift hours as well. Of course he took the chair at the AGM and at the very occasional board meeting. However, agriculture remained his first love.

Bill Dominey was just old enough to have served in the First World War in the ranks. Before the armistice he had risen to the rank of Quarter Master Sergeant and, owing to his slight boyish appearance, became known as 'The Pocket Quarter Master Sergeant'. He had the potential and training to become a skilled textile manager and during the 1920s had been engaged by the Marriotts to help run Marriott and Sons Limited. Marriott's soon realised that they had recruited a good man. Thus he had deservedly become Managing Director.

However, Bill was a great deal more than a Managing Director. He was an asset to the town in many directions. Apart from blankets he and I got to know each other as Toc H members. His roots in that movement must have extended back to the 1914-18 war. He and I have become good friends over the years and this book will owe much to him. Amidst his many commitments during the Second World War, he found time regularly to write to me giving news of our mutual Witney interests. He once told me that no one had ever walked out on strike from the gates of Mount Mill while he had been in charge. On one occasion some discontents had got as far as those gates; but he hastened after them and persuaded them to return to work.

To the best of my belief the two bombs just referred to were Hitler's last attempt at directly harming the town, although a number of incendiary devices and high explosive bombs continued spasmodically to fall upon the surrounding countryside. There was plenty of other indirect hostility and Witney suffered hardship and heartbreak with the rest of the country and the rest of the world. My mother's sister worked in London as a Civil Servant concerned with education. She was buried alive during one air-raid and, being fortunately rescued, came to Witney, with several broken ribs, to recover. When she went back to work her branch of the Board of Education had been transferred to Bournemouth.

London continued to bear the brunt of what Father termed 'terrible bombing' and he certainly knew about it as he continued to spend odd days in the capital on 'Weavers', blanket and Boys' Brigade business, with the occasional missionary meeting thrown in. Patrick continued his weekend work with the London Ambulance Service, an extremely hazardous occupation in darkened streets with bombs falling. It seems that everyone in Witney was doing at least two people's job and some a great deal more.

The Witney evacuees from London tended to show their appreciation of the quieter life of Oxfordshire by taking little notice of our air-raid alerts. I suppose, if those in London had 'downed tools' every time a siren sounded, not much work would have been done. However, people could die in other ways than by bombs dropped from the sky. A lady came for temporary refuge to our home. During the morning of the following day a telephone call was received by my mother. The official who spoke to her said that the lady visitor's husband had been killed the night before. The bomber he had been piloting had 'crashed on taking off and the bombs exploded'.

Witney was as conscientious over rationing as most other towns in the country. Rationing may have done some people good, providing they were the sort who over-indulged in peace-time, but most civilians felt the pinch. Hitler may have temporarily abandoned the idea of invading Great Britain, but we were even more than previously a country under siege, in that U-Boat attacks by the Germans were intensified — particularly in the Atlantic. So many of our supply ships were sunk that food and other essential commodities were in dangerously short supply. Witney met the challenge in various ways. Witney Mills Housing Society decided to break-up five acres of grass to put in potatoes instead. Turning land over to agriculture became general practice. The strict rationing of food caused people to be especially appreciative of any unexpected extra, which, of course, may well have come through some friend's skill, or unselfishness. One of the Boys' Brigade Officers, Mr Alfred H. Rowley, was by way of being a long-standing universal provider. When it came to a Sunday afternoon set aside for Sergeants' Mess, attended by officers and boys, Father entered in his diary, 'In the circumstances it was a wonderful spread'. On another occasion, when, unusually for him, he remained at the Mill for a meal, he commented on the fact that it was wonderful to be served with butter there. In war-time butter becomes a valuable 'essential fat'.

Miss Dorothy Bolton, the daughter of an Oxfordshire farmer, was Early's Welfare Supervisor and Canteen Manageress. She certainly was not the one to give extra food unfairly to a Managing Director any more than Alfred Rowley would have specially favoured the BB 'Skipper'! It seemed to one distant observer that restrictions in Witney gave rise to a spirit of fairness and generosity in the war. Later on, when I found myself in circumstances and countries where shortages were far greater than at home and the Red Cross came to our rescue, I felt this all the more.

Although in Witney when the warning sirens sounded during business hours people were apt to carry on with their usual occupations, it was different at night. When there was an alert then no chances were taken: able-bodied townsfolk reported to their 'post'. Once at the post, which might be the garage of that public-spirited motor engineer, Tom Smith, just down the road, the volunteers were expected to remain awake ready for action wherever required until 'all clear' sounded — and that was often not before next morning, when the day's work started again. There were also fire-watchers on duty in shifts at the mills and other establishments in the town.

The population of Witney must have become very tired in spite of apparent cheerfulness. There were no official rest periods for people suddenly called to duty. There was often worry about close friends and relatives, who were facing the unknown in other parts of the country or world. However, one gets the impression that there was also a feeling of camaraderie in the town during these anxious times. Nor was the rest of the world allowed to forget Witney's long service to other communities in keeping people warm at night. Years afterwards I heard that, during the period immediately before Christmas 1940, the Government was making an 'export propaganda film' at our Mill.

5 From Moscow to Greece

I joined the Navy to see the World,
And what did I see?
— sung by Fred Astaire

Although we had not volunteered as ambulance drivers in order to see the world, we did travel through a good deal of Europe, with a long stay in Egypt during the half-year following our departure by air from Stockholm on 8 October 1940.

It pleased me — and I hope him — to be able to greet my more politically minded brother with a telegram from Moscow on his birthday, 13 October. In Moscow we appreciated the great kindness of Sir Stafford and Lady Cripps with their two young daughters, Elizabeth and Peggy, who gave us twenty wanderers tea at the British Embassy. Incidentally, it must have been Sir Stafford and his staff who facilitated our journey through Russia. During our two days in Moscow we stayed at the Savoy Hotel and were shown round the city by a charming Intourist lady guide. She knew her Moscow well, but knew very little about the rest of the world. I remember especially seeing the Kremlin and Red Square with Lenin lying in his tomb. Cossack dancers and singers came and entertained in the hotel.

We left Moscow by rail drawn by a huge 2-8-4 steam locomotive heading south towards the Black Sea. After a fabulous, but by no means luxurious, journey through Russia, from Moscow gloom to Mediterranean warmth, we arrived at Odessa. There we visited the opera in company with what seemed to be a considerable portion of the Russian navy. The only man we saw in evening dress was the conductor. Needless to say, it was a wonderful show.

We continued our journey by sea to Istanbul, where we saw the Mosque of St Sophia, the Blue Mosque and many other wonderful

79

buildings: We also drank real Turkish coffee and for the first time I saw a display of bellydancing.

We crossed the Bosphorus by motor launch, then took train again to Aleppo, via Ankara, and passed through Syria among the bananas, sugar cane and oranges to Palestine and Haifa. The last part of this section of the journey was accomplished in motor cars. At Haifa we found ourselves at an establishment called the Carmelheim Mission, which was about to be modified to meet wartime needs and become a rest home and hospital.

We arrived on Saturday and the next day, Sunday 20 October, a fellow member of the unit, Kenneth King, who was always game for a good walk, and I set out in the morning for 'the place of burning' (El Mahraka) near the summit of Mount Carmel. It was indeed a good walk to 1,810 feet above the sea and twelve miles from Carmelheim. The story of Elijah and the priests of Baal — the dirty dogs! — has lived for me ever since. I could almost feel sorry for the wretched four-hundred-and-fifty priests and their hangers-on, dragged down that desolate height to be slaughtered at Brook Kishon. After our return down the mountain we took part in a Quaker Meeting. I cannot remember whether we said anything about Elijah's fearsome victory to the Quakers. However, our leader, Oswald Dick, reminded us that we should be grateful to the members of our unit still at home, who had striven so hard and successfully to see that we, the spearhead, were on our way to further useful and interesting work after this tremendous journey. Perhaps what Ken and I remember best about that journey was a sight we had of a small village thirteen miles away to the east, as we gazed from Carmel's height. It was the village of Nazareth.

On Monday morning it was train again to Kantara on the Suez Canal. Having passed over the waterway we continued by train to Cairo. The next day there was an air-raid alarm, so we knew we were back in a war-zone. While in Cairo we visited the Pyramids, the Mohammed Ali Mosque, the prison where Pharoah's wife had incarcerated Joseph and — incidentally as it seemed — were given instructions as to how we were to spend the rest of our time in Egypt.

After some hesitation by army and Red Cross authorities, we were told, I should think on the initiative of Oswald Dick, to report as ambulance drivers in Alexandria. Before we left Cairo he was interviewed by Richard Dimbleby about our journey and prospects. His excellent description of our doings was broadcast and heard in Witney as well as in Egypt.

At Alexandria we were stationed with ambulance cars close at hand in an army camp next to 8th General Hospital. During regular duty periods we needed to be on call to take out our vehicles and carry the wounded and incapacitated, and occasional member of the medical staff in a hurry. We slept and kept our few earthly possessions in a wooden-floored marquee, which a Staff Sergeant had helped us to erect. Near at hand were two bell tents used by Oswald Dick and his officers for administrative purposes.

The weather in Egypt being in general much warmer than the Scandinavian climate, we invested in new, lighter and smarter khaki uniforms. The soldiers in the rest of the camp must have been somewhat perplexed about our status. It may have been the new uniforms that prompted a friendly Australian soldier to stop as he passed our tent and say to me, 'Well, buddy, you fellows seem to be a fairly well trained lot! Where were you educated?' I couldn't help replying innocently, 'Oxford University'.

Whatever anyone thought about our origins, we had pushed ourselves into an essential and important job demanding care and sympathy. Neither we, not those in charge at the hospital, knew when we started a term of duty exactly what would be required of us. Sometimes we would have nothing to do except keep our ambulances in order. That was a very important and quite essential part of our work. There were some competent mechanics in our contingent and they made sure the rest of us knew how to look after the vehicle for which we were responsible. I shared responsibility with a fellow 'Old Boy' of Leighton Park School, Ralph Smith, for an ambulance we named 'Mrs H'. It must have had the lady's name and address painted on it, as I remember writing a letter of thanks to the donor for the wonderful gift of an ambulance to the Red Cross. One or two other people ought to have been thanked also. Oswald Dick had already drawn our attention to the work of our unit at home. Quakers and other generous people, including the blanket-makers of Witney, were also involved. Anyway sometimes a man's life depended upon 'Mrs H' being completely equipped and ready to go.

It was rare for us to be ordered out into the desert. More often it was a case of meeting a hospital ship — or some other kind of ship — that had got into trouble; terrible burns could occur during a naval battle. It was our task to get the sufferers from the ship to the '8th General', or to some other hospital, as comfortably and quickly as possible. Occassionally longer journeys were necessary to Cairo or Suez and we were sometimes asked to carry patients from local hospitals to Alexandria's main railway station for travel to quieter convalescence centres. I have in mind that Jerusalem was a possible haven for the wounded and war-torn.

As time went on demand for our services increased, because of Allied victories over the Italians in the desert and an offensive in Abyssinia. Sometimes we carried wounded Italian prisoners; sometimes fit prisoners helped us to load our ambulances at the port. It was fortunately only occasionally that we needed to take a patient who had been put into our ambulance straight back onto the hospital ship, where doctors, oxygen and almost every kind of hospital equipment were available (without this patients might have died on the car journey to hospital in Alexandria). Sometimes we were too late in taking this action and we then wondered whether we could have done more to save a life or give more comfort.

Although we had to be prepared to take out an ambulance at any one of the twenty-four hours on the clock face, we did find time for certain other occupations according to our various tastes and skills. My particular side line was teaching gymnastics to other members of the unit when asked to do so by Oswald Dick, who was rightly anxious that his men should be in good condition as a precaution against our needing to face more severe tests. My own weight rose to 76.6 kg (or nearly 12 stone).

In Alexandria there were plenty of opportunities for games with so many young men and women mobilised for something quite different. We played hockey, tennis, soccer and rugger, according to what we thought we were good at, in our free time. The more permanent European population was kind and welcoming to us temporary visitors. We were particularly welcomed by the Swedish family of Yberg to whom I had an introduction from Sweden. Mr Yberg had built up and maintained a very well-run match factory in Egypt.

We were also welcomed most kindly by Miss D. Jamieson Williams, the headmistress of the Scottish Girls School in Alexandria, and her music mistress, Miss Gwenyth Leggo. Miss Williams was the youngest headmistress I had ever met and, among her many duties and responsibilities, she found time to show us exiles from home round the neighbourhood, arrange bathing excursions for us and invite us to social functions at the school and at the Scottish Church nearby. Miss Leggo found out that Harold Cadoux, a Congregationalist from Oxford, and I were musically inclined. She, of course, was an accomplished musician and pleased us very much by inviting us to perform before fortunately uncritical audiences at the Church.

I am sure that none of our FAU party, who found ourselves in Alexandria, will forget the friendship afforded by Madame Hadad at Daily's Hotel. She allowed us to come and relax at her comfortable establishment when our somewhat austere camp life threatened to get on top of us. Even the good fellowship of the Sergeants' Mess did not equal the comfort of Daily's! It was Madame Hadad combined with Witney who gave us a Christmas dinner. Both were gracefully thanked by Michael Mounsey, the best linguist in our party and an excellent officer. Madame Hadad taught us French and arranged social evenings for us — her generosity went on to the end. We knew that the end of our stay in Egypt was imminent and on 20 March 1941 were told that the next day we would leave for Greece with eleven ambulances.

For some time Oswald Dick had been pressing the authorities to transfer our contingent to more hazardous work in Greece.

Historians will remember that towards the end of 1940 Mussolini had sought to help himself and justify Italy as a partner among Axis powers by attacking Albania. His troops were bitterly opposed, not only by Albanians, but by Yugoslavians, who were not loth to defend their independence against attack from these associates of Hitler. Then Mussolini had told Hitler that on 26 October 1940 he was going to start the conquest of Greece. Hitler was not impressed with the idea, perhaps because he realised that his colleague in war was no great military commander. At any rate the Greeks more than held their own against the Italian invaders. Doubtless partly because of this Hitler used the might of the German military machine to attack Greece from the north.

Britain was not favourably placed to help Greece, but King George VI promised the King of the Hellenes that our country would, as previously promised, render every possible support. Our country stood by that pledge and eventually, after years of terrible fighting and occupation, the invaders were to be forced to leave.

However, in March 1941 the prospect was bleak. As far as fighting was concerned, leaders of the Greek army had largely been schooled by the Germans, who now turned their expertise and overwhelming man and machine power against their former pupils. The FAU did not know all this, but I like to think that had we known we would still have gone to help.

By 15.10 hours on 21 March our party of just over twenty members, with ten ambulances and one utility van, were on board the troop ship, 8,000-ton *Damana*, getting to know how to make ourselves comfortable in hammocks. In my case, I discovered more than one friend among the RAF who, in addition to other troops, were our fellow passengers. One of these friends was a past member of 22nd London Boys' Brigade Company and another a member of the famous Methodist Boys' Club named Clubland. He volunteered that 'If there were a few more people like the Founder and Head of Clubland, Reverend James Butterworth, the world would not be in a state of war'.

Our ship then anchored alongside the aircraft carrier HMS *Eagle*. The band of the *Eagle* played, marched and counter-marched on her flight deck to give us a good send off! The following morning we found ourselves out in the Mediterranean. Our convoy was made up of eight cargo or troopships guarded by three destroyers and, on and off, by a cruiser and Sunderland Flying Boats. Precautions, in case of enemy action, included daily boat drill and the setting of a regularly relieved watch at strategic positions on the vessel.

It was rough enough at first to prevent about two-thirds of us service passengers enjoying to the full the three excellent daily meals supplied during our ten days afloat. The good-natured Quartermaster Sergeant was inclined to let the FAU off washing-up, seeing that we were 'unpaid volunteers'; but, of course, we helped. We also took our turn at 'look-out'. I was stationed with a Lascar seaman on the open deck at the extreme bow of the *Damana* at 16.30 hours and told to stay there until 19.00 hours. We had not long to wait before three planes appeared directly forward. I looked back at the Captain standing calmly on the bridge. There was no need to give an alarm! An earsplitting and blinding turmoil burst forth. I can particularly remember our view of the cruiser letting go all she'd got. However, I am sure the destroyers were doing their share. The troops on our own vessel also gave a good account of themselves with the available firearms — a four-inch cannon in the stern and two machine guns.

Three planes were involved in the first attack and we saw one of them, an Italian, coming towards us at about 500 feet. It dropped a torpedo, which narrowly missed one of the ships in the convoy. The second attack was made by three Heinkels: this time they approached us again head-on but dropping bombs from approximately 6,000 feet. One bomb exploded in the sea thirty yards to port of our perch; the following bomb from the same plane fell astern. The machine gunners thought they had damaged one aircraft. Before the end of our watch we saw the snowclad summit of mountains on Crete to starboard as the sun went down into the sea like a ball of fire at 18.05 hours.

We spent nearly six days sheltering in Suda Bay on the north coast of Crete, while nearby an important naval battle took place. The grapevine had it that the Italian fleet had ventured out and lost two cruisers and two heavy destroyers. An Italian battleship was also badly damaged before getting back into port. The British had lost two aircraft.

Not that life in Suda Bay was dull. There were frequent air-raid alarms; but after dark we were allowed ashore while not keeping watch. Then at 5.45 a.m. on Friday 28 March, six deafening detonations roused us from our hammocks. On deck we had visual evidence of what had happened. Two of our ships were out of action and liable to stay so for a long time.

During darkness an enemy warship had come as close as practicable to the entrance of Suda Bay. Six of the Italian crew had continued silently on into the bay in a small boat towing six torpedoes, which they released at almost point-blank range towards the two nearest vessels. Four of the torpedoes exploded aground. The fifth badly damaged a Norwegian tanker and the sixth had holed a cruiser, HMS *York*, which now lay with her stern obviously crushed on to the bottom of the bay. The six Italians gave themselves up after their exploit and in due course were brought on to the *Damana* as prisoners of war. There was a curious silence — almost of respect — as the six Italians were taken below. They had carried out their mission with considerable courage, and great skill. As far as we knew the only serious casualties were the two ships.

It must have been just about at this juncture that I was doing my daily dozen at a deserted spot on board, when an obviously senior Ship's Officer came on the scene and, looking at my uniform, abruptly, but courteously enough, pointed out that 'other ranks', were only permitted on the lower deck. Following this reprimand I believe I went off to take a spell at washing-up. Since I had already volunteered at least once for this duty it was no hardship. George Greenwood and I also volunteered for two extra hours of 'watch' (one of us at the bow and the other at the stern) from 22.00 hours to 24.00 hours to allow the two regular guards to take shore leave.

There was on the *Damana* an extremely efficient member of YMCA (Services), named Glaister. Since our sojourn on board seemed longer than expected he organised two concerts on the pattern of 'Gang Shows'. Four airmen, who had, I believe, taken part in one of Ralph Reader's scout shows in less interesting circumstances, bore the brunt of the entertainment. However some others, like myself, could not keep away. My sea shanties must have sounded quite classical compared with the remainder of the programme! I have a note in my diary, also, that Maurice Davis, Denis Applefort, Leslie Bloomfield (from the RAOC) and myself put on a tumbling and gymnastic item. Balancing became progressively more difficult towards the end of the show, because by then the *Damana* was once again under way. At 06.30 hours on the last day of March we were among the Greek islands and an hour later we drew into Piraeus.

Whilst unloading our cars, we noticed a number of British cruisers and destroyers in the port, while Greek and British troops mingled on the quay. We drove the thirteen kilometres to Athens where we were temporarily accommodated in a first aid post. We were obviously very welcome to the nurses and other Greeks. In this part of the world and, indeed, in all Greece, one was never quite sure on which side people were; however the British seemed to be trusted. The English King had said that he and his subjects would do all possible to help Greece and here we were to do it.

Apparently we had the choice of driving north west to the Albanian front, where there would be work at once, or going almost due north where there was, so far, little action but a German advance expected. We started off with Albania in mind. However, we were scarcely on our way when a tremendous on-slaught was unleashed by the Germans in Macedonia.

By the time we reached Larisa, a town still suffering from the effects of a recent earthquake and now being bombed, it was clear that we could be of more use due north; so, directed by Oswald Dick, we headed towards the advancing Germans.

It must not be thought that, amongst a good deal of turmoil the wonders of Greece went entirely unnoticed. I had found time in Athens to walk up to the Acropolis and to stand and wonder at the view of hills and islands from the south west angle of the Temple of Athena. I tried to convey the spirit of these overwhelming surroundings in a letter to my mother, who was a Greek scholar. As we drove north after leaving Larisa, we passed near to Mount Olympus, which, like the ancient Greeks, I could well believe was 'the home of the Gods'.

Brian Darbyshire and Kenneth King were our cooks and, wherever we were, they came up with something to eat at the right time. How we blessed them! When we needed to sleep — and had time to do so — we left our ambulances and took shelter well away from the road. When it rained — and in April Greece seemed as prone to showers as England — we got back to our vehicles and there risked being bombed or machine gunned. On the northward journey, sometimes along mountain tracks, we were frequently met by lorries and such like vehicles coming in the opposite direction. Smaller cars were sometimes to be seem, overturned, lying where they had run off the narrow road; but the army lorries, we understood, were for the most part driven by those used to London traffic. Bus drivers were magnificent in this situation both in the way they controlled their own vehicles and the consideration they displayed towards ambulances moving in the opposite direction. We found ourselves operating with Australian troops.

Mostly our job was to collect wounded from dressing stations and hospitals and take them somewhere temporarily safer further south. There were a great many casualties — some serious. Harold Cadoux and I were together in charge of an ambulance. I have a note that he was an especially good companion. In Athens we had made sure that we had a copious reserve of petrol; but, apart from keeping tank and oil-sump full there was a good deal needed doing to our cars in these rough and hazardous conditions. There were many distractions when a wheel had to be changed or a puncture mended. These distractions included the necessity of caring for our patients. Sometimes on our return journeys from our rapidly retreating 'front' the ambulance was so crowded that either Harold, or I, whoever was convoying rather than driving, needed to travel clinging to the outside of the coachwork.

Once, when Harold and I were sent to a hospital, we found it had already been evacuated. More often than not, when we got patients back to what we thought was a base hospital, that hospital would prove to be on the point of moving further south and we were requested to carry the patients on to another location. This job gave rise to greater anxiety for the FAU than had any previous experience during the war and I could not but admire Oswald Dick, who wore himself out seeking instructions, which when obtained were continually countermanded. He passed on news and advice to individual ambulances usually with some encouraging remark and sometimes through a seventeen-year-old Greek boy who helped with his local knowledge travelling in the same car as our CO. I admired that lad, too; he kept at the demanding and dangerous job until, exhausted, he could do no more.

As we worked bombs fell intermittently and machine guns spluttered from aircraft. I believe the RAF was outnumbered about ten to one by the Luftwaffe. I recall on one occasion that a vast cloud of German aeroplanes appeared in the sky. Before we had time to take evasive action two lone British aircraft roared into the sky over our heads from a nearby temporary air strip, in defence of Greece and ourselves. I remember thinking, 'there are some brave men in those two planes!'

Later enemy aircraft appeared and we left the ambulance. I found myself in a place rather closer than I would have freely chosen to a small aerodrome, as the Luftwaffe swept down. There was no time for any of the Greek airmen to reach their machines and get them aloft as the German airmen gunned the planes on the ground. There were explosions and metal seemed to be flying in every direction. I remember one piece passing me with a shriek or a bang (I can't remember which). I have often thought since, 'If that jagged bit of hardware had come six inches further to the left, I would never have heard it!'

I don't know why it was that when I plunged for cover, at least once I found myself on the top of a hill: anyway there I was watching huge holes, each with a circle of piled up earth encircling it, appearing silently and at intervals along the side of our road. Then I realised that the apparent silence when the eruptions took place was because sound travels more slowly than sight. The mind

1 Friends Ambulance Unit Training at Manor Farm, Birmingham, October 1939. R. E. E. is seated, in a blazer. Note Alan Dickinson, on the stretcher, in a Witney Point Blanket.

II Training at Manor Farm (a) the morning wash

II (b) stretcher drill

III (a) Gymnastics. R. E. E. is the instructor: his right arm is all that is visible.

III (b) Messing

IV Finland, (a) The Finnish party, early 1940

IV (b) The 'Garage'

IV (c) Mr Blom and Mr Linstedt, our Finnish Army interpreters

V (a) Vanrike Suomen, our interpreter, and R. E. E., 21 April 1940

V (b) The convoy of ambulances on the way to Norway

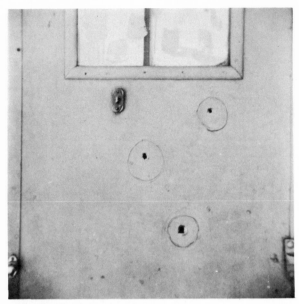

VI (a) Bullet holes in an ambulance

VI (b) The pass between Gädede and Godyard, 1 May 1940

VII (a) R. E. E. as a hospital patient in blues, in Alexandria

VII (b) Early morning PT in Alexandria

VIII R. E. E. photographed by Julius Kienzler (a
guard in Stalag VB) playing soccer: reproduced
from the *Gloucester Citizen* 6 March 1943

soon began to connect sound and sight as the stick of bombs came closer.

I also have an even more vivid memory of clinging to the ground in a still more exposed situation, as an aeroplane circled low spraying us with machine gun bullets. I have never lain flatter in my life and still cannot understand how those fellows up above managed to miss us. Perhaps they were as frightened as we were! In case of attack, I believe Oswald Dick's instructions to us were to get away from our vehicles, which were substantial targets, as quickly as possible with any patients we could move at once. We would be no good to anyone if blown up in our ambulance. Sadly enough that was a possibility: a driver in a vehicle just behind us — not an ambulance — was blown to pieces where he sat. That left just a bewildered feeling. One moment a man was laughing and chatting about the possibility of getting leave to England; the next he was not there.

Losses and sudden death were not confined to one side. I quote my diary of 21 April,

> Saw two German aircraft come down. One made a good forced landing. The other headed at low altitude — and evidently crippled — towards the German lines and, just before reaching them, suddenly turned sideways bursting into flames on striking the ground. Some of our chaps gave a hollow kind of cheer; but I think in our hearts we would all have liked to see those in that plane make a safe landing.

I do not know the ultimate reason for this obviously fatal crash. Maybe the damaged fabric had failed to hold together long enough to get the airmen 'home'. There was another theory that the escaping plane had happened to pass low over a hidden British battery. One fortunate, or well-aimed, burst of gun fire may have ended matters.

It must have been from the same, or from a similar, hidden battery that I was asked to pick up a lying case the following day. When I presented myself at this post, I was detained and questioned by the commanding Officer, who was puzzled by my unusual uniform and civilian 'papers'. In the end I persuaded him to follow me out to our ambulance, which good old Harold had more or less successfully concealed in the neighbourhood, and the captain became persuaded that we were genuine. All the same there had been some queer moments for me. The captain had been quite right to be careful. Apparently a few days earlier six Germans on motor cycles had been apprehended behind the British lines dressed in Australian uniform.

At this juncture we 'other ranks' began to realise what the higher command must have known immediately the Germans had commenced their attack from the north, that the Allied troops, vastly outnumbered and assisted by an only half-hearted Greek army, could not possibly hold back the huge efficient German fighting machine. We continued working harder than we had ever worked in our lives before and driving, mostly at night without any lights, often carrying far more than the regulation number of patients. I have a note in my diary that, on one journey, Harold and I had in, and on, our vehicle seventeen men, instead of the four lying cases it was designed to accommodate. The desperate condition of some of the patients and inadequacy of the roads and tracks to be traversed confirmed my belief that this was the most difficult job so far undertaken by members of the unit.

At first we had hoped we were conveying wounded to comparatively safe and permanent hospitals well away from the front line; but now we realised that there was no front line and that Greece was being over-run. Safety could only be expected by once again taking to the sea. Our job now was to get as many wounded as possible to some southern port with a view to our navy taking off them and ourselves.

Oswald Dick divided our party into two sections with about the same number of ambulances in each. One section was to get to the south coast as quickly as possible. Almost certainly both the drivers and wounded involved in that section would get away by sea before the whole country was occupied. Exactly how our Quartermaster, Ronald Joynes, led this section to safety I do not know. We did not meet again until after the war. His own and his section's journey to freedom was not without accident. He has told me that he waded ashore at Crete holding the diary from which I have been quoting (and which I had entrusted to him) above his head to keep it from salt water. We all owed a great deal to Ronald.

The rest of us in the other section, led by Oswald Dick himself, supported by Michael Mounsey and Duncan Catterall, were to go back towards the advancing Germans to pick up more wounded and after that try to reach the small Port of Kalamai in a bay on the south coast of Messena before the Germans did the same. We would almost certainly fail and almost certainly be captured. Oswald, being Commandant, was the only FAU member who could choose with which of the two sections he would go, whether to take charge of the escaping drivers or be taken prisoner with the rest of us. I am sorry that he is not still alive to read of my gratitude and admiration that he chose the latter course; but I fancy he knows.

In the case of Harold and myself, after our final northward ambulance journey, we got back to a hospital in Athens with twelve patients at 5.30 a.m. on 24 April. We spent the earlier part of that day in getting ourselves and the ambulance in order for a further last effort to escape with our patients. We were joined by three other ambulances and Oswald Dick in a staff car: then we were off in the early evening. We drove south west via Corinth to Argos, where we arrived at sunrise on 25 April. There we took cover from German air attack in quarries and ravines until night-fall. Then we continued our journey to the small southern harbour town of Kalamai, where we took cover again.

When it became reasonably dark naval vessels became apparent in the harbour and we joined a column of men in threes waiting our turn to leave. I calculated that there must have been about six hundred in front of us by the time the ships were fully laden and had to draw away. In an orderly manner and under military discipline we marched out along a road from the town, two files along one side of the fairways and one file along the opposite side, so that we should be out of sight from up above. It was one occasion since we left England that the FAU was reaping direct benefit from the 'drill' we had learnt at Northfield. I also believe that often we had enjoyed indirect benefit.

After we were clear of the town there was an air-raid and we were ordered to scatter. I found myself in an olive grove in company with a Lieutenant Stokes, whose wife was at the time living at Burford seven miles from Witney. I was able to bind-up his foot which was injured and we exchanged news of Oxfordshire and home. At 16.00 hours, we set off marching for the port again and at 18.00 in the middle of a village there was a determined bomb and machine gun attack from the air. I took cover in a ditch too near the road — a house being blown up within twenty yards. I stayed to help with casualties and eventually came on with them in

Bill Miall's and George Greenwood's ambulance, which had started from Athens after us and was evacuating a few patients. We dropped the worst damaged of these new cases at a hospital set up in Kalamai Town Hall, and brought the rest on to the docks, where we met the rest of the FAU party. No ships were able to call for us, the German land forces being too close. FAU and RAMC personnel returned to the temporary hospital, where there was plenty to do, and awaited capture. So ended 27 April 1941 — an eventful Sunday.

We found the Town Hall and an adjoining room filled with more than a hundred wounded — some were dying and the rest too seriously injured to be moved. We worked until Monday evening making the patients more comfortable and tidying up the surroundings under the supervision of a fierce New Zealand doctor, Major Thompson, who most certainly knew his job. There were in addition to ourselves one or two Greek lady nurses; but nursing facilities were negligible. For this reason we must have been asked to attempt treatments that would never have been countenanced in most other circumstances.

I remember one poor fellow with a ghastly suppurating open wound extending over half his back. It must have been the Major who told me to use my bare hands to squeeze out pus from his body. I did this at regular intervals (it seemed to me that pints of thick yellowish fluid exuded from the lacerated and inflamed tissues) — and the patient recovered: I heard from him after the war. I had just been carrying out doctor's instructions, but the experience left me with the feeling that, having already learnt about the workings of the human body through instruction in gymnastics, I could, if required, work as a masseur.

Harold Cadoux and I stopped work at 17.30 hours, as we were to rest before starting night duty. However, our repose did not last long: at 20.00 hours machine gun fire started outside (we learned afterwards that a New Zealander earned a Victoria Cross at this juncture by holding up the advancing Germans). Forty-two years later I have received gracious permission from the Imperial War Museum, London, to quote from the Official History of New Zealand in the Second World War 1939-45 as follows:

7930 Sergeant John Daniel Hinton
On the night of 28/29 April 1941 during fighting in Greece, a

column of German Armoured Forces entered Kalamai. This column which contained several armoured cars, 2 inch guns and 3 inch mortars and two 6 inch guns rapidly converged on a large force of British and New Zealand troops awaiting embarkation on the beach. When the order to retreat to cover was given Sergeant Hinton shouted. 'To hell with this, who will come with me?', and ran to within several hundred yards of the nearest guns. The guns fired missing him, and he hurled two grenades which completely wiped out the guns. He then came on with his bayonet, followed by a crowd of New Zealanders. German troops abandoned the first 6 inch gun and retreated to two nearby houses. Sergeant Hinton smashed the window and then the door of the first house, and dealt with the garrison with his bayonet. He repeated the performance in the second house, and as a result, until overwhelming German forces arrived, New Zealanders held the guns. Sergeant Hinton then fell with a bullet wound through his lower abdomen and was taken prisoner.

A footnote adds:

Hinton was in Stalag IXC, Badsulya, when the news of his VC came through. All prisoners in the camp were paraded and the announcement was formally made by the German Kommandant.

When comparative calm ensued a German Officer looked in to our, what had now become, prisoner of war hospital to take particulars. Our linguist, Michael Mounsey, enquired in German whether he could help; but the German soldier replied, in English, 'All right, boys, I was born in Putney', and told us to carry on with what we were doing. I should think that Harold and I went back to sleep until 22.15 hours, when our night duty started. During the night hours, one Greek sister was assisted by five of us medical orderlies in looking after about a hundred and twenty badly wounded men.

We were at Kalamai for just over a fortnight. Some of our patients died and others became well enough to be treated as fit prisoners and discharged to normal prisoner of war camps. I will mention one incident that occurred during the fortnight at Kalamai, which has remained both in my diary and my memory ever since. A German jeep brought a couple of our wounded — recently captured and in a poor state — to the Town Hall. We carried them into our hospital: then another inmate, a British lying patient and member of the RASC, noticed that the German driver of the jeep was having difficulty in restarting his vehicle to drive away. This patient managed to stand up arrayed in his under-clothes, or whatever else was serving him as pyjamas at the time, and flapped his way out into the street to help the German get the jeep going again.

I have a further note in my diary, written at the time, about the front line troops who had conquered Greece and captured us. I wrote, 'The Germans I have seen have gone out of their way to be courteous and friendly. Two officers brought us several bottles of beer and some cigarettes to hospital'.

I remember being told later by, I suppose, another German 'Front-liner', who had been involved in over-running several other neutral countries before Greece, 'When we go to a new country, we do our best to be friendly and helpful; but nobody likes us!' I did not know whether to regard the remark as pathetic or as a joke.

At any rate, as far as I was concerned the behaviour of our conquerors and guards at this stage was exemplary. German officers expected to be saluted, when we met them outside the hospital, and I was punctilious in obliging them. In fact, I believe I somewhat overdid this and seem to remember on one or two occasions performing the smartest and most correctly executed of military salutes to a number of beautifully uniformed Greek post-men and fire-fighters! The Greek population at this time and later, when we were confined in their country under less desirable condi-tions, was always as kind and generous as allowed.

When not on duty we medical staff could walk in the town. I once went for a hair-cut, sitting in one high chair next to a German soldier in another one. As I left the shop he and his corporal companion gave a good-natured salute, which gesture, needless to say, was returned in my best non-military manner. Later, after I had been out to buy some fruit and was returning to the clinic, I escorted a German officer, who was seeking a New Zealander, Captain K., and was on his way to our hospital. The German said, 'I am a friend of his. The other night I took him prisoner: then he took me prisoner: then I took him prisoner.' I found out, however, that Captain K. had recovered from a slight wound and left for a prison camp. I wish the two could have met, and, perhaps changed custodianship still another time!

During the days at Kalamai we became a small self-contained community. Cooking for the whole hospital was in the capable hands of Brian Darbyshire and Ken King. Of course we washed our own bed linen and bandages. I have a note that I massaged an Old Boy of 7th Jersey Company, the Boys' Brigade, which must have made both of us feel more at home. Once the Germans took some of us staff in a lorry for a swim in the Mediterranean. The same evening we took coffee sitting at the table of a café on the pavement and a Greek boy insisted on cleaning my boots for nothing while a German military band played tasteful music. The music surely must have pleased the Greeks as well as ourselves in spite of our prejudices!

Work in the hospital was still grim and arduous; but it decreased and on 12 May we were ordered to leave the next day taking with us not more than 10 kilograms of luggage each. We marched in threes to the railway station. The Greeks were generous with cigarettes and food on the platform and bade us a smiling farewell.

Twenty-eight English, Australian and New Zealand doctors and other medical personnel were transported by train from Kalamai. Our progress to Corinth must have appeared picturesque. Greeks rode with their baggage on the roof of our carriage drawn by a puffing 2-6-0 locomotive (driving wheels 18″ diameter) through lovely sunlit country peopled by strong country folk. We left Kalamai station at 07.30 hours and marched from the train into the prison camp at Corinth about eight hours later.

It was a real prison camp this time — thousands of us surrounded by barbed wire patrolled by armed German soldiers. There was not enough cover to house us all and we dug pits in which to sleep which was all right until it rained. We dug our own latrines and queued for meals. With care we could keep clean enough to avoid lice and fleas. For the first time since capture we could each send a letter home. I wrote my letter on an opened-up cigarette box, which in due course arrived in Witney. There was just enough mediocre food including what we supposed was horse. The water was really not fit to drink, although we boiled it and prepared other food over open fires. In spite of these disadvantages, when we could bring ourselves to think fairly, we realised that the Germans had taken at least ten thousand more prisoners than they had anticipated in Greece and more came in from Crete. They just could not deal adequately with so many of us near, and in, a battle area. My own belief is that the two successive German Camp Commandants at Corinth tried their best to make conditions tolerable. However, when Oswald Dick enquired about the possibility of civilian medical workers being repatriated he was merely fed with unwelcome propaganda and told that Germany was winning the war — a view which local evidence supported.

There was a hospital building but not enough patients to yield full-time medical work. All the same most of us prisoners found some useful employment and entertainment. I tried to keep fit by walking bare-foot (to save shoe leather) a good many miles round the camp. However, I would warn anyone else who ever finds himself in similar conditions that demanding exercise can be over-done. It would have been better to conserve energy. Most people had with them at least one book each to read and we passed these round. I read *Don Quixote* and the pocket Bible given me by my mother before we left for Finland. Parts of the Bible came to life when we were at Corinth and later at Thessalonica.

Several chaplains were imprisoned with the rest and about a thousand of us attended open air service on Sundays. We formed a choir of about forty enthusiasts and rendered such anthems as 'Guide me, O Thou great Jehovah' to Cwm Rhondda and 'The Lord's my Shepherd' to Crimond. As a choir we drew upon ourselves a bit of trouble, when we started practising another anthem — 'God save the King'. I can well remember the turmoil of flying rifle butts and German expletives as our custodians sprang down into the hole in the ground where our rehearsal was taking place! Apparently, according to the notes I made at the time, this interruption to our music-making did not discourage ten of us from taking German language lessons from a kindly Palestinian prisoner named Hans Gotier.

There were doubtful headshakes from some of my friends when I joined a party of volunteers to undertake civilian work in Corinth. I was advised to be careful not to involve myself in moving ammunition to be used in German guns. Anyway I wanted to see more of the town of Corinth, so took a chance. In fact we were set to help to clear out a school so that it could be used for German billets. It was not hard work and the job was soon done. Whereupon we were told by the German soldiers in charge of us to take it easy on the roof of the school, basking in the pleasant sunshine. We were rewarded for our efforts with various items of food supplied, I suppose, by the Greeks.

The German Commandant also arranged a prisoners' voluntary bathing parade, for three hundred prisoners, in the Mediterranean. We marched in threes to the shore, under the direct orders of our own officers; but also very much under the overall control of German guards with bayonets on their rifles.

Among several thousand young men of military age there were a considerable number of fine athletes. We watched or took part in some excellent international football. At the request of a British Sergeant Major I took one or two free-standing physical training classes. Some good hearty concerts took place and very likely some of the participants achieved fame after the war.

By no means every prisoner all the time accepted what one might call the foregoing 'privileges' and 'concessions' with joy and gratitude towards the Germans. For all of us, accustomed to freedom as we were, it was an uncomfortable, miserable and anxious confinement. We did not get genuine news from outside and our families did not get to know whether we were alive or dead. At times many of us were far from well. Consequently there arose a good deal of bad temper, complaining and insubordination. In charge of us was a Brigadier Parrington, who, I supposed, like Oswald Dick, could have got away with the navy but he had preferred to remain with his troops to be imprisoned with us. He put a notice on a board for other prisoners to read. I happened to be close to the board when this notice appeared. On request, I should think, I read it aloud to the hundreds who immediately gathered round but who were mostly too far away to read it for themselves.

These were the salient points set out in the British Brigadier's notice.

We, who are prisoners, have nothing to be ashamed of: we have been outnumbered and outfought by superior German forces. Some became prisoners only after being involved in a courageous rearguard action, which has allowed many others to get away.

The Germans guarding us seem, as far as possible, to be observing the Red Cross Geneva Convention. There is no call to

97

make matters worse by insubordination.

Some day the War will end and it will then be our task to win the Peace.

We remained at Corinth for nearly a month. Then news came that we were to go north. Most of us welcomed the prospect of a change. Any move, we thought, must be to less primitive quarters. How wrong we were!

The journey with which we were confronted would have been easy in normal times. Circumstances now made it extremely tough. We marched from camp soon after 02.00 hours on Saturday 7 June 1941. FAU members brought up the rear of the last of four contingents each consisting of about eight hundred men, so that we could help any whose physical condition bordered on collapse. We marched seven-and-a-half miles to one of the few parts of the railway system not wrecked by recent military action and took to cattle trucks. Our particular cattle trucks were designed to transport thirty-four men each, when not carrying cattle. During one part of our journey there were fifty-two of us and our kit crammed into one such wagon.

My diary reminds me that some of our medical personnel left us near Athens to look after Allied prisoners from Crete. We knew that bitter fighting had been going on there, because we had seen a number of the Luftwaffe's damaged planes come limping back over Corinth after dropping paratroops, or bombs, on Crete.

Railway bridges had been rendered unusable by explosives during the recent retreat and our train journey was interspersed by exhausting foot-slogging. It sticks in the mind that at one stage we walked forty miles at a stretch each carrying about forty pounds of kit. Prisoners do not lightly jettison their belongings. We in the FAU and RAMC patched people up with what suitable medical aids we still possessed and helped along those who were finding these forced marches too much for them. I tried to flag down a car containing a couple of German officers, which was overtaking us, to beg a lift for another prisoner, who had collapsed. Of course it did not stop.

The sixteen members of the Friends Ambulanc Unit taken prisoner at Kalamai were still together when we reached Salonica and, after a final march lasting an hour and a quarter, at 17.00 hours on 9 June, we entered the barracks, where those prisoners who survived were to be imprisoned for up to three months, I believe.

It is difficult to describe briefly and adequately what happened during those three months. Filth, starvation, misery and — to some — horrible sickness and death came the way of prisoners of war. There was apparently no semblance of adherence to the Geneva Convention. Doubtless this failure was not all the fault of the German soldiers on the spot. All were not equally cruel and heartless. However, it is difficult to understand the callous cruelty of the German Camp Commandant. I wrote on 2 August. 'A tragic day. Two hospital orderlies and one other walked within 5 metres of the barbed wire and were shot. Francis Welsh has died of his wounds.'

On 6 August I added that 'the Serb-orderly' had also died. Immediately after the first death one of our interpreters heard the Commandant congratulate the marksman, because there was 'one less dastardly Englishman to worry about'.

Some Cypriots tried to escape along a narrow drainpipe which they discovered ran under the barbed wire and offered a way out. As they squeezed along the pipe German guards discovered what was happening. They could have waited at the far end of the pipe and easily recaptured the escapists. However they shot them in that drainpipe: I saw at least one body laid out inside the wire as a discouraging exhibit for the rest of us to examine.

Another inmate of this terrible place told me that one night a light was struck by two officers who had needed to visit a filthy dirty latrine. To extinguish the light a guard lobbed a grenade into the building and killed both officers. I have to write of these disgraceful happenings in order to explain the destructive debilitating atmosphere of the place. However, even more than the violence, it was hunger, dirt and squalor that threatened life itself and sometimes led to moral breakdown.

Not all Germans demeaned themselves. I have a note that after the RAMC and FAU had been put in charge of the much-needed camp hospital, a German doctor came in and said, 'We are not here to fight each other. We are here to fight disease' — and against great odds that is what we medical personnel set out to do. One task of the FAU was to distribute throughout the camp of about four thousand men two anti-malaria quinine tablets per person each day. We heard from other prisoners recently captured in

Crete, how a German doctor had descended on the island with German parachutists and after landing immediately started to look after the sick and wounded, treating the most serious cases first irrespective of nation or race.

No praise can be too high for the British and other imprisoned doctors who organised us. The two I particularly remember were Dr Cochran and Dr Singer. Captain Cochran had served as a volunteer doctor in the recent Spanish Civil War. Lieutenant Commander Singer, a relation of the famous sewing machine company, had been serving aboard the cruiser HMS *Gloucester* when she was sunk in the Mediterranean. He was a very fine swimmer and succeeded in helping a number of his fellows to keep afloat for a matter of days before they became prisoners of war. Of course, they had scant clothing and no footwear when they struggled from the water. Captain Singer and his friends had, I believe, accomplished a similar forced journey to ourselves from Greece. When I enquired how they got on during the forty mile foot slog, I was told, 'Oh, that was no trouble, we did it with bare feet'.

At Salonica we were desperately short of medical supplies. Dr Singer was a surgeon; but there were to hand neither operating theatre nor instruments, nor anaesthetics. The supply of water was irregular and unfit for use without boiling. Only a few patients had pyjamas. There was not enough food of any kind, let alone special diets, and a shortage of nearly all dressings and drugs. Sanitary arrangements were less than primitive and we could not possibly keep bugs, fleas and lice from the indadequate hospital buildings, which contained no sitting rooms, only crowded wards for the lying. I have a note that at one stage there were in the hospital seventy-three medical cases (including, amongst others, four typhoid, four severe tonsillitis, three tuberculosis, seven diptheria and twenty-three dysentery) as well as thirty surgical cases. In addition to those in our hospital, twice a day there was a sick parade of those sleeping elsewhere in the camp who were damaged or unwell and needed what help we could give. According to my diary there were a hundred and forty-three such visiting patients on one parade. This was probably the average.

It is not often that prisoners have any say about where they live and work and on 28 August Dr Singer and six FAU members were sent away from the camp to look after other sick and wounded we knew not where. Those of us who remained in the hospital were somewhat better off than the rest of the four thousand or so in the camp, in that, firstly, we had a definite job to do and, secondly, the German doctor had insisted upon our being paid in Greek money for our work. The money would have been useless had we not been allowed to spend it on food. Brian Darbyshire who had been appointed our purchasing agent was permitted to go outside with a guard and another prisoner to buy in the town. Of course, he is an obviously honest man. All the same it is interesting that the RAMC as well as the FAU trusted him with their all-important food. The 'Quakers' seemed to be considered a bit different from the rest. For example, when on arrival at Thessalonica we had all been lined up and searched for guns and other incriminating possessions, the FAU was given only a formal cursory examination, with, perhaps the remark, 'Ach! Qvaker? Gut!' Needless to say the whole medical staff shared what food Brian was able to obtain. The only reason for our having extra food was that it helped us to do our job better — and indeed to do it at all.

Of course, we first-aiders did whatever the doctors asked us to do. At the start I staked out a claim to be a physiotherapist. However, it soon became quite impracticable to specialise, partly because an RAMC Sergeant who had been a professional masseur in 'Civvy Street' turned up, but mostly because there were more important things to do in just keeping men alive. All of us were starving. I believe my weight dropped from about eleven and a half to just about eight stone during three months at Salonica. Some others lost less, some a great deal more.

As the camp was 'transit' and outside Germany, the majority of prisoners remained in it for a comparatively short time. They came and went. We, who were working, did not know when we would be moved. I hope not many stayed much longer than three months. They would have died had they done so. I have a note in my diary that Dr Cochran said, 'All the FAU are useful just now; but Alan Dickinson is indispensible'. Alan's job in our hospital was working as Secretary and Registrar. He was a member of our party who later gave his life in Gefangenschaft — one could say that he worked himself to death.

Whilst I was there the number of patients continued to vary between two and four hundred. With treatment the majority became well enough to leave. When numbers fell they could be made up again by the influx of, perhaps, another hundred. At first, when operations were necessary, patients could be taken to the nearby Greek hospital, where were the necessary means. Sometimes, too, when it was sadly clear that a prisoner was near the far end, he could be sent to the Greek hospital to die. Finally we were even cut off from the Greek hospital while other diseases, such as typhus, were added to our illness list. It was heart-breaking, sickening work. Sometimes we knew the family in England of a very sick man who could not be left alone. We could scarcely do more for him than talk to him of home and 'after the war'. One wondered whether one would ever be in a position to write or speak to his friends. We would become very fond of a courageous patient and feel the same despair as he when he began to doubt whether he could get better. At times we had to be on duty twenty-four hours a day, feeling guilty if away for more than half an hour at a time.

Naturally all orderlies sometimes became sick themselves. I saved up my own real incapacity until near the end of three months and then did it properly being ordered to remain horizontal because of septicaemia, originating in a cut foot, and severe stomach complaints requiring surgery not obtainable in prison. Temporarily I was taken off all food. That could not go on; so a compromise was reached. I seemed to be getting better except for the necessity of undergoing a minor operation. I found I was quite capable again of helping to take temperatures in the ward, while our regular orderly was himself running a temperature of 100°F. The poor fellow lying next to me at this time died suffering from terrible sores. I had to discard my mattress, because it was crawling with bugs. Some kind friend took my clothes away to be treated in the camp delouser.

On 8 September there was a routine inspection of the hospital by the German doctor, attended by Dr Cochran and another of our doctors. Dr Cochran kindly came on in front to warn me that his German colleague was going to ask whether I would like to be sent on at once to Germany, apart from friends of my own nationality, for the necessary operation. I could only make one answer and, when the German arrived with the expected question, I thanked him very much and said, 'Of course I will go!'

I had no idea to which part of Germany I was to go nor whether the required operation would be carried out by our own doctors or by German doctors; but I was of little help to anyone as I was. Next day I found myself a lying patient in a fine German hospital train. German wounded, as well as I, were looked after by German Red Cross workers assisted by two kind and very efficient RAMC orderlies, whom of course I already knew, Jack Tattersall and Arthur Buckingham. It goes without saying that they had other duties on the train as well; but whatever they were, I believe Jack, Arthur and I regarded this as the most wonderful journey of our lives.

6 Gefangenschaft

As for my friends, they are not lost;
The several vessels of thy fleet,
Though parted now, by tempests tost,
Shall safely in the haven meet.
— Richard Baxter 1615-91

But what had Witney to say about our sudden disappearance from
the scene at the end of April? Here are parts of a letter from Father
dated 23 May 1941.

> We are still without any news of you. The Red Cross are of
> course on the look out, but don't seem to have heard anything.
> *The Times* yesterday printed a message from their Melbourne
> correspondent giving Sir Thomas Blamey's estimate of
> Australian casualties and adding, 'Seven doctors and one
> hundred and fifty other ranks of the Fifth General Hospital
> heroically remained in Greece to take care of the wounded'.
> General Blamey also reported, 'knowing that they had no
> chance of being saved,' — and that (my guess is), if you are still
> alive, accounts for your whereabouts.

Whatever Witney was saying and thinking about us, noteworthy events were taking place in the home town while we were
pre-occupied elsewhere. Perhaps we natives were not so far apart
as distance and the lack of regular postal service might lead one to
suppose. My family continued to write regularly, addressing
letters 'C.O. Agence Centrale des Prisonniers de Guerre, Geneva,
Switzerland'. I did not receive any of these until some time after
the stage we have reached, when we were about to arrive in
Germany; but I have them in front of me today. We had been
unable to get any letters home, although twice permitted to hand
in cards giving limited news.

104

In one letter from my mother she wrote that it did not seem to her that I was dead. She went on to tell me the news from, and of, Witney and the outside world, which I so desperately wanted to know. On 3 May 1941 she wrote 'Every day that passes makes us more anxious as to yourself'. She continued,

I had such a vivid dream on Wednesday–Thursday night, 23rd and 24th April. It was in a dimly lit School-room, or Class-room, and we were expecting Patrick [R.E.E.'s brother] to speak to us. Then, when he came, I wondered who it was, collar turned up, and it was you. I threw my arms round you and you felt strong and hard and full of vitality, 'Look at the Stars, M.', you said; but I would only look at you. Then you said, 'Go back to your world and let me go to mine'. But it seemed to me you meant 'work' not another 'life' and I waked as the siren sounded. I felt wonderfully cheered and comforted all day as if I'd really been with you, darling.

I had celebrated my thirty-third birthday in the Salonica transit prison camp by giving three cigarettes to each of the other members of the FAU; this was not particularly generous, as I was (and still am) a non-smoker. On that day I wrote in my diary, 'Mother and Father's Wedding Day and my Birthday. Though impossible to exchange cables, I know how our thoughts go out to each other'. I was right: that day father typed a letter to me. By then he knew officially that we were prisoners and the second card I had been allowed to send had come to hand. He said in his letter dated 7 August 1941.

The day before your P.C. came, a Mrs Stokes rang up from Fulbrook [near Burford] of all places to say that she had a letter from her officer husband at a camp in Germany in which he said, 'I left Richard Early in Greece, very fit; notify his people in Witney'. After tea the same day she very kindly came over for a talk. Good of him and her, wasn't it — absolutely beyond price. There is a great bond of friendship — and also of organisation among people who have relatives who are prisoners.

My parents had had a rather more eventful anniversary than I had. Father's letter continued,

Today has been a very busy one following on a number of

105

other busy ones on the same business. As the press has stated that Queen Mary visited us this afternoon there can be no objection to my writing about it. It was, as you would expect, arranged by the Baron [George Hayter Chubb, 1st Baron Lord Hayter, subsequently the oldest Member of the House of Lords, much loved relative, shareholder and personal friend of the Queen Mother] and was by far the worst thing of its kind I've ever been involved in. However everything has gone off very well, and the dear lady professed herself very pleased with everything. So I may as well close your birthday (when I am sure we have all been thinking of one another a lot) by giving you a few notes on what happened. Picture us waiting at the further end of the wool house. When she stepped in (on a carpet!) his Lordship presented Charles William Early [Chairman and Father's uncle], me and Patrick and your Mother. Then I presented your three sisters and Catherine and Eleanor [Father's nieces]. The retinue sort of presented themselves and we started in pursuit of H.M. and C.W.E. (he had agreed to show her through the wool house, but I had to sort of share it with him, owing to their difficulties of communication) [C.W.E. was over ninety and rather deaf]. The first few minutes were accordingly not very easy. After that, however, I took over and it became simpler. But I advise you not lightly to undertake piloting energetic royalty through Witney Mill and shout explanations over the noise of the stuff.

We had had two special staff meetings and a mass gathering in the weaving shed, and our people knew just what was expected and played up admirably. We had long lengths of wrappering laid in the yard to walk on. First of course the willey-shop, then straight into the spinning, then round to the warp-shop, across the bridge round the weaving-shed to the main entrance into the stock-house, down the length of it to the stocks (walking dry-foot on a length of collarcheck!), back across to the gigs and so up to the whipping room, where there was a special turn of cutting-out going on (which H.M. and I agreed neither of us could do) and a good White City sort of display of finished stuff and a table of archives.

All the way round the lady was wonderful — smiling to people and being introduced and shaking hands — and generally leaving everyone very happy. On entering a department the responsible man was waiting and was presented and had a handshake, Bernard Room and Albert Moss and Reg (Arthur being sick) and George Probets and Ernest Taphouse, and others. I caught Dorothy Bolton [Welfare Supervisor] at the door of the inner office, and made her be introduced. I turned away while they had a little chat, and when I looked round H.M. had disappeared and was chattering with D.B., Hedley and Willey Haley, with the place in a regular muddle of work and not prepared for her in any way. She had looked at a wages packet and the chart on the wall and I don't know what else.

Before that, however, and after the whipping room, we had got her onto a dais just in front of the office windows, and six old warriors were drawn up while one of them (Ernest Haley) presented her with a specially bound copy of *The Witney Blanket Industry* by Alfred Plummer. That wasn't enough for her though, and she said, 'Am I to speak to the others?' So they came up one at a time and were separately introduced and spoken to — Arthur Wheeler, Jimmy Martin, Fred Bridgman, Fred Middleton and last of all, with a special round of applause, Dan Fiddler. Total service of six 317 years (E.&O.E., as we say on the confirms). By this time you will have gathered that everyone had left work and gathered round the dais — including Newland Warehouse and New Mill. The only other presentation was a bouquet (4 guineas my boy and a pretty tasty affair) offered by Florence Buckingham, appointed for the job on the strength of being the leading shop steward. Then I said a word and called for three cheers which they gave in a very creditable way. She went to tea with the baron at Springfield, and Mother, Patrick and I were there. She and her lady and equerry were each *much* interested in you — he was a prisoner for three and a half years in the last war.

The next communication from Father was a letter dated 17 August. He referred back to the Queen Mother's visit to the Mill and went on.

Since then we seem to have had an uneventful time. Hitherto our life has been dull compared with yours — now I'm afraid you are taking a hand at the monotony business. One wishes that might be your worst trouble.

107

After QM's visit the lady-in-waiting sent me a delightful letter saying how much the visit had been enjoyed etc., and finishing, 'Queen Mary sincerely hopes you will soon get letters from your son and that you will have good news'.

While we were going round (ten days ago) (in the whipping room) I was showing the finished article and managed quietly to mention that in 1687 we had offered a pair of blankets to James II and in 1788 to George III and that we would like to follow precedent and forward a pair to H.M. This was graciously received (and in fact was mentioned last thing as we parted!) and in due course I had to get particulars of the size required. The Lady in Waiting wrote that those in use ('by the way the date on them is Queen Mary's Coronation year!') are $3\frac{1}{2}$ yards square. Work it out and tell me how you would go about finishing them. So after considerable head scratching I have writtern to say we propose to send a pair 102 × 120 inches (i.e. size 14) and venturing to suggest that one of them might be laid crossways if it is desired to get extra tuck-in. That has been agreed to, so now we have to put a chain of 14s to work, and no doubt the weaver concerned will be very bucked.

On 5 October 1941, Father reported again,

We sent Queen Mary the pair of Merino 14s we promised her — I should think as perfect a pair of blankets as we have ever sent out. Her Lady in waiting writes: 'Queen Mary is enchanted with the perfectly lovely blankets and commands me to thank you all most warmly for them. Her majesty expresses her appreciation and thanks to all who worked to produce this most lovely gift . . . ' and then, 'P.S. Queen Mary sincerely hopes that you are hearing regularly from your son and that he is well'.

Needless to say I was much encouraged by these words from the Queen Mother as I am sure were all those at the Mill who had worked on 'as perfect a pair of blankets as we had ever sent out'. The pleasure of reading about this gracious royal concern was only equalled by my feeling of happiness and relief at once again receiving letters from my family. I will draw mostly from my father's letters in telling of 'goings on' in Witney during the next four years; but parts, some of which I leave out, contained a great deal more than news. For example father reminded me more than once of the words written by Richard Baxter at the head of this chapter, and I will quote some of what he wrote before either family, or I, knew what had happened to the other immediately after the fall of Greece.

> I want to write to you; but it is not a sort of correspondence one wants too often, not knowing whether the other person is dead or alive, wounded or whole, prisoner or free. One rather finds the footing in which one holds one's loved ones. It is a great comfort to feel one has the biggest things in common with them.

He reminded me of what Paul wrote in his letter to the Romans, Ch. 8, vv. 35-9 and continued, 'It is a help even to have smaller interests in common, though we don't want to be monotonously unanimous!'

Here are some of the 'smaller interests'. On 18 September Father wrote that George T. Maynard was appointed Company Secretary, a post he was to hold in our old family firm for a third of a century: one of his first kind deeds was to send instruction on book-keeping to an absent member of the Board! Other news was that three more men, retired after about fifty years' work, had returned to give the firm a hand and take the place of some of us who were away. He continued, 'We are doing a lot of work and doing well. Everyone in excellent health and spirits — and that doesn't apply only to Charles Early & Co.'

A week later he said,

> Last night Ruth [my sister] gave a recital in the drawing-room for people in uniform. It was an experiment and there was the right number not to be crowded but to enjoy the comfort of soft chairs. Definitely appreciative of good music. I am afraid that the part that gave me most pleasure wasn't equally jolly for Ruth. She had explained La Cathedral Engloutie, or whatever it is, especially how it finished with the misty atmosphere of the open sea, and she had played it magnificently and come to that soft and moving part at the end depicting gently breaking waves. Just then old Looby [our alsatian bitch] in the hall outside thought she would like a drink. The door was open and through it came loud sounds of a splashing tide on the shore, competing with the piano for loudness. The piece finished with a hearty laugh, which is hardly its conventional ending.

Since 1902 the Boys' Brigade 1st Witney Company, part of Witney High Street Methodist Church, had served the town and particularly boyhood in the town. Father had been officer and, for most of forty odd years, Captain. He was also a long-standing member of the national and international Executive Committe of the Brigade, which accounts for the following news in a letter dated 26 November 1941:

> The past weekend I spent at Executive in York. Rather comfortable quarters, and a number of good friends of yours. Mac [William McVicker 'Secretary'] and Stanley [Stanley G. Smith, M.C., 'Brigade Secretary'] both asked if they could write to you, so I gave them addressed letter-cards. And Lord Home [Brigade President] has enquired about you so many times that I ventured to give him one too; he said he should send you a yarn, but I fear both you and the censors will have a job with his hand-writing. I had to go a day earlier for a BB Committee on post-war reconstruction. Peacock (London Secretary) who is a bit of a conservative and thinks such suggestions as dropping the original boys cap are unduly radical, calls it the committee of post war demolition. But I am afraid we are impenitent. Anyway neither he nor we have a shadow of doubt it will be a world in which free and voluntary institutions will flourish. You can put that in your pipe and smoke it as much as you like — duty free! [Which all P.o.W. tobacco was!] We are suggesting a broadening of the cultural sides of the work, and developing the club side too; all rather a satisfaction to me. Railway travelling nowadays offers a variety of overseas fellow-passengers which more than compensates for a certain congestion. They and the home product are a glorious lot of lads. The inspiration of being partners in a great job is, one can only pray, a thing that will not leave us when the job is finished. Surely we shall not let ourselves ever be possessed again by the ghastly spirit of unemployment. Is there anything worse than for a man to feel he isn't wanted?

He continues about the Boys' Brigade and relevant matters in the same letter,

> You will be glad to hear that Cyril Madden has been home for a fortnight after a year's absence (in the Navy). Mrs M and I

went up to his house for tea on Friday. He has had some rough times between here and George Harvey's [our Americal Agent], but is very cheerful. I hear that the Sunday I was in York he gave the Bible Class address [to 1st Witney] — an interesting yarn. He has been mentioned in despatches, and no doubt deserved it. Generally, the old BBs you know are getting pretty well scattered. They turn up from time to time all smiling broadly and in the pink of condition. Some of course are much too far away for leave — but I've no doubt they too are smiling. (What *can* one do with people who insist on smiling? If I remember rightly the same problem puzzled the same party, quarter of a century ago.)

Knowing father well and enjoying, I like to think, a similar sense of humour I, myself, and some others smiled as we dwelt upon these last remarks. We otherwise obtained our news from a loud speaker set up by the Germans near at hand. Through this means we knew about Japan's entry into the war at Pearl Harbor. I was therefore not taken unawares when father continued in like vein on 4 December 1941.

During the past week the Tea Party has grown bigger by the arrival of two new guests, a very tall man and a somewhat shorter one. I hear the little chap broke some crockery at the start, but the long 'un is as keen as mustard and will be a great help in making sure the others go the right way home. Meanwhile talking about parties . . .

My sister Ruth was at that time touring and playing classical piano music to the Forces in Devon. Having mentioned this, father turned, as if casually, to commenting upon our blanket customers in that part of the world. He spoke of Walton's of Exeter, where I knew the proprietor Mr Turner, as a BB Officer. He indicated that for present requirements Ruth might find more satisfaction in dealing with him than with Mr Hockley at Bobby's. In brackets he adds, 'What would happen if I put Maurice's name for the latter in this letter?' Of course, I remembered that our Sales Manager, unjustly I am sure, in moments of desperation, sometimes called the blanket buyer at Bobby's 'Hitler'. I began to wonder how that was relevant to our correspondence. In the next letter I was told a story which had possibly come father's way for inclusion in the

111

Boys' Brigade Gazette of which he was still the Editor. I am absolutely certain that it did not get into the *Gazette;* but I do not mind including it here!

> In the last war the average Tommy was more tolerant of pacifists than were some of the supposedly bigger bugs. A distinguished member of the Society of Friends was serving a prison sentence and got measles, which necessitated his being moved into a military hospital. The next morning the M.D., on his rounds, discovered what the patient was, and thought fit to harangue him in bed, 'What would have happened in nineteen-fourteen', he demanded, 'if everyone had behaved like you?' As he turned his back and marched up the ward, the soldier in the next bed was heard to remark, soto voce, 'Bloody fool. No bloody war of course!'

Towards the end of the letter there is a further reference to the blanket trade in Exeter, where Father asks,

> Do you remember Maurice Fyfield's nickname for Hockley of Bobby's of Exeter? If you don't there is no further point in this. Opinion here is that he will have lost his job before the year is out. [This letter was written in January, 1942.] His stuff has been definitely going wrong. Patrick rather thinks the concern of which he is the head will be packed up in the same period. I am less confident, my memory going further back than P's. But I think Hockley is nearly finished, which would be a beginning after which anything might happen. Forgive so much of the drapery trade.

In order to show that 'the penny had dropped', I included the following in my next P.o.W. folder home: 'Am interested to read in your latest letter that you think Maurice's Exeter acquaintance will shortly have to give up business. I can only add that I learn some of his humbler partners in business think it is time he closed his shop'.

I need to give the foregoing explanation in order that further letters from my father may be as understandable to the readers of this book as they were to us in Germany. However the following, about innovations in Early's weaving shed, does not require explaining. Father wrote:

I have a note in my diary about the new green overalls on the girls and women in Witney Mill and Newland Warehouse. A great improvement and likely to become a permanent institution. We have subsidised to the extent of about a shilling, otherwise they buy their own — and have paid cash, what's more. The money was got in by one or two stalwarts like Lottie Cox (a senior and a good weaver), who don't mind taking a colleague or two by the throat and telling them they may as well fork out and have done with it! I have now got Dorothy Bolton [Welfare Supervisor] and Arthur Parr [Weaving Shed Foreman] considering what we can do in the way of a badge system — e.g. long service bars — you can imagine it looks an improvement on wall-paper pinnies and old dance frocks etc., and I am sure will help self-respect.

It was not only weavers who showed their self-respect in those days. I quote from another letter written in January 1942,

I don't suppose that on the whole the rank and file of this country have as individuals ever enjoyed so satisfying a sense of self-respect and of being needed in the world. Without minimising much that is tragic, at any rate we have finished with the ghastly unemployment atmosphere when human beings were told they were not wanted. It is a pity that it takes a war to bring to young (and older) people a sense of vocation, of physical and mental opportunity and well-being, and of tackling the greatest job of a thousand years. Here for example comes a letter from Ted Winfield. He has gone through his final tests in Physical Training and is now Sergt.-Instructor in the A.P.T.C. (and married, which isn't your responsibility), and he writes 'Well, Skip, as I told you before I owe it all to the Boys' Brigade. I shall never forget what it has done for me, and I can assure you I will do all I can to help the BB, wherever I am or go'.

As indicated earlier in this story, Ted kept his word. With Ted Winfield in the army, senior boys had to take his place and continue the instruction given by adult officers in peace-time. The narrative continued,

Tommy Hedges now tells me he has got his crossed swords! Francis Hicks will be the best of all if he gets a chance. We took in BB new members last week and got twenty without any trouble — well hardly any; so our strength in the 1st Witney Company is about seventy. I counted thirty in the Club last night. Our fortieth Annual Inspection is to be early — 24th March — this year as we want to get it safely over before the indispensable 'Snip' Hicks is called up.

Of course Francis conducted physical training displays before 'call up'. The Company was inspected by Mr William McVicker (from BB Headquarters) before 'Snip' joined the army. He took part in the conquest of Italy and married a most charming Italian lady from Milan, who returned with him to Witney and became much involved in the Witney blanket industry.

The following extracts from letters written by my father had for me special interest. On 17 February 1942 he wrote about doings at the Mill,

> I am hoping to get the shop stewards formed into a small Council, to meet perhaps once a month. (We shall have to reassure the foremen about it; they, as you know already, have a weekly meeting with the family directors and I don't think foremen can helpfully be members.) I think you will approve of this. I have really no use for the little tin god business and 'you're not paid to think' and I'm sure you haven't.

On the financial side it was reported on 3 April,

> We have started a small new wages feature in business. It consists of a small weekly bonus to time workers based on the output of their departments. Thus in the case of the shed labourers, the tuners, the woolhouse men, each gang gets amongst them a penny per stockful or equivalent. It comes to, say, four shillings odd per man, which isn't much, but at any rate is buckshee on their time rate and has the merit that it is related to output and so adds a little sporting interest.

Wages and salaries were not to be discussed at the proposed council; but on 9 April Father wrote,

> Talking about pay, we are wondering whether our system of certificates for profit-sharing is the most effective way of doing it. Cash would be heaps more popular and when the amounts are small the large parchments are almost derisory! After all our

chief object is to stimulate interest in doing a good job of work. The encouragement of thrift is secondary, though possibly important. I feel thrift is an over-rated virtue and anyway should be encouraged by methods that are not suspect of paternalism. Getting a piece of paper rather loses its glamour when you have to pay income tax on it in cash! I'm afraid we shall have to settle it before we get your advice, but we will report in due course. (I wonder if about a year ago you just managed to get our cable in the course of which we filled up by reporting 'profit-sharing five per cent'. If so, it must have seemed a grotesque triviality in the midst of your desperate pre-occupations just then.)

Father went on,

Talking about business I am grateful for your remarks about our friend Hockley of Exeter. In the drapery trade they think he has used up some of his spring lines on the winter's business. But he obviously means to make a marvellous show. His business suffers from increasing competition and his advertising is less effective than it used to be. The three firms he controls are none of them too healthy and unless he has an exceptionally good summer season his business will go down.

These last remarks and similar ones that followed I used to read to the patients, whom it subsequently became my job to massage in prison hospital. We knew enough to recognise Rudolf Hesse referred to on 14 April 1942. (My brother Patrick had visited Germany shortly before the war),

Going into the dining room just now I noticed a p.c. portrait of your friend Hockley [the draper of Exeter] on the mantlepiece. It is one Patrick sent home a few years ago, when Hockley was just starting to work up his business — a good portrait, showing him in his trade clothes reading a paper with his chief assistant standing by. Funny episode the assistant leaving the firm and going abroad, wasn't it? Hockley is of course an enterprising chap, but like so many in his business he has, we think, expanded too fast and too far. All these branch establishments take a lot of keeping up. Unless the season's business turns out remarkably lucky he may find he has bought too heavily. And in the drapery trade you can't afford to have a bad year; shareholders after all, and in the long run, have an eye to business.

The final piece of news which closed the letter could not have been particularly interesting to the patients; but it was to me,

We haven't yet got the new Works Council formed in business, but I hope it will be ready for its first meeting in under a fortnight, and you shall then hear all about it — or something anyway. Meanwhile, the day after tomorrow morning, Mrs M. and I plan to escape to Cheltenham for a long weekend, and I admit I'm looking forward to it. Very much love to you.

Ever affectionately
J. H. Early

By 22 April Father wrote,

We are still getting the new Works Council together. I hope it will develop into something quite useful. The next time I write I shall probably be able to report its first meeting. Membership will probably be 19, consisting of 9 more or less elected by the rank and file, 9 appointed by the Management — and Dorothy Bolton as a sort of neutral Secretary. We are to keep clear of wages questions, leaving them to the usual channels and if necessary to the Union. At the first meeting I hope we shall discuss Production (elimination of lost time, waste and damages), Annual holiday (date and perhaps occupations), Profit-sharing (popularising), Suggestion scheme (good old chestnut) and any other business.

Sure enough a week later,

On Monday we inaugurated the Works Council by holding its first meeting, in the canteen. The workers' representatives are: four weavers (women), Sidney Godfrey, Joe Pratley, George Weller, Bernard Cauldrey, and Billy Beale [Engine driver of New Mill]. The corresponding nine appointed by the Management were: Howard Harris [Mill Manager], Will Haley [Assistant Mill Manager], Ernest Taphouse, Frank Gribbin [Departmental Managers], George Maynard [our new Secretary], Patrick and J.H.E. [Managing Directors], John Hudson [Warehouse Manager] and Herbert Godfrey [very much Foreman-Manager of New Mill]. I gather the 'rank and file' had rather a shock when they found the 'big bugs' were there in force, but we have stated that if any section wishes for a meeting on its own for any special purpose, it can be arranged. On the other hand, I rather feel they have got over their shyness, fear of foremen, etc., and realise they are as good as the next man and things have changed since the Crimean War. I started off with a rather long-winded prepared talk about the Council and what we hoped it would do in the way of helping to run the business on the lines indicated in my last letter emphasising the importance of health, accident prevention and comfort — indeed general co-operation including the proposal of a suggestion scheme. And so on. I referred to the profit-sharing and mentioned that since it was started the firm had made over to the 'workers' well over £30,000 (which I suppose rather surprised them, at any rate there was laughter when I said that of course that might not be much to some of them). I went on to say (gently) that I couldn't help wondering whether that sum was adequately reflected in increased interest and keenness. (The answer, as a matter of fact, I feel is that it certainly hasn't been, and that we need to make it more interesting and attractive — without necessarily making it more expensive.)

Father continued,

Well, we discussed a number of things — the date most generally acceptable for this year's holiday, whether anything could be arranged in the way of amusements for the week (the amenities of the east coast not being quite what they were, nowadays!), a draft of suggestion schemes, and so on. I suggested we should not settle these things till they had considered and discussed them and we accordingly adjourned till Friday, when they will be settled, with anything else that may arise. The Council will normally meet at 5.0 p.m. on the first Monday of the month. They also agreed that the representatives should be elected (by nomination and ballot) annually about May. Dorothy Bolton is the nineteenth member, being regarded as a sort of neutral and doing the Secretarial business. Wages are excluded from the business, as belonging to the Union, which I told them the firm wished to support.

117

Father concluded by saying, 'I hope this thing is going to become a permanent and very helpful feature of the business. If it goes as it should it may almost revolutionise the feelings and atmosphere of the place. I hope you will soon be able to take a hand in it.'

However, he could not forbear to add a note about sales!

On the selling side we have one customer who seems rather rocky — your drapery friend in Exeter. He has been talking shop within the last few days, in the hearing of the whole trade, in a way that certainly shocked his friends. When a chap has lost confidence in his colleagues and his business as badly as he seems to have done it hardly suggests stability and the prospect of successful trading. Bobby & Co., have still of course immense resources, but their competitors are already out-bidding them in several directions. Much will depend on the summer's trade of course, but their commitments are so large that anything may happen. One of their associated Companies is supposed to be *very* shaky.

Well, if Italy was the 'Associated Company' referred to above, it can hardly have been known what was coming to it in the shape of ex-BB Francis Hicks, who wrote to Father at this time saying,

Dear Skip, I expect you remembered me at Bible Class this Sunday morning. I led in bed as I have an innoculation Friday night, and my poor arm: I led a bed nearly all day yesterday but we have a good Cpl. in our billets: he brought us up a cup of tea in the morning as I did not get up for breakfast . . . I saw the R.S.M. over the P.T. instructors in the week and I have got to see him again when I have finished the course. I think I shall be alright: he was surprised when I told him I knew vaulting and I got one of the sergeants to put in a good word for me: they pick me out to stand in front of the class to give them the time so I'm doing alright at P.T.

Father remarked to me after quoting this, 'It looks as though another of your pupils will soon be marked for promotion, I fancy'.

I believe I thought, 'Poor old Mussolini! Snip Hicks is a devastating boxer!!'

I find that a good deal of my news from Witney concerned the

Boys' Brigade. The personnel were taking a full share in serving the community. Of the seven officers in the 1st Witney four, Harold Early [Captain], Alfred Rowley, Harry Dingle and Cyril Keates, were still at home and, among their many other duties, running the company. A great many of the boys, as soon as they reached the age limit, joined the armed forces; but Old Boys from previous generations rallied round and helped the Captain and Lieutenants to continue company activities in Witney.

As a prisoner trained for medical work I really had only one job and one full-time responsibility — that of looking after the wounded and otherwise sick — usually on the instructions of a doctor. Those in Witney had to make their own decisions and be prepared to work at any time of day, or night, on their own initiative and in many spheres. The four remaining officers were all businessmen, each of the three Lieutenants working in his own shop. When my family were buying supplies to be included in the limited number of carefully weighed Red Cross P.o.W. parcels allowed to be sent to me, often and quite contrary to my parents' wishes they would refuse to be paid. Their helpful and most effective concern for their imprisoned colleague will never be forgotten. However, I suppose I was even more grateful to the gallant four in Witney for carrying on with the BB work I had always had so much at heart.

In fact it was not in our own town alone that the 1st Witney was to be seen. We had in 1936 appeared fifty-nine strong performing Danish Gymnastics on the floor of the Royal Albert Hall as guest performers at the London District Annual Display and were to do the same again after the war. It was therefore not surprising that, one Saturday in May 1942, a small party from Witney found itself seated about the famous arena at 3.30 p.m. It is more surprising that the authorities had sufficient confidence to permit eight thousand British subjects getting together there at a time when the Luftwaffe was paying special attention to the capital. Father wrote,

> On Saturday Mrs M. and I went to London for Boys' Brigade Display in the usual place. Indoors one could not tell it wasn't the usual hour, and you can picture it just about as you have seen it a dozen times. Previously I was at a modest luncheon given by the BB Overseas Committee to representatives of

overseas churches now in England. About thirty of us were there. Stanley Smith and William McVicker spoke, and a Danish minister. Very well worth while I thought! I sat between the Archdeacon of London and the Chairman of the Y.M.C.A., in a European capital. I found he was father-in-law to a blanket maker of Witney! Meanwhile M. was at the Royal Academy, which I had to miss. We met in the Hall in good time to see the intriguing stages before 'the curtain goes up', so to speak. Old Scott Lidgett was sitting in solitary state on the platform, he is N. A. Lewis's parson, you know at the Bermondsey Settlement, and was to have the pleasure of seeing his Company, the 62nd London, win the Bugle Band cup. The guard of honour — *Daily Telegraph* drill finalists — was 1st Enfield and 1st New Barnett. Chairman was R. A. Butler, President of the Board of Education. I won't bore you with the programme in detail. It was pretty wonderful — not all of it perhaps quite the highest standard, but on the whole very fine, and some of it very moving. In fact if I got my own feelings across to you I am afraid your companions would wonder what you were blubbing about — which I take it isn't done in Stalag VB. I will just tell you one or two things that struck me. Perhaps the most remarkable (which you must work out for yourself) was the L.C.C., allowing that place to be packed to the roof. Among the items, Ground Pyramids were well devised and well put on; 1st Enfield drill (they won it) was a delight, and 'Free Standing Exercises and Partner Work' was put on by five South Essex Companies. They seemed to fill the floor pretty well, but they only numbered just over thirty. It made me realise what a show we must have put on in 1936 — which neither of us saw. I was talking yesterdeay after Bible Class to Alf, Harry and Cyril about it, and they were nothing loath to reminisce. They said the first three movements were just perfect for precision, a sort of dead hush fell, and the only trouble was that the bursts of applause in between drowned the word of command. They remembered the 'right foot sideways — place' and the little simple thud on the matting as fifty-eight legs shot out together. But we were in 1942, weren't we? Chairman's address was admirable and there was a rumour that he did it himself! 'P.T. Stick Work' might be worth thinking about, and then the Slough Battalion gave a fine crowd-scene Robin Hood-cum-Lion Heart show, full of colour and fun. We finished with massed brass, absolutely glittering, and playing like an organ with a pill-box 'drum major' [meaning a Boy not an Officer], and Old Gordon Wooderson conducting in white gloves. A slow hymn tune, followed by a glorious typical brass band March. The closing hymn was 'Father, who hast made us brothers . . . Take the hopes of every Boy'. The audience was 'requested to rise and sing'. I did the first, but I'm afraid I couldn't have done the second if you'd offered me 1,000 reich marks to try. We walked across the Park, trees and water looking their loveliest, had a most excellent supper in the (very modernised) old Paddington hotel, and got home to Witney at eleven-something. As a p.s. I may add that the *BB Gazette* had a full report printed in proof sheets — *the day before*. [But I am sure it was not half so good as this report, forty years after! R.E.E.]

We ought to let father say rather more about the Works Committee at Witney Mill before we end this chapter with the news from some other parts of the world that had special interest to those I knew at home. Here he goes!

It is the evening for the monthly meeting of the Works Council. The more I see of this the more glad I am that we have started it. It has considerable possibilities; for example we have formed a small Entertainments Committee to co-operate with the new Witney Social Centre and also to make plans on its own account, specially with the annual holiday in mind. As seaside excursions and deer-stalking in the Highlands are not particularly encouraged by the authorities just now, there is a call for the provision of sports and amusements nearer home. (Bowls on the Hoe, what?) So you can picture us footing it on the cricket field, Jack Hedges [our Groundsman] having no doubt carefully fenced off the square. The tea-party will, one may hope, at least leave us a rather more neighbourly and resourceful community than it found us. I want to get the Council to form a Health Committee also, to deal with such matters as general innoculation and sunray treatment. We finally launched the Suggestion Scheme, and also had another talk about profit-sharing and accepted the proposal that the starting limit for profit-sharing of two years' service and eighteen years old should be reduced to twelve months' service and sixteen years old. The alteration affects fifty five people out of our workforce of about five hundred, so should spread interest (the mental sort as well as the 6% variety).

In the same letter came reference to my sister married to Squadron Leader Donald Lee. Donald had played an extremely active part in the war in Europe and had at this juncture been seconded to America to instruct American pilots. At length Rosemary was permitted to join him. While still in England she had among a good many other activities been a breeder of dogs. One of her dogs had been called Bramble. The letter continued:

Do you remember ex-Governor Fuller of Massachusetts, who bought Bramble off Rosemary? She and Donald have just spent a week with them in Boston (going by air from Miami) and I will give you an extract from her letter on their return, written on 16th May. She is our best letter writer still out of prison. She says 'The Boston holiday was *terrific* and we are both exhausted! The Fullers' kindness was simply overwhelming and it was hard to thank them enough. We certainly were enjoying high life! Their house is stupendous, full of French and Italian antique furniture, the walls dripping with Rembrandts, Augustus Johns, etc., twelve servants of various kinds. But they themselves so kind and genuine, the ex-Gov. is really absolutely grand — so quiet and humorous and thoughtful. He is behind everything. . . . It was the sort of house where not only is your unpacking done and clothes pressed, but if you leave anything unwashed around it automatically comes back laundered the next day. I haven't time to tell you of all our doings during the week. They included 'Gone with the Wind' and another Theatre, a monstrous circus, a day in New Hampshire at the Fullers' farm (and seeing Bramble too) and being sent up to Maine for a day and night with Donald's Uncle and Aunt in a vast car — plus chauffeur! Some members of the family gave me a spray of orchids any evening we went out . . . Mr Fuller finally gave us each a book and me a marvellous great case of Elizabeth Arden, containing nearly everything you can think of plus a manicure set. And then, on the last afternoon, Mrs F. very coyly said she hoped I would not mind the suggestion but she would like to give me a dress to take back to Oklahoma! I was swept into a very nice little shop, and before I could check

122

her or hardly get my breath, she had given me three! — a green linen suit, a pale blue Shantung dress and a black silk with great red flowers on it, which will do well for Winter too . . .'.

Commenting on the foregoing Father said,

It must be the first time in history any member of our family lived in such surroundings. Perhaps the last too, for après la guerre they may not be so plentiful. Meanwhile it is interesting to know of such economic resources presumably available, via the tax gatherer, for tea party purposes. No particular business news, except that Hockley of Exeter is now, we are sure, in a bad way; competition increasing rapidly.

The following letter written on 9 June 1942 expanded upon this last piece of news,

I note you think as I do about poor old Bobby's bankruptcy. He's been a thorough bad hat, but we still have his portrait on the dining-room mantelpiece, where probably you will find it on your return. His latest associated firm, which started with such a flourish not long ago, is beginning to show signs of weakness. The nature of its chief competitor makes this inevitable. As regards the Bobby business nearer home — it is pretty clear that their East End business has absorbed such a quantity of goods that they have not enough summer lines to put in their West End windows. One can't face modern competition in that way, especially competition which is intensifying at the present rate. He may quit of course, and the shareholders in his firm will have difficult decisions to make in the interval before the creditors step in and take over the whole concern. But I mustn't worry you with business problems though I know you like to keep in touch.

Well, we in Germany suspected already that Hitler had taken on more than he had bargained for by attacking Russia and that Japan after a spectacular start at Pearl Harbor and the occupation of Singapore was being slowed up by the mighty intervention of the United States. Father's words confirmed our suspicions and there was little need to explain when reading them to other prisoners.

Just another word here about Rosemary and Donald Lee — I am anxious that no reader should imagine that they had an easy war. The contrary was the case. The well-deserved holiday in Boston lasted only a few days and training British pilots was a demanding job. However, most of Wing Commander Donald Lee's service involved flights over Germany and other parts of Europe occupied by German forces. On occasion he was billeted with his wife by an airfield near Witney. After one flight Donald failed to return and news came to Rosemary that her husband's plane had been shot down and Donald had last been seen descending by parachute into enemy territory. Some time later, having been unable to let her know until that moment that he had come unscathed to ground and had had to run for it, he walked into their room. This amazing escape was later in the war and is only one example of the strains and dangers which they and other young married couples were facing — some for as long as nearly six years of fighting. Sadly, it was not always that the loved one 'walked into the room'.

I had come to regard Gloucester and Gloucestershire as almost as much my home as was Witney and Oxfordshire. When I was a young boy at the Downs School, Colwall, Nr. Malvern, on occasion the Schools' 1st XV was taken to watch Gloucester Football Club playing Rugger against Newport or Oxford University on Kingsholm Ground. Mention in this book has been made of our visits to Cheltenham College to watch Gloucestershire play cricket against the Australians or some other visiting players. Except for Oxford University, Gloucester was our most accessible First Class Rugby Club and Gloucestershire our nearest First Class Cricket County. Gloucestershire cricketers had often played on Witney Mills cricket ground. In school days these things were important and Gloucestershire had for me since boyhood seemed very near Witney. After all, there were sheep to supply us with wool on the Cotswold Hills which were largely in Gloucestershire — and, particularly at Stroud, the ancient textile industry flourished as it did in Witney. There was a fellow feeling.

However that may have been, I had been thrilled when, coming into our Mill Office one afternoon in the early spring of 1936, I had found that a member of the Gloucester Football Club Committee had looked in during the course of business about buying some scrap metal. He had found Maurice Fyfield in the office and after their business had been concluded it had not taken the alert Maurice long to discover the position held by his visitor in the

Gloucester Club. Knowing the loyalty which good old Maurice bore towards all people and things concerned with blankets, I can imagine the kind of conversation which ensued. Maurice had often persuaded Gloucestershire cricketers to grace our Witney Mills cricket ground and he must have suggested that a Witney Mills player could well be offered the honour of running about on the famous turf of Gloucester's Kingsholm Rugby Ground! He probably said, 'You ought to give a "trial" to our Mr Richard. He's almost besotted about Rugby Football!' I suppose the Gloucester Committee man answered politely that he would bear this in mind. When I heard about it I expect I was grateful to Maurice but thought the matter ended. However, it was not, and a day or two later I received a card from Arthur Hudson, the Gloucester Secretary, inviting me to play right wing three-quarter in a mid-week game against Guy's Hospital. Almost unbelieving I had driven over to Gloucester and scored a 'try' against the doctors, which is what is expected from a wing three-quarter. I was rewarded by being selected to play at Kingsholm against the Harlequins the following Saturday. So it came about that for parts of three rugger seasons, on and off, I played for what I fully believe is the finest rugger club in the World. When, as a prisoner, I heard that Gloucester had been bombed, I would remember that tremendous pack of forwards clad in 'cherry and white', behind which I had often been given shelter, and thought, 'That man Hitler does not know what he is up against!' — very silly, of course, but prisoners and rugger players have curious thoughts. An International, Alan Brinn, the present Chairman of Gloucester's selectors, said recently 'This Gloucester Club is part of my life' — and so it became for me.

During my time with Gloucester three young ministers of religion were playing for the club, the Rev. E. L. (Bill) Phillips, the Rev. H. M. (Mervyn) Hughes and the Rev. C. C. (Kit) Tanner. Both Bill Phillips and Mervyn Hughes were rugger 'blues' and I am glad indeed that I know them to this day. I regard them with affection and admiration; but nowadays that is by no means only because of their prowess on the rugger field!

In 1939 Mervyn officiated at Bill's wedding to his Nancy, who was a Cambridge tennis 'blue', and I felt flattered and was very glad to be the 'best man'. Later than I, Bill, like myself, became a prisoner in Germany having been captured after dropping into

125

enemy territory as a chaplain to Allied parachute troops.

Kit Tanner and I did not play together very often, largely because both of us usually played right wing for Gloucester — and he was an international! However, on occasion, when I made way for him, I was included in the Gloucester XV in some other position on the field. I only met and got to know him on the rare occasion when we played together in the team; but I thought him a splendid fellow and a letter from home dated 19 March 1942 confirmed this estimation, although it filled me with grief. C. C. Tanner had become a naval chaplain and Father quoted the words of his mother,

> Surgeon Lieut-Commdr. G. N. Martin, who was medical officer of the Gloucester Club when my boy played for them and knew him well, says that when . . . began to go down Kit became possessed of super human strength. When the rescuing destroyer appeared on the scene my son made about thirty trips between it and the sinking ship carrying with him each time a comrade who was either a non-swimmer or an indifferent one . . . Kit must have swum for several miles in his journeys between the two ships. . . . One boy had an arm torn off, and people thought he was done for, but Kit brought him back and he was saved. By this time my son was completely exhausted; he lost consciousness while in the water and he died directly after he was picked up.

The foregoing is a graphic and moving account of Kit's sacrifice and final service to his friends. Reading it, it is hard to believe that his mother was not with him on the rescuing destroyer. She must have felt she had been and I guess the feeling was mutual.

7 Train to Württemberg

*'Thou preparest a table before me
in the presence of mine enemies.'*
— 23rd Psalm

It was weeks — and sometimes months — after posting that I received from Witney the letters just quoted in the last chapter reporting some of what was happening at home during the period in Germany which I am about to describe. However, I remember the various incidents now in the order of their happening.

The change in conditions affecting those comparatively few prisoners taken from Salonica transit camp and loaded on to a German hospital train on 9 September 1941 was abrupt and to us amazing. There was no other Friends Ambulance Unit Member beside myself on this train; but I believe that there were at least sixteen other prisoners in the coach nearest the engine, where I was in the front of the train. My diary reminds me that amongst the medical orderlies was Harold Butt a kindly, helpful and outspoken RAMC man from Australia who had in his spare time been a racing cyclist (he had ridden for his state). Other orderlies included Jack Tattersall, a Tramway's manager from Lancashire, and a New Zealander named Arthur Buckingham, whose family by coincidence had originated, he believed, in Witney. These three each held the rank of Corporal; but there was also William Paton, a Scot who in 'civvy street' was a nurse for the mentally handicapped. All these were on the train to look after the few prisoners who, like myself, needed special treatment. I expect they looked after Germans as well, and German orderlies on occasion certainly looked after us.

I found myself lying in an upper bunk with the sun shining in through an open carriage window. We were supplied regularly with food. The first meal was midday dinner consising of lentil,

127

potato and tinned pork 'mush'. I suppose this first meal provided more nourishment than a whole week's supply of food consumed by each of the unfortunates still in the prison camp we had just left.

The changing panorama to be seen from the windows of our carriage would have delighted any travellers. For men recently confined by barbed wire to an insanitary few acres it seemed a miracle of beauty. We understood that we were travelling north west and our journey would last about five days and take us through Belgrade on our way to Stuttgart. I did not know then, so well as I do now, exactly where Stuttgart was, so one gained the idea that we were on a kind of mystery tour! Most patients, like myself, slept well between unaccustomed sheets on our comfortable bunks. I awoke when breakfast (three pieces of bread-and-jam and sweetened tea) was served at 07.30 a.m. next day. I am not sure whether by that time we were in northern Macedonia or Bulgaria. (The Germans told us that Yugoslavia no longer existed but had been split-up again.) However, in whatever country we were, the outlook was peaceful. There were quiet farms and fields yielding maize, peaches, grapes, tomatoes and strawberries. Healthy cheerful countryfolk — the women wearing aprons over their coloured dresses with hair constrained by white kerchiefs — were to be seen working conscientiously on the land in the pleasant autumn weather as our hospital train sped gently past them. The war seemed far away.

Then at 12.30 p.m. came lunch of stewed meat, rice, carrots and celery with a slice of bread. Promptly at 17.30 hours, it was 'tea'. A Witney six o'clock 'tea' at home after the women and rest of the day shift had 'packed up' at the Mill could hardly have been better! The weather became cooler and more moist — more like England — and the country became almost mountainous, the hills covered with small trees, as we glided on. When we stopped at small stations, we could hear the tinkle of bells hung from the necks of cattle and see a few countrymen with what one of the orderlies called 'Jugo hats' on their heads. We noticed oxen drawing carts along the banks of wide mud-coloured streams as we emerged from the occasional tunnel: at times we appeared to deviate north east. Next we were trundling again north west over the plains. It is all recorded in my diary written at the time. Food, of course, was of prime importance to us. Some ate too much too suddenly and suffered for it. Thus it was that we came to Belgrade and saw the

Danube looking anything but blue. However, the sun re-appeared and lit up the whitewashed walls of many small houses and another kind of crop was seen — hops.

We became a most friendly party. Only one patient was running a temperature: he had jaundice. Jack Tattersall and I were, as far as I could see, the only Englishmen — remembering that Bill Paton was a Scot! The rest were New Zealanders and Aussies and, of course, German guards and medical orderlies. One of the Germans came from Berlin, but he had been born near to Lake Constance and could speak and understand French. At first I acted as interpreter; but it was not long before he and Lancashire-born Jack Tattersall seemed to develop a common language of their own! The German was good enough to tell us where we were and where he thought our train was likely to end up. However, we did not need to ask what country we were in, when the 'Jugo hatted' men near Graz gave way to others wearing shorts and stockings as we veered west through Austria.

At this juncture the second doctor on the train, a charming young German — even to us British — suggested that I should accompany him on a round of his patients in our carriage. On the way round he asked about the relationship of the RAMC and Quakers to the British Army. When he found our where I lived he also asked about Oxford. The doctor noticed that a few of the captive patients were suffering from stomach complaints owing to the sudden change from near starvation and lack of vitamins to the ample and complete diet supplied to us on his train. 'Ah yes', he sighed, 'we know that some of you suffered a good deal of malnutrition in Egypt before you were captured.' He genuinely believed this assumption was the truth.

Well, mistaken as the young doctor was in one respect, I myself began to feel so much better owing to the good food that I wondered whether I was going to Germany on false pretences. Good old Jack Tattersall reassured me by saying, 'I wouldn't allow a dog to continue in your condition without an operation!'

Jack was also loquacious — and apparently understanding — when philosophising with a German orderly, some of whose family lived in America. The German thought of Quakerism as an American institution, because an American Quaker had fed him when he was a child before America had entered the First World War. He knew, too, about Quakers feeding Germans in occupied

129

territories and in Berlin after that war. A patriotic Australian patient also invervened and together we talked about religion, Toc H, the Boys' Brigade, Hitler Youth and war. Jack, like the rest of us, I daresay, nodding knowingly when he did not understand the German.

Thus we travelled steadily on past Augsburg, Westheim and Ulm through Germany towards Switzerland — and we began to wonder whether we were after all to end up in a neutral country! We had not entered Germany quite in the manner we had, perhaps, anticipated when we joined up. We had possibly dreamed of a victorious entry into a conquered land. As it was, Jack Tattersall was moved to remark 'Can we believe we are all in an enemy country?' Once we recognised four fellow P.o.W.s working in a field. Occasionally we passed a bevy of German girls, who broke off from their labours on a farm to cheer and smile at the wounded warriors returning to the Fatherland. German and English looked much alike with uniforms discarded recumbent on bunks, as a lot of us were, in this train.

At this stage of the journey we began to leave Allied walking patients looking rather forlorn at various centres, and then at Ravensburg — only twenty-five kilometres from the Swiss border — we left our German patients. The German doctor told us that our final destination was to be nearby Rottweil in Württemberg.

On 14 September 1941, accompanied by the distant sound of church bells and a nearer brass band playing hymns to remind us that it was Sunday, we pulled into Rottweil Railway Station. My diary says that I 'probably dropped a brick by shaking hands with one of our German guards', as we left the train.

A half-mile ambulance journey and we found ourselves at a real hospital this time in a pleasant, old-fashioned, Black Forest town rather smaller than Witney. Rottenmünster Lazaratt was adjoining a convent and we understood that before the war our part of the building which was now surrounded by barbed wire and guarded by German soldiers had been a home for the mentally deranged. Our windows were rendered impassable with iron bars, useful for keeping both lunatics and P.o.W.s inside!

To the joy of us newcomers, we found Dr Singer and several other good fellows, who had been transferred from Salonica, already in residence. Brian Darbyshire, George Greenwood and Duncan Catterall — the last named an officer — were also on duty

130

to receive us. Three more of the FAU, Bill Miall, Harold Cadoux and Ken King, were on the premises, but laid up with jaundice, a prevalent disease amongst us prisoners.

The conditions in this war-time prisoner of war hospital compared favourably with some civilian hospitals in peace time. Facilities for operations were adequate. One room was converted into an operating theatre; another was used sometimes as a church and sometimes as a hall for entertainment. For the first time since we were taken prisoner we were able to enjoy hot baths and get really clean. On arrival all my clothes and other kit were taken away to be searched by the Germans, cleaned and deloused before return. I wrote at the time that the food was almost as good as that to be expected in a hospital in London or Birmingham. The high quality of food could largely be attributed to Red Cross food parcels having been received. Ever since our arrival at Rottweil I have felt tremendous gratitude towards all the devoted Red Cross workers concerned in getting us those food parcels. They saved thousand of lives.

I was put to bed on a sheet-covered mattress under blankets, that were not quite up to the Witney standard, but again adequate! These blankets — or perhaps it was only one to each bed — were doubled inside a linen bag, which was regularly washed in the nuns' laundry next door, where some prisoners gave a helping hand.

On the day after arrival Dr Singer, with smile as wide as ever, came round with Captain Stanley Gilder, known as Dr Gilder to us medical staff. Dr Gilder was one of those who had failed to get away from northern France. He had probably stayed behind to care for wounded prisoners as he was doing now. With these two was a German doctor, Dr Essig, who was making a routine inspection. In general Dr Gilder was in charge of the English-speaking personnel, but he seemed to be able to get the Germans, including the nuns next door, to help us in any way they could. His kindness, tact and flair for language made him the most influential individual in the establishment.

The two English doctors studied my condition as doctors do and told me they would operate in just over a week's time. Accordingly, the day before the operation, I was moved into a room next to the theatre. George Greenwood and Bill Miall were the orderlies in charge of our small ward, in which there were two Maoris from

Auckland, an Arab and another Englishman besides myself.

As for the operation — under these comparatively excellent conditions I imagine that there was nothing to worry about. I am not sure whether Dr Gilder or Dr Singer wielded the knife, but my diary reads, 'Remember wondering, as blanket of unconsciousness approached, which girl friend, or parent, would have the honour of being last in my thoughts'. However, in fact I believe the last thought was, 'There's nothing for it but to trust the Doctors now!' Next I remember Reg Haldane saying, 'Well he took a long time to come out of that!' Reg Haldane was the RAMC theatre orderly and like several acquaintances at that time was to become a lifelong friend.

During the next few days the Maoris kept the rest of us in our room cheerful with singing and back-chat. The remaining FAU men came in to see me from time to time and we prepared a statement to go to the German authorities:

24.IX.41 Prisoners of War Hospital, Rottenmünster.

On behalf of a section of 7 members of the 'Friends Ambulance Unit', I take the liberty of explaining to the German Authorities matters concerning our Membership.

We are all associated with the religious Society of Friends, which is known in Germany by the name of Quakers. We are civilians and volunteer members of the British Red Cross; we wear the field uniform and possess the identity papers of the Red Cross and are supported solely by voluntary contributions which have nothing to do with the British Military Authorities. Our members do not receive any payment and do not carry weapons.

The Association was founded at the start of the war, in order to enable young Quakers to perform a humane service in the spirit of the Quaker ideal. After three months of hospital training in England the Association offered its services to the Finnish Red Cross. These were accepted and we worked till the end of hostilities on the Ladoga Front. Afterwards we helped with the evacuation of the area which was handed over to Russia.

When the war in Norway broke out, we transferred our work to the Norwegian Red Cross until the British retreated. We then crossed the border into Sweden, where we remained till a

132

journey through Russia, Turkey and Syria brought us to Egypt. In January 1941 we put ourselves at the disposal of the Grecian Red Cross. We were accepted in March and travelled to Greece. During the British retreat we found a temporary hospital overcrowded with British wounded and looked after by a small Grecian staff. We decided to work at this place, which was occupied by the German troops on 28th April 1941. We continued working in Kalamai for several weeks, followed by three months' medical and surgical work in the field hospital of a prison camp at Salonica. Now seven of us have been assigned to the prisoners of war hospital here at Rottenmünster and travelled here with a transport of sick and wounded, while the other nine continued to work in Salonica. This letter is written on behalf of those other nine members also.

As members of a voluntary relief organisation, we take the liberty of drawing your attention to the fact that we wish to be released to our own country under the protection of the Geneva Convention. The expenses involved in transport will be settled by 'The Friends Ambulance Unit' in London, the British Red Cross or the 'Society of Friends'.

R. D. Catterall P.o.W. No. 16495

The foregoing is a translation of what I believe Brian Darbyshire wrote in German. Duncan Catterall, our FAU Officer in the hospital, signed it. He has since become a well-known and extremely skilful specialist medical doctor in England.

We now believed ourselves to be in a situation from which we could report the location of every member of 'the captive band' taken prisoner at Kalamai and should let the Red Cross and our friends in England know our whereabouts. We therefore on 19 September 1941 had sent a postcard to Das Internationale Komitee vom Roten Kreuz, Genf, Schweiz, saying,

Will you please cable Cadbury Chairman Friends Ambulance Unit Bournville England at his expense: Seven Members Cadoux 16404 Catterall 16495 Darbyshire 16498 Early 16587 Greenwood 16497 King 16493 Miall 16496 now working prison hospital Germany may receive letters and parcels Address full name gefangen numeren followed by Stalag VB Germany. Remaining nine still working in country of capture. Would you be good enough to let know cable has been despatched. Yours faithfully R. D. Catterall.

Almost as soon as our party arrived at Rottweil, and indeed before, we began to wonder about the possibility of repatriation or, for members of the FAU, transfer to a civilian internment camp. After all, we in the FAU were civilians. I wrote down my own views at the time as follows,

(i) For those working in these conditions (in Rottenmünster), envied by less fortunate RAMC (working elsewhere), if easily replaceable it *may* be our duty to accept an opportunity to get back to England for more hazardous, arduous or responsible work instead of spending the rest of the war in this safe retreat.

(ii) It would not be playing the game to try and escape while we are negotiating with the Germans to give us special concessions as Quakers. If the Germans refuse repatriation then we can think again.

(iii) Don't force anyone's hand before we know what FAU in London, German Quakers and International Red Cross (all of whom have been approached) are doing for us.

(iv) Be careful not to do something just for sake of change. There is useful work, of a kind for which we joined the FAU, here (in Rottweil). We did not join to spend the war in quiet study and meditation in a civilian concentration camp (i.e.) Quite likely there are women to do the nursing there and we would not be in much demand.

The foregoing thoughts show how little I knew of 'the outside world' — especially the remarks about 'a civilian concentration camp'. Had any of us ended up in some such establishment the chances are that we should not be writing our memoirs now. Anyway for my part, I was never offered a passage to England or any other change until the Allies took possession of our hospital at the end of nearly four more years!

From now on the part I was to play in the war was very well mapped out, and looking back, even after forty years, I still feel great gratitude towards those who made my own work possible.

The hospital soon made sure that I was fit to go into action again. I sought the sooner to recover usefulness by extra physical activity including walks round the small square with buildings on two sides and barbed wire with a German guard marching along outside on the other two sides. I found that a regular walk round the path keeping as near to the wire and to the buildings as possible was excellent for the health. I also discovered that one round of the little square, so to speak, meant travelling 135 yards and that during an hour's recreation I could comfortably walk three-and-three-quarter miles. I came to these conclusions by keeping a close eye on my wrist watch as I walked and not quite such a close eye upon the German guard who had his bayonet at the ready.

Imagine my surprise, during, I believe, my second afternoon's exercise of this kind, suddenly to find myself grasped by the wrist on which was the watch I was studying. A figure in grey uniform was addressing me, in hostile and excited German. One does not argue in a foreign language with a man who has you by the wrist and is carrying a rifle and bayonet; but I did indicate that perhaps we could go and find an interpreter. That was not difficult; as Sergeant John Southall, who, unlike myself, understood German like a native, was close at hand. The guard still kept hold of my wrist; but John and I were able to explain to the zealous German that I had been neither training for, nor immediately attempting, escape from the hospital. On the contrary in a way I had voluntarily put myself inside it to try and relieve suffering according to my Quaker persuasion. The interview ended in smiles all round: all the same I could not but feel exceedingly grateful to good old John Southall, and we earned for myself the nickname of 'Der Sportsman' from more than one of our German guards.

It was at this stage that we were allowed to go and fetch from a loft our somewhat battered and charred belongings, which had been extremely thoroughly searched and de-loused. Of my belongings I can only remember that one, a leather fur-lined waist-coat, was missing. It had been a present from my brother before our party left for Finland. I assumed that some German soldier was now to wear it on the Russian front and I could hardly feel jealousy. However, rumour had it that Moscow was about to fall to the Germans. I doubt if we believed that; but we who had been on a Russian front in war-time knew the conditions that would prevail there now winter was setting in.

By 24 October snow was falling heavily in the Black Forest district. Dr Gilder had asked me to share the duties of masseur with the officer's batman, Dick Whirity. Dick and I found that we shared a birthday; we still exchange greetings on 7 August. Dick was an extremely skilled lightweight boxer and when, a lot later,

Witney sent us out some boxing gloves, he kindly instructed me in the noble art. His interest in physiotherapy derived, as did mine, from his acquaintance with physical training and development. To start with we shared the massage cases. However, in our spare time, he looked after the domestic needs of the officers and I looked after a ward. As time went on I became definitely appointed hospital masseur by Dr Stanley Gilder and more or less held down the job for the remainder of the war.

To start with my work, outside the ward for which I was particularly responsible, consisted of massaging with my hands; but my province was soon extended to include the leadership of gymnastic classes for those recovering from wounds and for those who had lost limbs. Towards the end of our three-and-a-half year stint in Germany I was to be made responsible for maintaining and operating remedial electrical equipment in what I eventually called 'my massage room'. Until we were captured I had little special skill in physiotherapy. After I was taken prisoner I really only followed the instructions of careful and devoted doctors in dealing with our long-suffering patients!

One or two of our patients succeeded in escaping from the hospital during the time we were in residence. As far as I know none of these reached home. Usually they were brought back temporarily to the hospital (so that we could see that they had been caught) before being taken to another prison camp. In the case of the RAMC it would have been considered desertion had a medical orderly escaped while on duty in this prison hospital. Whatever I wanted to do I felt bound by the same rules as the RAMC in this respect. In fact I once contrived to get shut out of the place and almost had to bribe the sentry at the gate to let me in!

Some of the long-term patients who were declared by doctors to be unfit for further service were sent home in occasional batches. So were some doctors and other purely medical personnel before the end of the war. Amongst those sent home was Dick Whirity, who was good enough to meet my parents in London and give them an eye-witness account of doings in Stalag VB. Just before the end of the war Dr Gilder himself was also to go. He, also very kindly took the trouble to give news of me to Mother and Father. Such kindness was very much appreciated.

As for the FAU, some of our number were at intervals moved to other Stalags and most of those got home before the virtual end of the war. I had been asked to do a special job, so there was in my mind no question of my moving separately from the bulk of the British medical staff and patients. In fact, all of us in this category were transferred to another prison hospital at the nearby town of Nargold on 28 December 1941 and brought back again on 12 February 1942.

There was another and sadder way to leave the hospital. I will quote exactly from my diary of 31 October 1941.

On this frosty and snowy morning twelve of us under Captain Gilder and Sergeant John Southall marched to village cemetary for the burial of Charlie Sutton, who died after a long illness (pneumonia and T.B.). He came from London (Kennington I believe), where he lived with his sister. Eleven Germans paraded and fired a salute. It was a respectful ceremony with short prayers read by Captain Stanley Gilder. There were beautiful wreaths from English, French and Germans.

When it came to care of the sick and wounded the German point of view was much the same as our own. Here is another word-for-word extract from my diary on 12 January 1942.

I started a free-standing gymnastic class for one-armed men. Dr Gilder is arranging for George and Brian to see the German Dr Rhomer about possible move of other six FAU Members to a civilian camp. On hearing our position as Quakers explained Dr Rhomer said, 'Pity the whole world doesn't think like that!'

And on 13 January I wrote,

George and Brian saw Dr Rhomer German doctor in charge of hospital today and explained that six FAU wanted to be transferred to civilian internment camp on grounds:— (i) to study (ii) there was decreasing medical work in hospitals and they could well be spared (from our Stalag VB hospital) (iii) more chance for repatriation either during, or quickly after, the war. Dr Rhomer was friendly and George and Brian like him. He asked about FAU history and work and said he would write to ask if they might be transferred. George also mentioned that Dr Gilder needed a masseur (in this hospital VB) and that I was very willing to stay here.

And perhaps I may add more from the diary covering the

following three days — 14 January,

> Good walk (on parole under supervision of German guard) 2.0 p.m. to 4.10 p.m., wonderful snowclad pine wood: we saw deer skip across the road in front of us and horse-drawn sledges and children tobogganing: rather a job to get through (in addition to the walk) sixteen massage cases, one individual excising, two heat treatments and four gym classes (including one for leg amputees and one for those who had lost an arm).

And 15 January, 'George Greenwood's 26th Birthday.'

And 16th January, 'Joe Teraoka, Swiss Cottage, London, always a friendly companion and his interest in music and knowledge of German most cheering.'

I will not immediately quote more from the diary but would like to add something more about my friend Joe Teraoka. He was Japanese, but brought up in London. He spoke cultured correct English with just a trace of a cockney accent. He was an RAMC orderly, well established at Rottenmünster before any of us FAU arrived there. When I started work in the hospital it was my good fortune after leaving the 'sick-bay' to sleep in a bunk immediately above his. So we had the opportunity to get to know each other extremely well.

Returning to the day of the evening of 28 October 1941, I had written,

> Joe saw me saying my prayers and said it was the first time he had seen a man do that for two years. An interesting conversation followed in the room about Heaven, Hell, Christ and Miracles, Buddha, Mahommed, toleration between sects (or lack of it) and King George IV's bulging stomach.

When Japan came into the war on the German side, the Germans interviewed Joe and asked whether he would like to be released from prison to help the Axis powers. Joe explained that he had been brought up in England and was a British national; he would most certainly prefer to remain in prison on the British side. This was accepted and he returned to his medical duties in Stalag VB.

There were other incidents demonstrating personal goodwill to me during these early days at Rottweil which remain in my mind and heart. I have no need to use my diary in recalling them: here are some of them.

138

At first when we FAU members were the 'new boys' at Rotten-münster hospital it was agreed that the FAU and RAMC should inhabit different rooms, because the FAU tended to eat more than our fair share of food. Perhaps those who have never been half starved for a prolonged period will be unable to understand this. Anyway the agreed arrangement, although established, did not last long. While this segregation of the FAU and the RAMC was being observed, I must have been still off-duty owing to the recent surgery and was feeling considerably the worse for wear. Temporarily I was housed among complete strangers mostly of other nationalities. Imagine the pleasure it gave when, on awaking the first morning in this foreign environment, I found standing by my bunk the big, kindly and outspoken RAMC Corporal, famous as an Australian Interstate cyclist, Harold Butt. He had brought in a wonderful sugared hot cup of tea from our own RAMC quarters.

The second incident at about the same time concerned the shovelling of coal. A small contingent of us prisoners were marched to Rottweil railway station to unload a truckful of coal to be delivered to the hospital. I cannot remember how it was that I had been selected for this job of shovelling coal from a railway waggon into nearby road conveyances. After a time I began to wilt and the German guard, who was standing near in complete uniform and carrying his rifle, took the heavy spade from my hands and completed my part of the work.

The third incident was quite different and must have been some weeks if not months later. The Germans allowed medical and other working personnel to leave the hospital and play matches on a local soccer ground. By this time I was fit enought to hold my own in the British XI, which often played against the French. In these limited Internationals the British team usually won — perhaps we had rather more real footballers available than the opposition! I was no soccer player. Although right-footed, I usually played on the left wing in order to increase the power of my left foot. Dick Whirity, as well as being an excellent boxer, was a very good footballer and played centre-forward.

One afternoon, when I seem to remember a considerable number of our walking patients had been escorted to the field by our guards to watch our prowess against the French, I found just after half-time that I had scored two goals. We were winning comfortably and, when the right winger sent a slow centre across the goal mouth it would have been easy enough for the centre-forward to complete the movement by putting the ball into the net. However, the generous Dick allowed it to trickle on towards me on the left with the words 'Go on, Richard, you put it in and get a hat-trick!' There was really no difficulty about my consummating the only hat-trick I have ever scored on any soccer ground! Then Dick Whirity went on and finished off a hat-trick for himself. I would like again to thank my Australian and German friends as well; I hope they will read this book!

Rottweil did not seem all that remote from Witney, especially after my firm had managed to get through to me a beautiful brown Witney blanket with four darker bars at each end — a Forbar in fact! With pride and in comfort I slept under it for the rest of the war. Another treasured possession was an all-wool pullover. The donor of this was my schoolboy and lifelong friend, Alan Paine. The pullover was made by his famous firm, which has done so much in exporting from Godalming, Surrey. I wrote to tell Alan that I was wearing his wonderful gift night and day.

Another connecting link was a good supply of books sent very often from Blackwell's of Oxford on the instigation of my fellow members in Witney Reading Society. Witney Reading Society had been founded, largely by Witney blanket makers and Methodists, in 1853. My family paid my subscription to the Society during my absence and passed on my heart-felt apologies for non-attendance. I used to receive messages of good cheer from book meetings — and books bought on my behalf. If one wishes to read a great many books, learn to act in plays and make music, there is nothing like contriving to become a prisoner of war! Not all the requested books and sheets of music came from members of the Reading Society. The Red Cross and other friends helped from more than one country; but my brother regularly sent *The Countryman*, published not far from Witney: it was one of the publications which the censors allowed through to us. I have it in mind that they did not also allow me the opportunity to read the *Boys' Brigade Gazette*.

Jerome K. Jerome's *Three Men on the Bummel* came safely to hand in spite of its containing the remark, written in AD 1900 'Hitherto the German has had the blessed fortune to be exceptionally well governed; if this continues, it will go well with him. When his troubles will begin will be when by any chance something goes wrong with the governing machine.' Added interest was that Jerome had taken his *Three Men* on a visit to the Black Forest and the River Neckar: in fact that river flowed within a hundred yards of Rottenmünster and before we left I had swum a mile up and down it, supervised by a guard, of course. Jerome K. Jerome was a philosopher as well as a humorous novelist: he had served as an ambulance driver during the First World War.

Imagine, also, what a joy it was for a captive blanket maker to be able to read not only Jerome K. Jerome's lively books but *The Crowthers of Bankdam, Inheritance, Dover Harbour* and *Captain Hornblower* — to mention but a few; for there were books about medicine and physiotherapy as well. There was also *Brush up your German*. After reading the books ourselves we used to pass them on to George Greenwood, who was building up quite a sizeable and extremely interesting Kriegsgefangener Library. George, like the rest of us, made the most of his latent talents and some of the books he offered to his clientele came from Witney Reading Society. One book, which I did not hand on to the Library, was from George Maynard, Early's new Company Secretary. It was about accountancy, and I studied it myself and eventually brought it back to Witney. As well as books, there were priceless letters from members of the Society. I particularly remember those from Bill Dominey, rival, and very skilled blanket maker of Witney, who sometime later became a most valued colleague. These letters about Witney and home meant a great deal to one who was away for an indeterminate period. Here is part of one letter from the Reverend Woodman Treleaven. He had been one of Witney's Methodist ministers and a member of Witney Reading Society in bygone days. After reading it I could almost feel that I had visited the old town myself!

Lately my wife and I have had a delightful short holiday. We were for a few days with Marjorie Leigh in Corn Street, Witney, and then with Alfred Butler at Burford. The beauty of Witney stood out like a lovely thing spot-lighted against a dark background. I met your father and mother and many other old inhabitants looking only a little time-worn. George Wickham [a local draper], as nervous and explosive as of yore, sat in his usual seat in the Choir [of which he was Choir Master] on Sundays and Charles Miles [a gardener, whose bass voice had once been described by a knowledgeable musician as the finest in Oxfordshire] added volume to the tasteful playing of the new Organist [a fine musician, banker and charming Member of the Reading Society], Frank Lane. Viewed from Fulbrook, the beautiful Cotswold stone, framed with green, made a restful picture. I wondered whether you would like to be reassured that so much that is beautiful in the old town is awaiting your return and so many sound kindly people will welcome you.

Yes, I was reassured about what I knew already by such letters as this.

For me and doubtless for other medical orderlies another consolation was that we were doing a useful job. However, there was other joy as well as sadness and humour. It was not to be expected that our mixed party consisting of a considerable number of high-spirited young medical workers, divided between rooms well away from the patients on the fourth floor, would always live in undisturbed harmony. In one room there might be a preponderance of those from the Antipodes. Another room might consist largely of Indians. In our own room to start with at any rate, we were mostly Friends Ambulance Unit. Occasionally there were disagreements, and one room would raid another with no more dire intent than to dismantle the bunks beautifully made for the night.

One evening there had been a certain amount of what our custodians would call disorderly behaviour on the fourth floor and we were expecting an attack from Australia next door. We, therefore, carefully arranged a bucket of water above the doorway, making sure that, when the door was opened, the bucket would be left securely hanging but upside-down. We set the booby trap and then waited for the sudden entry of Harold Butt, the large cheerful Australian, and some of his compatriots from the other room.

For some minutes there was complete silence. Then, as we expected, the door was flung open and water descended over the head and shoulders of . . . the German guard. He was elderly — too old, I suppose, for the Russian front — and dripping wet, he looked round at us standing like perplexed statues. His eyes were somewhat unconventionally aligned and he was too surprised even to let his hand grasp the revolver on his belt. Then we all started to talk at once trying to explain matters in our imperfect German. I believe that Brian Darbyshire, our expert in languages, eventually

142

got across the sentiments we had difficulty in putting into words. The German smiled and nodded as he made a dignified retreat, doubtless much relieved that he had not discovered a complicated multiple escape attempt! There was no more horse-play that night!

All were not so fortunate in the news they received from home, or from other parts of the world, as I was. One of our patients was obviously made very happy one day at being handed the first letter he had received here from his fiancée in London. A quarter of an hour later Dr Gilder had to break to him news just in from the Red Cross and obviously after-dating the letter, that this girl, whom he was to marry, had been killed in an air-raid.

Christmases came and went during our stay near the Black Forest. Thanks to the Red Cross we always had something special to eat at these times. We also enjoyed special services. The first I remember was conducted by that amazing all-rounder Stanley Gilder. During that Christmastide he interpreted for us the address as it was spoken by a French Protestant Padre from nearby Villinghan, so that we English-speakers might understand better.

Another Christmas Day later on, I was walking round inside the little square recreation ground already referred to and the German guard was, as always, proceeding rather gloomily with his rifle slung over his shoulder along the outside of the barbed wire. I was pretending to myself that I was walking the half mile from my home to Witney Methodist Church, as very likely some members of my family were doing at about that time. In view of the day, I paused to wish the man in grey outside in my best German 'A Merry Christmas!' He took the greeting seriously and stopped, as I had, in his progress along the wire. 'Yes,' he replied, 'and to think that more than two thousand years after Christ showed us how to live, we treat each other like this!'

I do not know what Hitler and a number of others on either side would have thought about such fraternisation: but I — and I was by no means alone — formed friendships with the opposition which in some cases proved lifelong. After the war, when we invited one German soldier, who was I believe a chemist in Rottweil, during peace-time at any rate, to a Rottenmünster reunion in England, Dr Gilder, in a kindly speech of welcome to overseas visitors said, 'If we had all been Prisoners of War there would be no more wars'.

A picturesque exaggeration; but we understood the truth he

conveyed by his remark. At another service Stanley read a Prayer recently used on 11 November at the Boys' Brigade Memorial Service in Witney.

One day a message came up to the fourth floor from a German sergeant, who had brought for treatment to our hospital some prisoners from another camp. He announced that he had some time to wait and wondered whether any of the medical staff had some music with which he could while away a few minutes. Through the thoughtfulness of my family, the Red Cross and a friend in Switzerland, I had accumulated a few songs and even oratorios. Therefore I went down to the ground floor and asked Sergeant Leopold Vetter, the gentleman concerned, whether we could not try out my music together. We proceeded to do this very much to my advantage. He was a brilliant pianist and I believe I can still sing by heart in German *Die Beiden Grenadiere* and with a bit of revision *Dichterliebe* by Schumann, as he taught me. Leopold Vetter lived in Germany near Switzerland. He was considerably older than I was and must be near the end of his mortal span by now. I received no reply to my last letter; but some of us enjoyed meeting him again after the war.

My own interest (although no great skill) in music led to other friendships which lasted on into peace-time. Lieutenant Maurice Rowland of the Royal Artillery Corps was a most helpful pianist and together we rendered *The Two Grenadiers* in English at concerts given by the British medical staff organised at first of course by Dr Gilder, who also produced some excellent plays. 'Rowley' and I still exchange Christmas cards. The French prisoners enjoyed *The Two Grenadiers*, because the song ends with the tune of *The Marseillaise*, sung I need hardly say full blast towards their part of the room. However, when, after coaching from Leopold Vetter, I changed to singing it in German there was almost a revolution!

Another excellent pianist was Robert Maréchal, a young Frenchman, who was training to be a Roman Catholic priest. He was a real friend as well as a good musician. Somewhat late in our gefangenschaft, I was asked to sing a bass solo from *Messiah* at a Church of England service. By this time there was a Roman Catholic priest in the hospital (one of the French prisoners) and I remember that both Bobby and I went to ask this Padre's permission for Bobby to play the piano accompaniment at our Church of England service. Of course permission was granted; the fact that we were all prisoners together united sects and sometimes religions.

Robert Maréchal and I got to know each other very well before the end of the war. After the war he completed his studies and became a priest and missionary in Burma. His eventual departure from this life grieves me but fills me with admiration. The Burmese village, where he worked, was molested by murdering brigands. The brigands started to loot the small township and kill the inhabitants. Thereupon Bobby, using his full authority as priest, gathered all the men, women and children available into his church. This done he stood at the entrance barring the way to the evil-intentioned brigands in protection of his flock. The murdering band came on, killed him and ravaged the church. His was an heroic death and I do not believe such sacrifice is vain.

Returning to the end of 1941 and beginning of 1942, during which period Japan and America entered the war, our hospital was sometimes visited not only by the International Red Cross but by thorough-going German 'High ups'. One day we were told that we would all be called at 5.45 a.m. the following morning, because a German General was coming to inspect. Such visits were taken very seriously, partly because it was advisable to hide away incriminating documents such as, in my case, the copy of *Brush up your German*, which included a local map. My diary tells me that we were not actually called at 5.45 a.m. because the German soldiers responsible for getting us up were at that time confined to the cellar during an air-raid alarm. Anyway, before the inspection we had to make sure the great man had nothing to complain about. No one was more thorough than our cheerful naval surgeon Dr Hugh Singer, who had even at this stage been responsible for saving the lives of more than one patient. Before the General appeared Dr Singer entered our ward and seeing that I was tidying some spare blankets came hurrying across the room to lend a hand. I could not help reflecting that, even from Dr Singer, I did not really need help in this particular task! However, I remembered quoting to the Lieutenant Surgeon a day or so previously a sentence I had once read, 'There is nothing that the British Navy cannot do'. He had cheerfully agreed that the statement was correct; although my quotation may not have been word perfect.

It is noteworthy that when, after his tour of inspection, the General had expressed his complete satisfaction with the state of the hospital and the way the patients were looked after, Dr Singer took the trouble to come round and personally thank each one of us for our support.

One of my massage patients, named George Savory, like a few others, suffered from what we called 'a dropped foot'. In other words he had no power to raise his foot forward and upwards to make the angle between lower leg and foot more acute. In order to walk at all he needed, say, a string from his toes to just below his knee to hold his foot approximately at right-angles to his leg. I massaged George furiously and hopefully to help him regain the use of the necessary muscles in the front of his lower leg. That was of no avail, but we could get the muscles to work by using electricity.

In view of the foregoing our doctors concluded that the nerve from the brain which should have operated the muscles concerned was for some reason out of action. This was reported to the German medical authorities and they offered to take George to a German civil hospital to investigate further and operate themselves. This offer was accepted by Dr Singer. As George Savory's masseur I was interested and asked permission to accompany Dr Singer and our patient to see what was to happen in the outside hospital. I was very pleased when the Germans agreed that I might see the operation. This is what my diary reminds me happened forty years ago

2nd February, 1942. Left with Dr Singer and George Savory to attend operation in German hospital at 8 a.m. Anaesthetic, Ethyl-Chloride followed by Ether, was administered at 9.40 a.m. and operation was concluded by noon. Three German Doctors with Dr Hofmeister in charge performed the operation. Two German orderlies and three Sisters assisted in the theatre. Incision about 12" long was made in right buttock and extended down the back of the thigh about 3" deep. The sural nerve (about the same diameter as a pencil) was traced until it was found where it was calloused to the bone on one side and attached by scar tissue to the muscle on the other side, where a bullet had passed through the groin. The consequent restriction of the nerve caused pain in the foot and lack of any power to lift it. The Surgeon released the nerve from the muscle — but not, for fear of severance, from the bone. Now we must wait and see

146

how much benefit comes from this action. I thought the Germans took very great care.

There was at the hospital in 1942 a quiet young patient from the British Army named Alan Lorimer. He must have been delicate before being taken prisoner and our own doctors, in consultation with the Germans, who usually had the last say in these matters, must have agreed that he should be kept at Rottenmünster instead of being sent to a Stalag where medical treatment would be difficult if it became necessary. I believe he was suffering from a lung complaint which became worse, but do not remember more about his condition. He had a pleasant baritone voice and took part in our 1941 Christmas concert. A good friend to Alan was Chief Petty Officer Fred Bosomworth, who slept in the same room.

Alan Lorimer had not the necessary physique, nor perhaps the necessary temperament, to withstand austere conditions in a prison hospital a long way from home — even though in his own way he entered into whatever fun was going on. After some months he began to fail and became bedridden. Then the time came when I remember Dr Gilder saying sadly, 'I am afraid Alan is going to slip through our fingers'. The Chief Petty Officer stood by him to the last and did all he could to comfort and befriend his room companion.

One day Fred had been absent in another part of the building, very likely to get something for his friend. When he returned he found that Alan was smiling and cheerful and greeted him with the words, 'My mother and father have been here. I hoped you would be back before they left'. Fred received the news seriously and sympathetically, saying that he was so sorry he had been away and missed meeting the visitors. Had they really come into the room? 'Oh yes,' replied Alan, 'and some of the family as well!'

Alan did 'slip away' soon after these incidents. Who is to say that his family did not pay him the visit of which he spoke?

8 Dream of the future

The phantom sky line of a shadowy down,
Whose pale white cliffs below,
Thro' sunny mists aglow,
Like noonday ghosts of summer moonshine gleam
Soft as old sorrow, bright as old renoun,
There lies the home of all our mortal dream.
— Henry Newbolt

Those whose destiny has led them to part from family, friends, life work and home for an unknown length of time will understand Sir Henry Newbolt's words. I was fortunate to be kept in touch by wonderful letters from Witney and from other parts of the world. There was also something more than words alone uniting us. We at Rottenmünster acted plays and listened to music about the happy return, dreamed about it, held services about it and prayed about it — with deep longing.

Here is a typical letter from my father written in his distinct hand on a special 'Prisoner of War Post Form' instructing him not to forget to write my P.o.W. number and to 'write very clearly within the lines to avoid delay in censorship'.

Mrs M. and I are having — and enjoying — a week at the 'Rising Sun', Cleeve Hill. As I write I look out over that superb stretch of England from the Cotswolds, on the edge of which I sit, to the familiar contours of your old friends the Worcestershire Beacon and the rest of the Malvern Hills. The downs about here are glorious and even the efforts of the Reception Committee can't spoil them. A day or two ago we had the monthly news letter of the P.o.W. Relatives Association in which is printed your letter (part of it) about attending the operation. I am glad, as I think your remarks (given in full) will cheer up a good many relatives. The same passage with other titbits (e.g. your boxing lesson from Dick Whirity) is circulating from hand to hand round the firm in carbon copies. We are glad the sports parcels have got through and have hopes for the rest. Your letter of 14th May to Patrick is our latest. Your Reading Society messages are in good time for next week's meeting. Chief news from Newland House is the taking of two swarms of bees. M. hopes that they are not both from her own hives — 'Summat for nowt' preferred!

C.W.E. [Charles William Early, aged 92] is back from holiday — still keen on Woolhouse, but much older and more delicate than you left him. Not that you'd think so to see him cock an eye over a sample of wool! Don't refer to this of course, but give him another P.C. soon — the other gave great pleasure. Very much love from us both. J.H.E. P.S. Another set of boxing gloves left some weeks ago.

In his next letter, typed from our Newland, Witney, home on 24 June 1942, father speaks about my sister Ruth, the musician of the family.

Two days after I wrote you last, Ruth joined us at Cleeve Hill. We had a message asking her to ring up London and the result is that she has signed a fresh contract with ENSA with a party for straight music, half a dozen of them, the only one whose name I know, besides Ruth, being Gladys Ripley, contralto. I confess I am heartily glad to think of her being off jazz. Talk about chopping faggots with a razor. She had actually had lessons in it from Billy Mayerl. Old Solomon seems to have taken the kindly view about it that one must get a job somehow if one can and plenty of musicians hadn't got one in their own line.

Ruth's concert party did in fact include a conjurer, 'as a concession to the low brows', and was to travel and perform in a good many sea ports as her party circumnavigated Southern Africa on its way to the Western Desert.

Next comes in the same letter a paragraph about the allocation of shares in our private limited company of blanket makers, following my Uncle Edward Early's death at the beginning of the war, and the letter continues.

You will have gathered from our profit-sharing this year

being 3½% that we are not making large profits. The Profit Sharing Certificates are being handed out this week. We are adding a slip saying 'The enclosed Certificate bears interest of 6%. Keep it in the hope of adding others to it. It comes as a small token of the Firm's appreciation and thanks'.

Our firm's loyal USA agents were called Workman and Hunt and, when father ended his letter by speaking of them as follows, I think anyone who has carefully read his foregoing letters can interpret.

On the drapery side of our business we are still a good deal bothered by Bobby & Co. We don't see much of their travellers nowadays: they only call on us as you might say casually. Our own representatives do far, far, more than they. But their competition in foreign markets is still tiresome. Hockley, the General Manager, will quite certainly get the business and himself into the bankruptcy court. What one asks oneself again and again is not whether it will happen, but when. (Wasn't it Charles II, who, on his death bed, apologised to those around for being such a unconscionable time a-dying?) Just now his business seems to be taking a fresh lease of life and, for the moment, one must face the fact. But, in addition to our own firm, he has Workman and Hunt to deal with and it would be hard to say which is the greater their (Workman's) manufacturing recources or the resolution they put into their business. Both I think, are unlimited, near enough. What Hockley apparently doesn't realise is the accumulation of resentment which is growing throughout the whole drapery trade. When he has to face his creditors it will be a stormy meeting. This week I can't tell you when that will be. Only that I am *dead certain*. But enough business gossip! All our love to you, ever thine J. H. Early.

Even before starting this book the reader will almost certainly have known that Witney has been famous for making blankets, or whatever blankets were once called, for upwards of a thousand years. To start with blanket-making was accomplished by literally thousands of skilled individuals, often banded together by family ties. By 1685 Robert Plot, first Custodian of the Ashmolean Museum, Oxford, was able to say that there were in Witney sixty

150

Master Weavers, who between them owned one hundred and fifty looms giving employment to 'three thousand poor people, from children of eight years old to decrepit old age'. In more recent years, following the Industrial Revolution of the eighteenth and nineteenth centuries, four family firms had emerged, employing about a thousand town — and country — folk between them. Apparently the war-time government of 1942 came to the conclusion that the Witney blanket industry would operate more economically if still further concentrated. Accordingly two of the firms in Witney were ordered to close down their factories; so that all the actual manufacturing could be accomplished in the Mills of the remaining two. In his letter of 20 July 1942 father describes this move.

Smith and Phillips have appealed in vain against the 'Concentration of Industry's' recent decision to close them down. It seems very hard lines though of course there are bound to be hard lines for a great many people, and it won't be a joke for any of us. S & P will still take orders and be allotted materials, but will have to get us, or Marriott's, to do the making. I don't know that they will lose much of their identity, or good will, in the trade; things are too abnormal. But getting going again will probably be the pinch, and there I am very sorry for them. We shall need to be as helpful as possible. Meanwhile we have cancelled our advertising arrangements — not a great sacrifice, as the expenditure would have been of doubtful value anyway — but we hope they will take it as a gesture that we don't wish to take advantage of the situation.

This 'concentration' was a foretaste of the future. After the war, Smith and Phillips got going again all right, as did other concentrated manufacturers; but now, in 1983, Early's of Witney are the only blanket making firm in the town. Marriott and Sons merged with Early's in 1960 and, between the end of the war and the time at which I write, Smith and Phillips also closed and Major Jack Lawton-Smith became a director of Early's and other excellent employees from his firm also came to lend him a hand. The Witney branch of James Walker of Mirfield, having been concentrated with Marriotts during the war, also got going again afterwards but is now closed down. Mr R. N. Peace, the son of Walker's manager in Witney, opened an excellent shop in High Street, where Witney blankets and other bed clothes are marketed most successfully.

I like now to remember that a good many blanket makers in Witney and in our own firm must, like Jack Smith and myself, be descended from grand old Ursula Marriott, my seven-times-Great-Grandmother, who, when she had lived a 104 out of her 106 years, was in 1727 credited with above 150 living descendants.

Father's letter about business and trade ends with something quite different — a new youth centre to be run professionally under the auspices of our High Street Methodist Church. He concluded with the words, 'To a certain extent it will, I suppose, be a rival firm to the Boys' Brigade, but there should be room for both and they should help one another. If approved, the Board of Education would pay for most of it'.

I record this last excerpt, because during the war there seems to have arisen a changed attitude to social work. Previously social work tended to be left to amateurs working in their spare time. Much more now the Government began to pay social workers and club leaders. In the first uniformed youth organisation, the Boys' Brigade, founded in 1883, the officers, and indeed the boys, were largely expected to raise necessary cash. Most later youth organisations were the same until 1939-45, when the government began to help financially much more. Nevertheless, when father eventually retired from his entirely amateur BB work and was presented with a kind and generous gift by his 1st Witney Company engraved, 'James Harold Early Esq., J.P. in deep and sincere appreciation of over forty years Leadership from Officers, N.C.O.'s and Boys, 1946', he was considerably moved and in responding said, 'Chaps! I am so very grateful; but you know I have never had a better paid job'. However that landmark in his life was still four years ahead when, in August 1942, he went on to write about the Worshipful Company of Weavers:

> A week last Saturday, being St. James' Day was Weavers' Common Hall — Service in the Kings Chapel of the Savoy. Last year, when I was Upper Bailiff, I got them to have for the Anthem 'Jesu, Joy of Man's Desiring'. They had it again this year. You can imagine the organ alternating with the choir of boys only. One of the loveliest things I ever listened to.

Yes, I could remember that wonderful piece of music and it was appropriate that, just after the service, father received a note from

Ruth, who was in London on her way to join her 'African Concert Tour'. I am sure 'Jesu, Joy of Man's Desiring' was in her repertoire for the Western Desert. Father 'nipped' out from his business meeting for a farewell lunch with her. Having told me this, he closed his letter with a few remarks ostensibly also about business:

> As to the blanket trade, Hockley, of Bobby and Co., Exeter is, of course, giving us a good deal of anxiety just now in the east-end business — though perhaps no more than we are giving him elsewhere. We are seeing a good deal of Workman and Hunt's friends. More and more and more. We had two in for the evening yesterday, charming boys (one, Ritchie, told me his Grandmother's name had been Early!) W. & H.'s marvellous help and determination is the best business news I can give you in these grim times. They are a great firm.

Father did not test the censors by overplaying this kind of business news and there was a gap before the follow-up came.

> Talking about business, we are still speculating a good deal about Bobby & Co., Ltd. Definitely too many branches to be healthy. It would be wrong to pretend it is not a very anxious situation for those of us who are concerned in their future. It is. But all one's experience of the drapery trade goes to show that an East End business and a West End business running together don't mix well. Add to that a large branch in the Southern suburbs, and it is a job in the long run to know (since supplies are after all not unlimited) where to offer your best line of goods. And when your trading methods have put a whole lot of other concerns into Queer Street all over the town, you look in vain for a single helping hand when you need it. At least one of Bobby's associated firms is as sick as muck. Enterprise and bluff and clever publicity will carry a firm a long way, but once you start to flag and the market starts to have doubts about you, then the seeds of collapse begin to sprout. Hockley is a smart managing director, but compared with Workman and Hunt he is a midget. You can take it from me W. &. H. are working in the closest collaboration with our own firm. The two businesses are now practically one and the same.

This kind of 'business news' continued to flow from Witney for a considerable time to come. Presumably the German censor was

not acquainted with the real and most excellent Bobby organisation, which, under expert leadership in the real drapery trade of
Great Britain, had co-operated with Witney blanket manufacturers for generations. I used to take father's letters with me while I
made rounds of the hospital massaging, or helping with other
treatment in the massage room. I believe that reading them to the
patients helped the treatment! As time went on, however, the
German censor apparently realised that a second meaning could
be read into some of Father's remarks and that even the use of
initials could be conveying illicit news. I was interviewed by the
Germans and told to write home and stop anything being written
that could not be understood by all. I wrote home emphasising
that the use of initials, i.e. Mrs M. for Mother, and P. for my
brother Patrick, should be discontinued. The hint was understood
and no more news of the same kind as heretofore came through.
Needless to say further letters from Witney were all the more
welcome, because they wasted no space in talking about Hitler. As
a foretaste of things to come, when we got home, I received the
Beveridge Report and one got the impression that the country was
determined to make sure that not only education, but medicine,
surgery and full-time work would be available to all after the war
— and one hoped for some method of negotiation between nations
instead of fighting. During the war there was unstinted co-operation between employer and employee and a determination among
the more far-seeing that the scourge of unemployment should
never return and that just as strikes and lock-outs would bring no
permanent solution, war could not either. 'Forty years on' one has
to admit that we have not as yet won the peace; but I believe we
have glimpsed how that may be done.

There were diverse means of obtaining news from the outside
world. We heard the German version from a loudspeaker blasting
out, amongst some excellent Teutonic music, the news several
times each day. There was also an adjustable radio set in one of the
German staffrooms on the ground floor. One British officer found
that he could gain private access to this radio set and tune in to the
BBC. Unfortunately, he was discovered doing this by the Germans
and sent away from the hospital to be imprisoned elsewhere.

Blanket making was a great common interest I shared with
Witney. The whole textile industry of Great Britain — very much
including the Bobby group of stores — was doing a splendid and

loyal job. Its doings occupied a very fair proportion of my P.o.W. letter space. On 5 October 1942 father wrote about doings at the Mill

One or two interesting things in business today. This afternoon I had a short welcoming talk with the first batch of Smith's [one of the Witney Blanket firms partially closed down for the duration] Weavers — eight of them — who had started work for us at 8 a.m. I told them they were welcome and, if they felt rather pushed about, well, so were we; that they would be treated just the same as our old hands (only I didn't say hands); and that they could take all their troubles from wet feet upwards to Miss Bolton [Welfare Supervisor]. Big Ben is just booming out 9 o'clock. I wish you could hear him. She had already had them along to the canteen for dinner and they were impressed by our low prices. Then at 5 o'clock we had the monthly Works Council — first Monday each month — no accidents to report. One suggestion adopted: to cut the trees which are shutting the light out of part of the weaving shed — a simple and useful brain wave! Suggesters of adopted improvements are surprisingly pleased with their payments-on-the-nail of five bob. With regard to time-keeping we are going to let one clock do all the work in the weaving shed and have the other one under a glass shelter against the office wall for non-shed people. No clocking *out* except for odd times. A number of other topics of course, and then the 'premiere' of the sun-ray lamps downstairs. From the stairs one could see the ambulance room flooded with intense light looking whiter than daylight and quite unbearable at close quarters without dark specs. There were a number of us who wanted to try it, including four 'nighters' and myself. We just stripped to the waist and stood with specs on between the two lamps for a single minute each. Later the period will be extended to three minutes. Dorothy Bolton will of course have to organise suitable relays and it will all be done in work hours. I am afraid this tedious narrative will seem much ado about nothing, but I confess I am rather pleased and intrigued over the thing. Anyway the two precious lamps cost £20 apiece!

As a matter of fact I was very interested in 'the two precious lamps'. I had similar equipment to look after at Rottenmünster in my massage room. (Of course, it was not *my* massage room! The

155

doctors and other nationalities used it as much as I did.) When not engaged in routine duties in a ward I was usually massaging people in their own rooms or taking gym classes for the temporarily or, sadly enough, permanently disabled. I ran into trouble from Dr Stanley Gilder for overdoing this. He found me teaching a somewhat war-worn little Arab to stand on his head. However, the doctor did not let me down in public!

We had in our physiotherapy room, as at Witney Mill, various electrical contrivances. There was an infra-red lamp and an ultra-violet lamp. If one did not keep an eye on the place, other orderlies and some almost fit walking patients were apt to drop in and switch on the ultra-violet in attempts to produce on their bodies a healthy looking seaside tan!

In the massage room, one proof that I was really taking responsibility was that I cleaned the double-glazed windows and swilled walls and floors. The previous much more skilled operator of electrical equipment was a young soldier named Jack Palmer. He had far more medical knowledge than I had, and was promoted to more all-round duties. During the last period of the war he decided that when he got home he would study to be a doctor. Indeed, after the war he became a much-loved and public-spirited GP, and amongst his many other duties found time to spend a week as Medical Officer in the 1st London and 1st Witney Companies Boys' Brigade Camp in the Isle of Wight. His son also followed in his footsteps as a skilled doctor; but I also have noted that this son, a good many years after the war, has been described in the press as 'the Great Jonathan Palmer', because of his prowess as a top-class racing motorist.

As previously indicated my mail was by no means solely between Rottweil and Witney. Some was to and from Denmark. I was in touch with kind people I knew in this adjoining country to Germany. Letters from Denmark could at that time not go far beyond dwelling on personal matters. However, I learnt from our Physical Education Professor, Svend Holtze of Fredensborg, that when there was a dearth of tobacco after the invasion of Denmark on 9 April 1940, he and some other Danes succeeded in growing tobacco in their own gardens. I only learnt afterwards that when at first the Danes put up some kind of resistance to the overwhelming man and machine power King Christian X of Denmark personally gave orders to stop the fighting. By doing this he must have saved thousands of lives — both German and Danish. That did not by any means give to the Germans control of the independent Danish Vikings. Svend and Norah Holtze were in touch with the Danish underground movement. Young men operated an illegal paper and printed it in their gym-apparatus room at night. At times they had saboteurs staying with them when those fled from the Gestapo. It would have been a death sentence had they been caught for hosts as well as saboteurs.

When Christmas came round, I learnt later, some Germans put up a Swastika flag on the pole above Copenhagen's towering City Hall. This gesture by no means cowed the Vikings. At once King Christian X demanded an interview with the German Commander and told him that on Christmas Day, of all days, that flag in such a position would give great offence to all true Danes.

'It must come down!'

The German angrily snapped his heels together and barked 'Heil Hitler! Germany has conquered Denmark: of course the Swastika will not come down!'

'In that case', said the King quietly, 'a Danish soldier will cut that flag down.'

'If he does; I will have him shot!' shouted the Commander.

'Then', said Christian X, still calm, 'you will add regicide to your many crimes; for I am the Danish soldier who will cut down that flag.' The Swastika came down.

It is a terrible experience to be occupied by enemies and terrible crimes were committed in Denmark, partly because the Germans prevented the Danish police from keeping order. Many innocent Danes lost their lives. Alexandrine, Christian X's Queen, was a German princess by birth and she said at this juncture that she had never before been ashamed of her native country, but she most certainly was now. Sometimes, when a German was killed, the invaders would seize indiscriminately a dozen Danes who happened to be in the locality and shoot them. As the Danes walked out to their death they would sing a hymn or a verse from a hymn. That must have taken even greater courage than marching out to die. I understand that one of the hymns that could have been sung went to the tune 'Ascalon', a Silesian Folksong written in 1842. The Scottish words below were written by Benjamin Rhodes 1743-1815; but of course the Danish heroes sang in their own language.

My heart and voice I raise,
To spread Messiah's praise;
Messiah's praise let all repeat;
The universal Lord,
By whose almighty word
Creation rose in form complete.

A servant's form He wore,
And in His body bore
Our dreadful curse on Calvary:
He like a victim stood,
And poured His sacred blood,
To set the guilty captives free.

But soon the Victor rose
Triumphant o'er His foes,
And led the vanquished host in chains:
He threw their empire down,
His foes compelled to own
O'er all the great Messiah reigns.

With mercy's mildest grace,
He governs all our race
In wisdom, righteousness and love:
Who to Messiah fly
Shall find redemption nigh,
And all His great salvation prove.

Hail, Saviour, Prince of peace!
Thy Kingdom shall increase,
Till all the world Thy glory see,
And righteousness abound
As the great deep profound,
And fill the earth with purity.

Fru Svend Holtze, Norah, whose husband was our much-loved
and admired gymnastic instructor, is an English lady from Cum-
berland. She had taught us Danish Folk Dancing before the war
and most kindly wrote to me from Denmark when I became a
prisoner. She told me, when we met again afterwards, about the
father of one of our Danish partners in the dancing classes. He was
in charge of the royal gardens and woodland surrounding

Fredensborg Palace. One day he came across a German officer riding his horse along a royal drive. Very angrily, he told the rider in no uncertain Danish that only the King of Denmark was permitted to ride that way and ordered him off. He uttered his words with such ferocity that the German was glad ignominiously to quit the wood, where Danes were allowed by their king to walk as they wished.

I should just add to the foregoing that it was Grethe Maag, daughter of the determined, skilled patriotic head gardener, who took pity on an old dancing partner by also writing to me regularly during my captivity. She was engaged to another Englishman on Svend Holtze's course. They married after the war was over and my wife and I have always enjoyed great affection for them both.

To speak of 'my wife' at this stage of the story is premature; but now, as I write, she helps me in my descriptions of those sad and difficult times in her country. Her own work, then, was in a large Copenhagen store. From time to time German soldiers used to come into the store, usually to replenish their wardrobe. She had before the war taken the trouble to know a certain amount of German together with English, largely learnt from us students beside her native Danish.

One day, early in the occupation, a German officer, who had certainly not taken the trouble to learn the language of his unwilling hosts, bustled into the store and asked to speak with someone who could understand German; as he had some purchases to make. 'Our Frøken Madsen' was fetched and, on her arrival she said to the would-be customer, 'Do you speak English?' The whole shop stopped to listen!

There were various ways in which the Danes could, between 9 April and the end of the war, inconvenience their unwelcome visitors. If the German authorities got to know about a specially awkward Dane, that Dane's house might attract a visit from German soldiers after which he would never be heard of again by his friends. One day a couple of Danish telephone engineers called at the German headquarters of a town and explained that there seemed to be a fault in the telephone system and they had come to put it right. The Headquarters' staff were pleased that the hitherto indifferent telephone experts were at last anxious to help and invited them in to attend to the defect in the system. So the Danes came in and connected an extra line, whereby a Danish watch-committee could listen to all incoming and outgoing calls. Each time the committee learnt that the Germans were about to arrest a suspect, it would make sure that an ambulance was sent to the threatened Dane's home to carry him to safety before the Germans knocked at his door.

Denmark was the oldest independent kingdom in the world at the start of the war and remained so at the end of it. Poland was a new independent country, but since 1945 can hardly be termed independent. Yet it was for Poland that Great Britain had declared war. While writing this book I have remembered that on 1 May 1943, the Germans insisted upon Captain Stanley Gilder joining in an 'International investigation' to inspect corpses said to have been those of Polish officers in the parts of Russia, or Poland, recently occupied by the advancing German army. When the doctor returned eleven days later, we respected a request he made not to be questioned about his journey. Forty years later he has very kindly given me permission to publish the following letter, for which I asked him.

> I will tell you roughly what happened about Katyn. I went with a quite pleasant guard to Berlin and was put in a transit house on the banks of the Spree where I met two nice U.S. Officers and a paranoid South African Colonel, who was convinced that I was a German stooge. We were interviewed by German Officers — I protested formally and was told it was an order to go to Katyn. Next day we flew in an old Junkers plus a few British N.C.O.'s to Katyn via Breslau and Biala Podlaska (8 hours) and were put in a funny old building in Smolensk, the usual rotten block of flats the Soviets construct. However, we were entertained in the local officers' mess and handled with kid gloves.
>
> Next day the trip to Katyn (15 to 20 miles) was harrowing. Thousands of Polish corpses in mass graves all shot through the back of the neck. No reasonable person could doubt that they were shot by order of top Russian government — the action of our Foreign Office in boycotting the Katyn Memorial was contemptible and the refusal of some M.P.s to proclaim the truth was disgusting. The only comment I made at the time was that it didn't matter who did it — both the Nazis and the Russkis were entirely capable of this crime.

160

We went back to Berlin next day and were kept in the transit house for several days because the Germans wanted someone to do a radio talk on it. Naturally we refused, but the paranoid Colonel asserted that he was the Senior Officer and therefore nobody else must speak for us. We were sent back to camp except for that Colonel. What happened to him, I don't know.

I think I realised at that time how vile the human race is collectively and nothing since has changed my opinion (one expressed well by Sir Thomas Browne in *Religio Medici*). Fortunately there are individuals who restore one's faith in man as a person and fortunately also God gave us a sense of humour to laugh at the pompous asses who pretend to control human affairs. Every now and then I meet someone who makes me feel ashamed of my shortcomings and I see a glimmer of hope. Meanwhile one does what one can.

Dr Gilder did all he possibly could at Rottweil for the sick and dying of many nations. None were more grateful to him than Russians transferred to us from a hospital near at hand. The Russian prisoners received no Red Cross parcels unless we could give them some, as we did at times. Most of those who came to us would have died of TB had they needed to stay elsewhere. Some died in our care despite our doctors' efforts. I have good reason to remember this, because in April 1943 I started on a thirteen-week stint of night work looking after Russian TB's.

Stanley Gilder is a brilliant linguist and spoke to the Russians in their own language. He taught me enough to be able to pretend to understand them and offer some words of comfort. He could sometimes save their lives. Some of these Russian patients were farmers and shepherds from the Russian countryside, where, unlike the rest of us, they had never been exposed to tuberculosis and never built up resistance against it. When a poor fellow died during the night, I remember feeling ashamed that he was not still with his family looking after his farm in south Russia.

It was a queer feeling being the only man in the hospital whose duty it was to be awake. Of course there were the German guards conscientiously walking up and down carrying their rifles outside the barbed wire and probably a German sergeant dozing in the office downstairs.

One night I was hurrying along a darkened passage in response

161

to an unusual sound and ran into a rather solid and immobile body. I thought this might be one of our mental patients. 'Get back to bed!' I said sternly: it was the German Sergeant Stuhlinger. I fancy he was as surprised as I was when he switched on his torch. We both stepped back, grunted and then went on our premeditated ways. On another night the excitement was a violent earth tremor, which must have woken most people in the hospital; a proportion of the personnel hastened down towards the cellar thinking that it was an air-raid. Being awake already, I had my doubts about the air-raid theory and stayed with the Russian TB's, which indeed was my duty; but it may well also have been the safest course. My memory is of the Russian patients' loyalty and helpfulness to each other and to whomever was trying to look after them.

I still have an 'Army and Navy Stores' stick-on label from a tinned Christmas pudding sent me by my family to Finland in the Spring of 1940. There is a note on the label that the pudding concerned was eaten at 2.00 a.m. on Good Friday 1943 — just after it had been delivered to me at Rottenmünster. How many hungry people and countries had that pudding passed by before it caught me up?

Still another night it was my job to have nine Russians, recovered sufficiently to be moved to a regular P.o.W. Camp, ready for transit in the small hours. Using Red Cross parcels, I was able to make them nine beautiful cups of tea, sweetened with condensed milk, before they left for a prison camp, where they would certainly not receive Red Cross parcels. The German guard responsible came in to the ward and watched the preparation of the nine. He kept hanging about looking longingly at the cups of tea and he didn't get one. Perhaps I thought that the kind and generous people in England who had sent those parcels did not intend them for people who were not prisoners. After forty years I just can't remember my thoughts!

Even sadder occasions were when, as too often, one of our Russians died in the night and it fell to me to call the doctor and then help the German sergeant to carry away the poor emaciated body.

At Rottweil there was, before we were relieved in 1945, another short deviation from my usual routine as hospital physiotherapist. That was when I was sent with Dr Pridis and, of course, at least one German guard to accompany some Indian mental patients, adjudged unfit for war, to a port for repatriation via Sweden and England to India. Dr Pridis and I were not required to go all the way to India with them! It was by no means a comfortable train journey. At one stage we shared it with German troops on their way to the Russian front. However, having left our patients near a northern port, by dint of bribery with Red Cross cigarettes, our German guards were persuaded to bring us back via Vienna. Being P.o.W.s we were not permitted to walk on the pavements in the Austrian capital — only in the road. On entering an inn for refreshment, and greeting the barmaid with a courteous, 'Grüsz Gott!' we were somewhat startled when she clicked her heels together, raised her right hand and barked, 'Heil Hitler!' That made us smile, of course; but we did not smile when in a German town we found ourselves part of a crowd outside another inn, which had the night before suffered from British bombs; several civilians had been killed.

In peace-time the six-day journey from near one side of Germany to the other and back again would have been of immense interest. Imagine what it was like for us during a war after three years mostly spent in one building! On 1 September 1944 our small party was fifty kilometres from Krakow in Poland and we were told that the Russian forces had advanced to within sixty kilometres of that town on the other, or eastern, side. We persuaded ourselves we could hear the guns. When we got back to Rottweil we were told by two Americans wounded and recently taken prisoner in France that French territory was almost completely occupied by the Allies; so we imagined we could hear the guns on our side of Germany too.

At about the same time Father, who was not given to over-optimism, wrote saying, 'I think I hear the bell for the last lap'. He also told me that after he had gone to the front door one day and stood for a moment before shutting it, a passer-by, whom he couldn't put a name to, stopped and asked after me. I expect Father said I was doing well. 'O, ah!' said the other as he turned away down Newland, 'You'll soon have him back now!'

The German radio on 5 September reported that Antwerp and Brussels were in British hands and that the Bulgarians were requesting terms from the British, Americans and Russians, who were entering their country. In view of this news we were not all that worried when Geneva cabled that Red Cross parcels were to be reduced to half a parcel per man per week. Later on, for some reason, the Germans stopped our Red Cross parcels altogether. That could have been because they found that even when rations to us from their Commissariat were reduced we still fed better than a good many local German civilians.

By this time the Reverend Paul Guinness, with the rank of captain and a prisoner like ourselves, had been seconded to our Prisoner of War hospital as Church of England chaplain. He did a good deal more than arrange, and preach at, Sunday services, and proved himself a good member of our International community. He had a room to himself and soon found occasion to real aloud there one of a series of plays by Dorothy Sayers about the life of Christ, to a group consisting of Roman Catholics, Church of England and other sects from several countries. He was a tall, splendid-looking man and could more than hold his own with most of us when playing deck tennis! Deck tennis was a suitable game for restricted space in confined quarters. I made a note on 15 September that the Padre compèred community singing and insisted that I ended the evening by singing 'Jerusalem' with the rest of the twenty-five in the congregation joining in the second verse. Somewhat to my surprise I found I knew the words — having heard it sung so often, I suppose, at Witney, and other surrounding Women's Institutes! A few days later there is another note in my diary indicating that, unlike some of the rest of us who were told what to do, the Chaplain had to work out his own programme and persuade as many of the rest of us as he could to co-operate. He had only his own conscience and beliefs to keep him going. His influence towards the end of the war made a great difference. Near the end of September reliable news came that the Siegfried Line had been penetrated — and we calculated that the Allies were about sixty-three miles from us.

By 4 October we had no doubt but that we were hearing the big guns as the front approached us tantalisingly slowly. Allied aeroplanes were almost continuously overhead and sometimes came down in flames. Just as well they knew where our hospitals were, we thought! I write hospitals in the plural; because on one side of us was what must have been the very primitive hospital for sick and wounded Russian prisoners and on the other side a hospital, set up in the Convent, for Germans — partly staffed by the nuns, of course. I worked out that since capture I had taken a share in the treatment of soldiers from about twenty countries — including a wounded German soldier, whom I had carried into the Convent next door on my back. At this stage, I find that on 5 October 1944 my diary says, 'German radio reports Russians south and north of Belgrade and Allies massing in Holland, where they have already pierced the German border in a big attack'. I had in my diary added, 'The suffering in this hospital makes one long for the end of the whole wicked business'.

There were frequent comings and occasional goings of patients now that the ground fighting was so near to us. A number of long-term patients not fit for further service left us for repatriation. Because his service in the war was and would only be medical and surgical Dr Gilder, after a long and self-sacrificing period of leadership and humanitarian work, had by now also been repatriated by agreement through the International Red Cross. However, he didn't forget us and I understand that, when he arrived in England, he had the kindness to write about ninety letters giving first-hand information about those left — with no censors to interfere! — to our close relatives — 'absolutely priceless', as my father said, when Stanley wrote to my parents.

On 30 October 1944 I wrote in my diary, 'Brian showed me the way to prepare and administer a new drug discovered at Oxford since the war began. It is called penicillin'.

We all had to do what we could when and where help was needed. I sometimes found myself in the operating theatre. The diary continues on 2 and 3 November,

> Good mail from Witney dated August and September. It is evidently the opinion in England 'it will be over by Christmas'. Brian Darbyshire and I on reading in mother's letter that Mounsey, Miall and Whitehead are repatriated decided today that, if we were at home, we'd probably be doing something less useful than we are here. That is particularly true of him; for he is now permitted to 'assist scrubbed up' at operations in the theatre.

The sound of guns came closer and was almost continuous from the section of the Front nearest to us: the German radio announced, 'Big British attack in Holland'. There was lots for us orderlies to do in addition to any specialised skills we had developed. The long-term patients, now repatriated, had, while they remained with us, been able to take off our shoulders what you might call 'domestic duties'. We now had to wash clothes and scrub floors ourselves!

Our walks, on parole and with a guard, continued and very often included a visit to the 'Farm', where the farmer and his family used to call us in and give us milk, or cider, according to our taste. We became fond of the kind Württemberg family at the farm and were very sad when the farmer and father of the family, Herr Bilger, died suddenly while tending his sheep in the snowy Black Forest winter. My diary records that on the way back to Rottenmünster I 'talked with Padre helpfully for me'. Both inside the hospital and outside food was more scarce. I wondered if that had been one cause of this unexpected death?

By this stage in our 'gefangenschaft' it became difficult to realise that there was any other kind of life available. I felt apprehension at the thought that in a few months — weeks perhaps — I would be expected to take responsibility for my own and other people's actions in Witney. I may have been somewhat reassured by the following incident which showed that we long-serving prisoners did assume a certain authority, which was nothing to do with rank — indeed Brian Darbyshire and I had no rank at all.

I had been 'filling in' with a short spell of night work and wrote in my diary on 16 November 1944,

> Sergeant Jones tells me this is my last night of duty in present spell (since 17th October). A change is as good as a holiday! Have twice had to speak to British officers about making a noise after 'lights out'. At 23.00 hours last night I heard a burst of song in an officer's voice I knew well. Then I heard another officer interrupt urgently, 'Sh . .sh . . sh . ., Richard's "on"!'

Anyway, I returned to 'my massage room' the next day and back to full-time physiotherapy. A Captain Richard Birchenough joined me in looking after the various ultra-violet, infra-red and other electrical equipment — very good-natured of him, as I believe he was a skilled professional in civilian life. So our fourth Christmas as prisoners came and went. Air-raid alarms and consequent descents by patients and orderlies to the cellar became even more frequent as the German front line retreated towards us: the guns began to sound like thunder. Sometimes, walking back

166

from the 'Farm', we needed to take cover from the RAF. Glancing across from one ditch to another, we squeezed down as much out of danger as possible, remarking that it reminded us of our military days!

My diary records on the last day of the year 1944 that,

> I was accused of sabotage by the Stabsartz [or head German doctor], because a solar lamp in the massage room burnt out before its time. If this occurs again I'm for 'strafing'! Don't mind that; but, if I'm to be 'strafed', I might as well earn the honour myself. Therefore now all treatment in the hospital involving German apparatus I undertake myself. This is interesting and takes me amongst many nationalities.

On 5 January 1945 the repatriates included our friendly young barber, Sweeny Webb. He most kindly took with him a small wooden Black Forest doll, which I had bought in Rottweil for my mother. He faithfully delivered it to her in Witney before her birthday on 12 February. During the first two months of this year a few more of our 'long-timers' were also repatriated and some others were adjudged fit enough for regular Offlags, or Stalags, and left us that way. However, a far greater number of newly wounded Allied prisoners arrived at Rottweil railway station from the nearby battle line at various times of day and night. There were so many of these newcomers that occasionally we had to put two in a bed. Often, they were in very poor shape and few were fit immediately for massage or electrical treatment. My time was, therefore, not so fully occupied as that of some other orderlies and it was usually my lot to meet the newcomers at Rottweil station. This was an interesting job, as a number of these patients were wounded from the fighting zone not much more than forty miles away. Our visits to the station sometimes coincided with visits from the RAF up aloft, and the RAF became better and better at bombing the railway. Fortunately each time there was a raid when I was at the station we managed to scuttle across to the air-raid shelter on the other side of the station yard.

On 15 February my diary says, 'Great rush for the shelter when raid announced; but once inside, the crowd was as friendly and joking as, I imagine, a London crowd would be!'

Another place where nationality did not seem to make much difference was at the 'Farm' with the Bilger family. After the loss of the father of the family, one son, who was in the German army, was reported missing. I believe we visitors from nearby Rottweil were almost as anxious to know whether he was alive as was the remainder of his family. We were before the end of the war able to rejoice with that family when news came through that he was a Prisoner of War in America.

With the end of the war for us in Germany obviously approaching, and no Red Cross parcels, we were very short of food; so were the Germans in the countryside around us. It was not a repetition of 'Salonica starvation'; all the same the lack of protein caused considerable lethargy. Our electricity supply at Rottenmünster was cut off from time to time and we spent so long in the cellar that I obtained permission to administer physiotherapy while we were down below, although electricity cuts sometimes interfered with us underground as above ground. Occasionally my massage programme was so much interrupted that I could not complete it.

Several bombs came uncomfortably near to Rottenmünster and windows were smashed, so that we learnt that it was wise to leave them open in wards and living quarters. On cloudy, overcast days the RAF usually kept away; but, according to my diary, 13 March was different. I wrote, 'Sun came out first time for some days and after half-an-hour Air Force was here and we had four hours in the cellar. Twelve civilians killed in nearby cottage and schrapnel on roof'.

14 March 'Many times in cellar and Germans said we were not to go on conducted tours during fine days'.

15 March 'Long spell in cellar; but Germans relented about walks — a lovely day and I took my first bathe of the season'.

1 April (Easter Day) 'Front appears to be moving in right direction. Several times to cellar again. Padre conducted good Service. Wrote two letters'.

2 April (Easter Monday) 'Gusty, sunny weather . . . pleasant short walk with Arthur, the guard, one Indian, two Serbs and one Pole'.

5 April 'Brian thought he heard guns and saw flashes in Stuttgart direction last night. I think there have been more continuous air-raid alarms than ever before'.

16 April 'Rumours that Allied troops are only twenty miles away begin day and three thousand Red Cross parcels (not rumour) end it'.

18 April 'Am very glad Russian prisoners next door are being given a Red Cross parcel each. We're eating a great deal more than I'd choose to eat if alone'.

On 20 April, which was Hitler's birthday, I went on the last walk it was practicable for us to make to the 'Farm'. Frau Bilger was kind and generous to the last and insisted upon our accepting a bag of flour. I was able to respond with the gift of various small keepsakes and a promise to write after the war. I walked towards Rottenmünster alone and met crowds of German soldiers all, except one officer in a car and a motor-cyclist, on foot. German civilians were also on the move with push-carts and horse-drawn vehicles piled with household furniture and other possessions. It was the fourth time since 1939 that I had seen men, women and children, sad and vacant looking, leaving their homes during a military defeat of their country. I liked it none the more.

I heard machine-gun fire and bridges being blown and rejoined our escorted party. The German guard, obviously very much alarmed, hurried us back to the hospital, where almost at once there was an air-raid alarm and we had to get patients that could be moved down to the cellar. After half an hour we were allowed upstairs again and found French Moroccan troops in possession. They were also clattering past Rottenmünster outside — some sitting on the top of their tanks laughing and cheering. There must have been limited resistance only in our little town and the wave of conquest had passed over us.

We wondered what would happen next. We were not recommended to leave the hospital for fear of possible snipers who might have been left behind by retreating German forces — and a counter-attack was possible. Some of our walking patients took the place of the German guards outside the barbed wire. My diary indicates that German soldiers were to be seen scrubbing the floors, which had been our job previously. I continued to massage those patients in the hospital who would in these new circumstances submit to such treatment!

A senior French officer visited Rottenmünster on 23 April and arranged for almost all the French to leave at once for repatriation. Those of us who lived further away needed to wait a little longer.

My diary records on Wednesday, 25 April 1945,

A very good day! The Sisters of the Convent next door

entertained all mobile British, Italian and Serb patients and other available personnel to an excellent mid-day meal in the Convent Hall, after we had attended a pleasant short Service in the Convent Church conducted by our own Padre.

Later in the day I went with the doctor now in charge of our hospital, a Major, to attend General Dumas, commanding the Artillery of 1st French Army, at his billet. When our Major had told me that the French General had a bad back he confidentially added, 'I want his help in getting us out — so do your best when you massage him!' I am sure we all three did our best!

Quoting from the diary of 26 April 1945, I recall,

Usual, day's massage (plus the General) until noon. Then things began to happen. French ambulances turned up and offered to evacuate some of the hospital. Before these were away American ambulances arrived to take rest of Americans and British. The Major allowed me to fulfil 15.00 hours appointment with General Dumas. When I got back, 16.00 hours, most of the others had left and I was in one of the last ambulances. Two American Negro drivers took us speedily and safely to 51st Evacuation Hospital, near Stuttgart.

Responsibility for patients is now transferred to somebody else.

We were kept hanging about and, in our sensible moments, could realise what a huge job the RAF had — to get so many prisoners home. It seemed that we were all to be treated as hospital patients until after a medical examination.

Brian and I found ourselves separated from most of our friends of the last four years. Some of these had left Rottenmünster before us in French ambulances. The Americans fed us well and, at 20.30 hours on 27 April, I was transported in a car with three Americans, three Indians and one German wounded soldier to a field hospital established on an evacuated German airfield. I cannot remember much about it, beyond noticing a large coloured portrait of Adolf Hitler, wearing uniform, in the building where we were fed. Some-one had taken the trouble to throw the contents of a tin of oil paint into his face. The Americans had not as yet completed their organisation here and we were now 'parked in a coldish tent on stretchers' until midnight. Krailsheim, the little adjoining town, and the aerodrome itself were 'v. badly knocked about'.

Next day a pilot told me it was unlikely any UK planes would arrive to take the fifty or so of us British to England, owing to the weather. There seemed a good deal of rain, mist and mud about. On Sunday 29 April about twenty of us attended Service conducted by an American Lutheran Padre. We sang very heartily!

On Monday 30 there was snow, on and off, and we thought no suitable plane would risk it. We thought wrong. At midday dinner — a good one — we were told a plane would take us to England in ten minutes' time — and at 13.10 hours we were off.

The crew of our Dakota consisted of the pilot, the co-pilot, the radio operator, an engineer and a lady nurse. Additional passengers were twelve stretcher cases, twelve walking patients and a doctor who had also been a P.o.W. I asked where we were going and was told, 'to Malmesbury'.

It was a misty, bumpy journey and at 16.00 we looked down through a break in the clouds and saw Beachy Head. We were home.

9 Home in 1945

To ev'ry land the wide world o'er
Some slips of the old stock roam,
Leal friends in peace . . .
— Harold Boulton

As we passed over the English coast I glanced round the inside of our aircraft. At that moment all the other passengers were looking outwards and downwards towards the land some of us had not seen for five years. There were a number of other planes moving around our own. They reminded me of goldfish in a spacious tank. Then, over Haywards Heath, our ear-drums told us that we were descending. Less than half an hour later we landed gently at Malmesbury in Wiltshire as promised.

We were helped out on to English soil by RAMC personnel, who allowed us to do nothing unaided. After a short coach journey we were checked-in, given a cursory medical examination and deloused at a general hospital near Swindon. Supper and a cinema show followed and we were each allowed to send a Red Cross postcard home. About midnight we were taken by lorry to the railway, put to lie down on bunks in a hospital train and looked after by wonderful Red Cross nurses as we travelled through the night stopping at Oxford station and continuing on to Worcester, where we arrived at 5 a.m. on 1 May. We were then taken by charabanc to the County Hospital, Hereford. On the way we made a short stop seven miles from Ledbury and heard an 'English' cuckoo and smelt hops and other May-morning English scents for the first time during five years.

On arrival at the Hereford Hospital — a nissen hut affair — we were firmly put to bed with our ex-patients and kept there all day. My diary says,

172

Not a bad start in England. Sleep, food and charming nurses! Mr Avory Jones of Red Cross visited and promised to ask his office if he could give Brian and me 25/- each to get home with. A lady Doctor promised to recommend us as fit for 'leave'.

The second full day in this country started by hearing on a radio set owned by the man in the next bed the words 'Hitler est mort'. I needed to translate to the owner of the set who had not, like myself, enjoyed the advantage of familiarity with French as well as with German during the few years past. Later that morning we heard the fall of Berlin announced. Meanwhile, Brian Darbyshire was working hard to get our forms of discharge. Finally they arrived in time to let us leave the following day.

My war-time diary ends: 'Good fun today replying to telegram from family, viewing Hereford Cathedral, serving (and eating) meals, bathing, cleaning equipment and dancing with the nurses in the evening. Generally preparing for the great morrow'.

The return to the family and Newland House, Witney, sur-passed all expectations; but one felt with some trepidation that real life with all its responsibilities was about to start again and that five years of education and experience in blanket-making had been lost. That may have been so; but all of us — prisoners from more than twenty nations at Rottweil — had learnt a great deal as well and could share our knowledge and conclusions about life and politics with our farflung homelands covering a great deal of the world — and Stalag VB, of which Rottenmünster was only a part, was but one prison camp among many in the vast German Reich. There was much wisdom behind the remark made by Stanley Gilder years later to the effect that had there been more Prisoners of War treated as we had been at Rottweil and more Germans behaving like the guards and native doctors there, wars in the future would be impossible. However, different prisoners and different guards had behaved very differently in some of the other prison and internment camps in Germany as well as in other countries. Deep feelings of those experiences remained as well.

I hardly know what effect the war had on myself. To judge what effect it had upon others is still more difficult. I have not during my life been much given to nightmares. However, I suffered one quite recently more than forty years after the conditions causing it at Salonica have mercifully disappeared. This particular night (forty years after), we had been looking at a Second World War film on television. I had not given it undue attention and it had nothing to do with prison camps. Early the following morning I found myself at Salonica, apparently in that camp again. I don't know how I knew this; but I could sense that some of those terrible hopeless walking skeletons were with me. I felt greater horror than ever I had felt forty years previously. It was the evil spirit once again. I struggled out of bed on to the floor crippled by cramp, still believing I was at Salonica and groaning out loud, but conscious enough of my present environment to realise that someone else — not of Salonica — was asleep close at hand, someone I knew well. What relative could she be to me! I was not married forty years ago! Then I began to come back to the 1980s and looked across to the other side of my bed for reassurance. Yes, there was my wife as calm and beautiful as ever, where she had been by my side, all the time. All was well; but the horror of that dream lasted the whole day. I wonder how many of the thousands from that transit prison camp have suffered with dreams like that during the last forty years. Some of my friends have not survived; others of us will retain the horror of 1941 — not so far under the surface — until the end of our time.

Whatever some prisoners suffered — and a great many had an incomparably worse time than those who, like ourselves, were often protected by the Red Cross and Geneva Convention — the fate of a few of those in charge and guilty of horrible crimes must have been worse. I have before me a cutting from the *Daily Telegraph* of 6 October 1980. It is headed 'Nazi camp's "beast" kills himself in Brazil hide-away'. There is an illustration of a good-looking young man, apparently a German sergeant, early in the war. Another picture is of the same man about forty years later, shortly before he plunged a knife into his chest and killed himself in Brazil. (He had attempted suicide on five previous occasions.) In this second portrayal we see that he died not only looking like a beast but like a weak, wretched bloated beast exiled from his own country. I am glad that I do not know much more about this 'Human Beast', nor of the German court that in 1966 found him guilty of the death of 152,000 other human beings. However, other incidents come back to me rather more clearly.

Soon after a friend of mine and fellow prisoner was captured, he was interrogated by a German officer about the activities of the

174

unit of which he was a member. The young soldier told the officer all he believed would be permitted by his own side. Apparently this was not enough to satisfy the questioner. The officer wanted more information. This my friend refused him; so the officer turned to the German guard who had marched the Englishman in for examination, and said, 'Very well, take this man outside and shoot him.' The guard marched him out and my friend prepared himself for death. He told me that he said to himself, 'Ah well! Life was good while it lasted'. To his surprise the guard said, 'Don't be so silly, of course I won't shoot you!' So started my friend's gefangenschaft and he worked with the rest of us to the end of the war. After that I know he made a real success of his chosen profession and married a helpful and charming wife. The two were regarded with respect, affection and gratitude in the English county where they made their home. Then, quite recently, for no apparent reason he took his own life. I have wondered since whether that German officer had his way in the end after all.

Three more war incidents which, though I was not present, I believe happened — a small unit of British soldiers was operating in an exposed situation near an isolated building situated in its path. Progress was barred by a German sniper, using a rifle, located and well concealed in the building. Several British soldiers had already perished. The British held several prisoners taken as the unit advanced and their (the British) Commanding Officer made it known to the sniper that he would shoot the prisoners dead, one at a time at intervals, until he gave himself up by coming out of hiding. As the rifleman did not immediately give himself up, the British officer proceeded to implement his threat. After two prisoners had been shot dead the German sniper came out and was taken prisoner. Then the advance continued.

A much admired and loved schoolmaster of mine, Captain E. C. Coxwell in the British army during the First World War, told me, when I visited him in later years, that one day in France (I imagine in the 'trenches') he was on a tour of inspection and came on a British sniper hidden in a safe but elevated position. The captain asked him how he was getting on. 'Very well,' came the reply. 'Get up here, Sir, and have a go yourself!' The Captain got up beside the sniper and borrowed the rifle. It was easy enough to spot an unsuspecting enemy soldier and get him in the sights; but, having done that, he just could not squeeze the trigger. My schoolmaster friend got down from his perch and walked away. Perhaps that is why some of us are pacifists.

I am, of course, old enough to remember the first 'Armistice Day' on 11 November 1918 and it happens that I am writing these words on 'Armistice Sunday' 1982. The day the Armistice was signed at 11 o'clock in 1918, my mother was walking through Witney in the afternoon. Our town was rejoicing over final victory and the cessation of hostilities. Owing to the shortage of men in war-time a few women police were doing duty and one was stationed in Witney. She was somewhat aloof and reserved, which was what her job demanded. Perhaps owing to this, Mother greeted her and probably spoke about the general relief the population felt that the terrible World War was over. She must have been very concerned indeed when the young constable gave way to tears and said she had just been told that her brother, who was in the army, had been killed on the last day of the war.

I cannot say that the foregoing thoughts came to me on arrival at home in May 1945. Some were old memories and others were only relevant years after. Immediately I did not know what to say and do, when the kindly people in the house next door put flags out through the windows to welcome the returned wanderer. When it came to the following Sunday and my parents and I were getting ready for church, I recalled that I had attended service in Germany the Sunday before and it didn't seem far away. 'Yes,' said my father, 'but it would be virtually impossible for you to get back and do the same again today!' We were in a different world.

Returned Prisoners of War were recommended to take at least six weeks' holiday. I supposed I should do the same and try to become acclimatised; however, I spent a day in London in order to resign from the FAU. My memory is that Oswald Dick, my CO at the time we were captured, with a fellow textile manufacturer from Gloucestershire, David Tod, were in charge of the small Friends Ambulance Unit HQ party in London. Not long before they had had plenty to do as ARP wardens when London was being bombed. This HQ staff had also undertaken priceless work in keeping our families in touch with us exiles.

I was told that I was completely free to return home and recommence my pre-war job. As I was technically not a returned P.o.W. but a returned 'Interned Person', I would not qualify for extra rations during my six weeks' holiday. That did not worry me much since — whatever I was entitled to — my mother was to make sure that the Witney authorities supplied ration cards to cover the extra for a P.o.W.! On leaving the FAU Headquarters I visited 'The Cheshire Cheese' and ate a lunch I had dreamed about for the last four years. Then I walked to Paddington station so that I could go some way to understanding the devastation suffered by London and by the whole British nation during the same period.

Although I did not at once get back to weaving, it was impossible to live in Witney and not be involved in blankets. I had given away the 'Forbar' Witney blanket sent me in Germany to another returning prisoner on the grounds that there were plenty more at home! About a week after coming back I found myself selected to play for Witney Mills Cricket Club against, I believe, an Oxford team — and cricket comes into this story again.

As already mentioned, our family firm of blanket makers had generously continued paying my salary during hostilities. However, I was not doing this job of my own choosing in order to make a good thing out of the war. Therefore, I had mentioned to my father that when I got back I would even things out by some repayment. I had also made a will, which would have had the same effect should I have failed to come back. Knowing the problem to be solved, father had written to me on the death of Charles William Early, when he had reached his ninety-fourth year, suggesting that I should buy from C.W.E.'s executors the Cricket Field on which my Great Uncle had allowed the firm and others to play cricket for generations. I was very glad indeed to discharge my debt by doing this and handing over the hallowed turf to the firm. When I eventually returned, I was also very glad to pay for the conversion of the extremely solid air-raid shelter, which the government had erected on the perimeter of the ground, into changing rooms with adjoining washing and bathing facilities.

In spite of the foregoing efforts to deserve something better, I was bowled out first ball — I can still remember the look of distress on the face of the kind-hearted bowler at having so unceremoniously disposed of a recently returned prisoner. Well, I suppose my cricket gradually improved and I began to take part in Saturday games as before the war. However, I gave cricket a miss one Saturday early in the season. Possibly arising out of the visit to the Mill of Queen Mary, when in 1941 twenty-five veterans had taken

177

part in a presentation to the Queen Mother, Master Harold realised that there were available twenty-two men and three women, who had worked fifty years or more each for the firm. Therefore a sizeable Half Century Club could be formed. The first meeting of the new Club was held on Saturday afternoon in Newland House garden, just after the Second World War ended in Europe. The *Witney Gazette* reported as follows:

> Mr Harold Early said he thought it was fitting that the older people present should be the guests of a firm that was itself not quite new. Ever since 1669 when Thomas Early was apprenticed he and his descendants had followed the same trade, father to son, in the same little place for two hundred and seventy-six years — one of the oldest firms in the world. They were there that afternoon to commemorate rather a noteable achievement by twenty-five of their number who had been associated with the firm for fifty years, some of them a good deal longer. . . . Many of them looked back to their first days at work, boy and girl days. They knew they were starting work in an old firm and perhaps they had said to themselves, 'This funny old business is over two hundred years old; I don't suppose it will last my time!' But it did last, somehow or other, and the years went on and so did they, working together and grumbling and criticising and having, now and again, a bit of fun as well. . . . A lifetime of work is a great offering for a man or a woman to make — indeed, it is a great gift — something that can hardly be paid for. So that afternoon, in asking the members of the new Club to accept some tokens, together with a cup of tea, 'The Firm is not paying a debt, but is at any rate recognising that a debt exists!' Framed certificates of long service were then presented to the founder members, and the pleasant and memorable party ended with a performance by a conjurer and ventriloquist, and a Punch and Judy show 'which appealed specially to the veterans!'

So, in 1945, The Half Century Club was founded with twenty-five stalwart members. Since then it has grown in number to more than sixty members. However, we have had to ease the rules for entry owing to the raising of the school-leaving age to sixteen and the fixing of the usual retiring age at sixty-five for men and sixty for women. At present Half Century regulations allow men to qualify after forty-eight years service, if they retire at pensionable age, and women to join after forty-six years service. However, some members of the old firm still complete their fifty years service and wait until that time before joining the Club and receiving his, or her, certificate and gold watch. Such a one is Mr John Stanley Sparrowbank, who started work in the spinning department in August 1932. I believe he was the one hundred and forty second member of the Firm to be welcomed into the Club during and after 1945, when he joined us, accompanied by his sister Nellie, at our Christmas meeting, 1982.

Like several other Half Century Members, including myself, Jack's service with the firm has been interrupted by, and includes, war service. During bitter and one-sided fighting he failed to get back to England from Dunkirk in 1940 and became a prisoner for the rest of the war. At first he was imprisoned in Poland on very meagre rations and then, still near the Eastern border of Germany, he worked on a farm, where he received kindness similar to that accorded to us at, what I might call, 'our farm' in Württemberg. However, he came back to England in very poor shape and it was 1946 before he started spinning again at Witney Mill and playing cricket again for Witney Mills Cricket Club.

Just at first we ex-prisoners wanted nothing better than to be allowed to recommence our various peace-time occupations and to pick up the reins exactly where we had laid them down five years previously. We soon discovered this to be impossible. Conditions in England had changed just about as much as our own outlook on England and the rest of the world. I set up my own bachelor establishment, not far from the Mill in West End, Witney. West End is the 'old fashioned street' mentioned in Leonora Harris's famous poem and song, 'There's an old fashioned house in an old fashioned street, In a quaint little old fashioned town'.

Outside my house German Prisoners of War were repairing the road and pavement. At first, wrongly I daresay, I thought it tactful not to take much notice of them. They seemed to be working well under the authority of Witney Town Council. However, after a time I discovered that they were making personal remarks about the new inhabitant of what I called 'Tilt House' outside which they were doing a very useful job. Evidently they did not expect that an insular Englishman would understand. This particular Englishman had acquired just enough knowledge of Germany and

Germans to have a pretty good idea of what was said and to be able to add a few words to theirs. Far from taking this amiss the prisoners seemed glad to find someone with whom they could speak in German.

A few mornings later one of the Germans, named, as I found out afterwards, Heinz Koselack, asked me whether I could arrange for a football match to be played between the Germans and a local team. There was little difficulty in this, because our blanket firm owned a ground and a good many of us had played soccer not so long ago. There were also members of the Boys' Brigade to help. It was not all my footballing friends who were willing to play. After all, until a few weeks before, Germans had been killing British and British killing Germans. At Rottweil we had played football with and against the Poles, Serbs and French, but never against the Germans. My memory is that we had a good game and I believe the Germans won by a small margin.

Having had experience of what such things could mean, I invited the prisoners' team to Tilt House after the game and stood the visitors a 'footballing tea'. The following week I received a letter from Heinz Koselack on behalf of himself and his comrades saying 'thank you' both for the game and for the tea. Heinz added also that he and the rest of the team realised that I had gone out of my way to help, because I had been a prisoner myself, knew what it was like and felt real sympathy. This was quite true; but neither he nor I expected that these considerations and perhaps a similiarity in character would lead to a forty-year friendship at least. I happen to know of another lifelong friendship formed with Heinz. Frank Clack played football before the Second World War for the Boys' Brigade 1st Witney Company. Frank was a lanky lad, quick of eye and limb. Lieutenant F. C. Keates, Sports Officer of the Company, is justly credited with first suggesting to Frank that he play for 1st Witney in goal. He proved an excellent keeper and by the mid 1940s was playing in the First Division in goal for Birmingham City. Later he kept goal for Bristol City. There is no hero like a football hero and Heinz, knowing of Frank's Witney connections, ventured to go in after a game and meet Frank in the Bristol dressing room. So started a Witney-East-German friendship which has lasted to this day.

A more unlikely friendship from a human point of view was that between the musician Leopold Vetter, and my mother's sister, Dr

Patricia R. Elliott. Auntie Patty had for some time before the war been the doctor looking after sick children in St Andrew's Hospital, Singapore. When the Japanese attacked, she was certain that the city could not possibly be adequately defended and would fall into Japanese hands. She refused to leave 'her children' and was interned — sadly enough not being allowed by the Japanese to continue caring for the children. She was imprisoned until the end of the war against the Japanese and suffered great hardship, which must have been largely the cause of her death soon after release. She was granted time, however, to return for a last few weeks of life in England and stayed with us at Witney. While with us she asked me to tell her the name and address of one of my guards, who was by now suffering shortage in his conquered country. I told her of Leopold Vetter and she at once sent him and his family a food parcel from this country. She sent several more before she died. In letters and when I met him once again later Leopold Vetter used to refer to this unexpected friend as 'the good aunt Patricia'. I am asking the publishers of this book to use on the jacket a drawing she thought out and executed while interned under conditions at least as cruel and disgraceful as anything described in the story I have written.

Of even more concern to me than German friendships was my connection with Danes and Denmark. This dated back to the visits involving attendance at gymnastic courses in Fredensborg during my summer holidays before the war. While taking part in these courses, I had fallen under the spell of the four beautiful Madsen sisters. They were among a number of young ladies who came in from the royal town of Fredensborg to help at our Danish dancing classes and partner us male students during our efforts to master this somewhat exciting form of folk dancing.

I do not know whether my admiration for the Madsens was obvious to my fellow students — mostly young schoolmasters. However, I was warned that the four lovely sisters had an elder brother — a huge Viking of a man fiercely jealous of their honour. Now, forty years later, I am in a position to assure readers that Albert Madsen and indeed his wife Elizabeth may be Vikings, but they are exceedingly kind and helpful Vikings! However the Madsen family had nothing to do with my first visit to Denmark after the war. I don't know whether four years' virtual segregation from the fair sex was still affecting me, but it was on behalf of the

181

Boys' Brigade that Harry Shirley, the Scottish Secretary of that Organisation, and I were asked to attend meetings of the Friviligt Drenge Forbund, or Danish Boys' Brigade, at Aarhus in Jutland during the early spring of 1947. We were accorded the honour and pleasure of meeting Holger Tornöe, who founded the FDF in 1902. He had been a great friend of Sir William Smith who, nearly a hundred years ago as I write, founded the Boys' Brigade in 1883.

I cannot remember a great deal about our few days in Denmark in the spring of 1947 and hope that Harry and I represented the BB adequately. We travelled from Harwich to Esbjerg on a Danish ship. The first meal aboard demonstrated a welcome increase in nutrition over the rationed fare then available in the British Isles. We were told that the Germans had been careful not to take too much food out of this prosperous and well-fed democracy. That was partly because they wanted to make sure there was enough for their lately occupying forces — doubtless with a bit left over for export to Germany. I have also to admit that I enjoyed marching through the streets of the University Town of Aarhus in a column headed by magnificent FDF bands.

The address at one of the services was spoken by an FDF chaplain, who had been engaged in the sad and demanding duty of visiting in prison the few Danes who had behaved traitorously during the occupation. These included the still fewer Danes whose actions had led to the death of one or more of their compatriots and who now awaited execution.

What ever my reasons for going to Denmark during the freezing cold spring of 1947, I cannot hide from myself the over-riding reason for undertaking another three weeks' gymnastic course at Fredensborg during the following wonderful summer. At Christmas 1946 I had sent a card to Gerda Madsen expressing my regret that she had not heard from me at any of the previous four Christmases, because I had been abroad. To my relief I found out that, although her three sisters had all become married during the war, she herself was still single. What neither she nor anyone else told me was that when various Vikings had started taking her too much for granted, she warned that she did not intend to marry until a certain Englishman of her acquaintance did the same. Had I known that, I do not suppose it would have taken me until two years after release to find my way back to Fredensborg. I need not continue describing here the romance. However, if any young man wants a word from me about how to woo and win a beautiful Danish girl, I will be glad to advise! After the marriage service in Fredensborg Palace Church, where Gerda had sung in the choir as a girl, everyone had the opportunity to speak at a magnificent family wedding feast such as only Danes can lay on. Of course, the bride looked wonderful and, during his speech, father said, 'I am sure she is as good as she is beautiful'. Thirty-five years later I can aver that he was absolutely right. His confidence has been fully justified and is still being confirmed. I had married the finest woman in the world, who up to that point in her life had lived in the world's second finest country.

We were not the only international couple who were obliged to await settled times before becoming married. A year or two after our own wedding I found that one of the skilled 'fitters' who came over from Oxford to attend to our heating system at Witney Mill was, like myself, an ex-prisoner. He was Henrik Schulze, a German, who had been a P.o.W. in this country. When his turn came for repatriation he had preferred to remain here in England and marry, instead of going back to his native Germany. He must have been a good craftsman and had joined Alden's, the well-known specialist Oxford engineers.

Henrik and I soon discovered that we had a good deal in common, but he had married and made a home in this country of his capture. He had also learnt the English language. When we now meet at the Mill the conversation is apt to start by my saying 'Grüsz Gott!' He replies courteously in German, but I soon have to apologise for my lack of linguistic skill. Whereupon he says in English 'Don't worry; we understand each other'. Wars and prison camps sometimes lead to friendships and if there were enough friendships of this kind there would be no wars.

Henrik and I frequently have the opportunity to meet and greet each other. It has been different with Heinz Koselack's friendship with Frank Clack and myself. Frank and I have never met Heinz since he returned to the continent and became most happily married in East Germany. However, Heinz writes excellent letters and we have much in common. Here is a composite letter made up in fact from several letters received from Heinz Koselack during the last three years. They were written in German and a good friend has translated.

Dear Richard and family, In 1946/7 we worked on the highway in Witney and now I thank you for your Christmas card and kind wishes. It is a considerable number of years since I was a P.o.W. in Witney and, to be quite honest, that was not a bad time. Every now and then I tell by friends about those wonderful people of Witney. Thank you also for the postage stamps — I am particularly pleased with the one from Guernsey. You see, I stayed in the Island of Jersey for over a year. It is a pity that I am in the German Democratic Republic. I would love to see the old friends in England again. Unfortunately our freedom is still restricted these many years after the war. We are not allowed to visit our friends in West Germany or in West Berlin. Our children are all well. I can still remember your sister [Ruth]. She played the piano at a charity concert with us P.o.W.s in [The Sheldonian Theatre] Oxford. Please give her my regards.

Are you in touch with any other former P.o.W.s? As I write this letter the name of Mr 'Jimmy' Green comes back to me. He was responsible for street maintenance in the town [Engineer and Surveyor of Witney U.D.C.]. He was a fine man, but must be dead now. There are, however, other things one does not forget as long as one lives, such as our game of football against the workers of the blanket factory and the gathering afterwards at your home. I should like to thank you again for the unforgettable memory of that. Are you still involved in the manufacture of blankets? How is our football pal, Frank Clack? Is he still working in your factory? He is a wonderful man, a real sportsman, unassuming and always content. Please give him my best regards. During my time in Bristol, I was very proud that I knew this player. His performance as a goal-keeper was of a high standard.

I am now sixty years old: I am also a grandfather and am glad to say have enjoyed good health apart from a gall-bladder operation four years ago. I try to improve my health by distance running.

I understand that you want to write a book about the war years, 1939 till 1945. Please say that I am of the same opinion as you in that war does not bring any good to mankind. The evil part is that it is man who is out to destroy his fellow man. The continuing advance in technology brings ever more dreadful and cruel weapons of torture and death. I myself have spent my best days, one could say my youth, in war and captivity, from the age of 19 to 28. Now I am living in the other part of Germany; we only have opportunity to cross the frontier to the West after we become 65 years old — in practice after retirement age. It is sad that we have no relatives in this eastern area. However, we are not hungry. It is a human peculiarity that we 'look up' to people who are 'better off'; but we should also remember those who would gladly change places with us. The little man has to be satisfied with the consequences of a great war. Only a handful of people decide the fate of mankind, millions of people, through their policies.

At our factory a big plant is being built — partly by Englishmen; so there are some of your fellow countrymen here with us. Unfortunately they are screened off and we cannot speak to them as I would like.

Pity I do not live in the Bundesrepublik. I would surely have paid (you) a visit by now. That would have been a wonderful occasion! However, let us hope that it will happen one day — fate may be kind to me! I have always hoped to see the name of Early's on the collective English Stand at the Leipzig Fair. If it so happens that you have to visit Leipzig, we live only an hour away. We would be delighted if you could come home at Sandersdorf one day. Although the name of our town has 'Dorf' in it, our place has 15,000 inhabitants; so it is not a village but is about the size of Witney.

My dream has always been to visit the Channel Islands again and also Oxford and Witney. Many, many regards to your dear relatives. We wish you health and contentment. Remember me sometime with some Channel Island stamps!

Regards from my good wife to you both!
From your friend
Heinz Koselack

10 'Our task to win the Peace', 1984

Industry to Temperance marry,
Then we may weave truth with trust.
— Ode to Peace, 1748

The reader of the previous nine chapters may well consider that we have reached a suitable stopping place. The war was ended. Some of the participants had settled in past opponents' territory. Lifelong friendships had been formed between those who had recently been adversaries. The narrator had become married to the girl of his dreams from another country. Yet the story is not finished, although in the natural course of events a good many of the leading characters have passed on

Mention has been made of Jack Palmer, who virtually handed over the 'Massage Room' as a going concern to me at Rotten-münster in 1942, or thereabouts, and of how he came and served as Medical Officer in our Boys' Brigade Camp at Whitecliffe Bay, Isle of Wight, a few years after the war. However, he and his dear wife Dorothy showed great kindness to many others. I will quote from correspondence sent me by another kindly soldier, Julius Kienzle, at one time serving at Rottweil in the German army. He was somewhat older than most of us.

In January 1965, Julius Kienzle received a letter written in German on the notepaper of Docters Caldwell, Camm and Palmer practising in Sussex. Translated it reads:

> Dear Kienzle! It is now twenty years since we were in Rottenmünster and I hope that in May we will have a weekend reunion in a hotel in England. Many of my old colleagues would like to meet you and I would like to know whether you and your wife will be able to come to England.
>
> We would also like to meet Feldwebel Stuhlinger. Do you

know if he is still alive and what his address is?

With best wishes for the New Year.

Jack Palmer

After the reunion had taken place at Brighton the *Rottweiler Rundschau* reported on 15 May 1965 as follows:

Big-hearted German at prisoners of war reunion. Former British P.o.W.'s held a meeting in Brighton to which medical orderly Julius Kienzle accepted the invitation.

Julius Kienzle was called to join the Army in 1939. When the P.o.W. hospital in Rottenmünster was opened in 1941, he was transferred from Konstanz to Rottweil. Because of his peacetime job he was employed as apothecary and also learnt the secrets of pharmacy. After the previous pharmacist was sent to the 'Front' Julius Kienzle was put in charge. While issuing medicines to the medical and surgical wards of the hospital he often met the English doctors. Later, after a period at Adres near Calais in June 1942, he was employed in orthopaedics making artificial limbs for German and foreign soldiers.

Several years after the war, during the song festival of 1956 at Göllsdorf, Julius Kienzle received an unexpected visit from an English doctor, who had been a medical orderly at Rottenmünster. It was Jack Palmer. Jack was on his honeymoon and had included a one-day visit to Rottenmünster. After that nine more years went by until, on 30 January 1965, Julius received an invitation from the English medical men to a get-together marking the twentieth anniversary of their return from prisoner of war captivity. So it was that Julius Kienzle stayed in Brighton on the South coast of England. After the journey via Stuttgart, Paris and Dieppe he crossed the channel to Newhaven. There Doctor Jack Palmer was on the quay ready to take his German guest to the Marine Hotel in Brighton, where the other hosts from various parts of Great Britain had already assembled. Some time was spent exploring the rocky coastline of the Channel and on Inland trips. However, it was the getting together again that was the most important feature of the visit.

What happened during the official meeting at Brighton was recorded by an English paper called the *Evening Argus:*

187

Doctor Jack Palmer from South Chailey, Sussex, who was a skilled medical orderly at Rottenmünster, said at the meeting 'I went to the place where I was imprisoned again. I asked the Catholic Sisters if they knew Mr Kienzle who had done so much for us during the dark days of our imprisonment. They told me that he had his own orthopaedic business near the hospital and I was happy to see him again. When we were organising this reunion on the twentieth anniversary of our liberation in 1945, it was a matter of course to invite him as our guest'.

Dr Stanley Gilder, formerly from Eastbourne and now at Amersham, added, 'Herr Kienzle was a soldier in Hitler's Army; but he fought many big battles for us. He was employed as Apothecary. He went to great lengths to obtain the medicines we needed. He must have taken many risks to help us'.

A further tribute came from Mr John Southall, a businessman from Birmingham, 'Kienzle's Christian humanity was a light amidst the Nazi brutality. He took photos of many of us, so that we could send these to our relatives back home'.

Mr Kienzle, who is married with three sons, said in German, 'It's a great honour to have been invited to this meeting in Brighton'.

Julius must also have sent a letter of appreciation to our Queen after he returned to Germany from Brighton. I do not know what he wrote to Her Majesty, but I have a copy of the reply he received. A Secretary at the British Embassy at Bonn acknowledged, 'On behalf of Her Majesty Queen Elizabeth II, I am thanking you for your letter. It was very kind of you to write to Her Majesty about the reunion of Prisoners of War in Brighton'.

This meeting at Brighton was the first of several almost annual meetings between past Rottenmünster men — with families mostly acquired since the war — at such English centres as Torquay in Devon, Bournemouth in Hampshire and Burford in Oxfordshire. The series culminated with a reunion at Rottweil in Württemberg in 1973. Jack Palmer was the instigator on the British side at any rate. I should think that Julius Kienzle was the same for those living in and around Rottweil. Anyway, here is a letter dated 6 May 1981 about that get-together.

My good friend Richard Early and your good wife Gerda! Many thanks for your kind lines. I hope you are both healthy and happy. I have recovered from my illness about which I told you. Unfortunately, I have had back trouble for the last eight weeks. It is wear and old age. I have had hot fango compresses and they made it better. I will be eighty on 17th September this year and I hope that I will keep well till then.

Yes, Dr Gilder said once that, if everybody had had an experience as a P.o.W., there would not be another war. However, the big nations like many others, are getting ready fast, because they are all afraid of the others. If the world would disarm and the money saved spent on social services, that would lead mankind towards Christianity.

As you want to write a book about the war time, dear Richard Early, I am gladly prepared to help you. The best of luck! My three sons are married and we have five grandchildren.

Best regards to the Harrison family and the other friends of days past. Dr Palmer came to visit me three times with his wife and children. Sadly he died too young in 1979. He wrote many kind words to me. We have lost a good friend in him. I was also sorry the interpreter John Southall died on his way to visit Dr Palmer in London.

> Greetings to you both from your friend.
> Julius Kienzle

With the help of several others I will tell the tale of 1973. The British party arranged in alphabetical order, as it was by the kind organiser Jack Palmer, consisted of:

Mr & Mrs Richard Early
Dr & Mrs Stanley Gilder
Mr & Mrs Reg Haldane
Mr & Mrs Ernie Harrison
Miss Paula Harrison
Mr & Mrs Doug Moors
Dr & Mrs Jack Palmer
The Misses Penny & Clemency Palmer
Masters Jonathan & Jamie Palmer
Mr Joe Teraoka
Commander W. T. Plant

The eighty-year-old Commander was the only adult male participant who had not been imprisoned at Rottenmünster, and it was regretted by all that Mrs Joe Teraoka could not come; but she was with us in spirit.

It can be judged from the foregoing that seven of us were past inhabitants of Rottenmünster, thirteen were relations and one an elderly and sympathetic friend.

We crossed the Channel, which Hitler had failed to do in the opposite direction, by hovercraft from Dover to Boulogne on Wednesday 11 April. We then travelled in two minibuses, one driven by the Palmers and the other by Ernie Harrison and Doug Moors, past such famous landmarks of the First World War as Vimy Ridge and Verdun, where we spent Wednesday night. On Thursday we crossed the Rhine at Strasbourg to Baden Baden: then along the frozen Schwarzwalder Hoch Strasse, where it was snowing, we approached Rottweil. Julius Kienzle, his wife and family were on hand to meet us. We were escorted to, and made welcome at, a small neat house. After a good meal together at Gasthof Linde Post, Horgen, we were distributed for the night to various private dwellings. Gerda, Joe Teraoka and I stayed in a most pleasant home.

On Friday 13 April, we came back to Rottenmünster after twenty-eight years' absence — a queer feeling: the place seemed little changed. The German medical doctor in charge of mentally deranged showed us round the premises we had once occupied. Then Sister Oberin Apronia — and many other kind and charming sisters — stood us a wonderful meal in the Festsaal of their Convent next door. I was able to take from my pocket the programme which had been printed for us recently freed prisoners, when we had been equally well cared-for in the same place on 25 April 1945. Afterwards, we bowed our heads in the wonderful Münster Church, which dates back to the eighteenth century. Dr Gilder presented Sister Apronia with twelve 'Peace' rose plants for the Münster as a memento indicating our affection and gratitude.

At 16.00 hours we were received by Herr Oberburgermeister Doctor Regelmann — the combined Mayor and Clerk of Rottweil — whose term of office extended over twelve years at the Rathaus, or Town Hall. There we had a panoramic view of Rottweil from a high tower, which it had not been practicable for us to scale during our previous residence in the town! The Mayor also arranged for us to visit the Town Museum and listen to a most interesting talk about Rottweil's history from Roman times to the present day.

190

Doctor Regelmann appeared to possess a close fellow feeling towards ourselves: he had been a P.o.W. in England during the latter part of the war.

On Saturday we enjoyed a glorious outing arranged for us by Julius Kienzle. We drove to Constance and, after lunch there, were amazed by the breathtaking view of lake and snowclad hill country under glittering sun. Perhaps we ex-prisoners were more moved than we admitted by excitement arising almost unconsciously from the knowledge that during part of the outing we were travelling over the escape route attempted by some of our friends. We had a wonderful view of the Rhine waterfalls. On Sunday we visited the beautiful city of Stuttgart and could scarcely believe that it was the same wrecked city which we had seen when we left Germany in 1945. However, that Sunday was really made noteworthy because of what happened in the evening.

Alexis Konjevic was a Serb. His country, Yugoslavia, was dismembered early in the war by the Germans and he had become imprisoned with us at Rottweil. We had shared our English Red Cross parcels with him as with the Russians. He was an expert clock-maker and had, in addition to his medical work, repaired and kept in working order our ageing time-pieces during imprisonment. Immediately after the war he settled down in the nearby clock-making town of Schwenigen and set up his own watch and clock business, becoming married in the process. That evening his charming wife and twenty-seven-year-old son at first entertained us in their own house and then took us all out to a meal at the Bethovan Beerkeller. He had not forgotten those Red Cross parcels in earlier days! It was a generous and kind action by Alex and his family, which has been remembered over the years.

April 16 1973 was an especially interesting day for Gerda and myself and I will quote from the 'Rottenmünster News Letter No. 3', issued by Reg Haldane shortly afterwards.

> On Monday we journeyed to Calw to visit a blanket factory, which is in fact nineteen years older than Dick's place in Witney. We were very warmly received by one of the Directors, Herr Fritz K. Döttinger, the Managing Director, and, after being regaled with coffee and cakes, were conducted on a tour, which culminated with the presentation of a cushion to each of us.

191

I had known about a blanket factory somewhere near at hand, during the short time we had spent at Nargold after Christmas in 1942 and was now intrigued by the thought of finding out more and meeting these German blanket makers. It was extraordinarily good and trustful of the Calver Decken-und-Tuchfabriken AG to show round a rival blanket maker and his friends from a lately enemy country. We met the President of the Calw Company, Herr Rolf Sannwald. He was also President of the German Blanket Manufacturers Association. When we were introduced I was able to explain that a Managing Director of our Blanket Firm in Witney, Mr J. Brian Crawford, was similarly President of the British BMA.

The Calw Company could indeed trace its origins back to 1650, when several families weaving in their own houses combined to create a joint fulling, dyeing and finishing mill. This Calw combination at first made various textile articles, but did not then weave and finish blankets. The three present Managing Directors of the public company formed in 1905 are related to the founding families but not directly descended from them. The manufacturers of blankets in the mill started comparatively recently; but some of the present mill buildings are two hundred years old. At the time of our visit about 60 per cent of this factory's output was blankets and 30 per cent of the mill's production was made of wool.

Herr Fritz Döttinger kindly and helpfully showed us round his mill himself; both the mill and the operatives were much like what was to be found at Witney Mill and there seemed to be an excellent spirit. I was very grateful that we blanket makers could get together for an hour and a half. Years later we still correspond.

By now it was certainly the turn of us from England to do some entertaining. That evening, when we came back from Calw factory, we found that Jack Palmer had taken great trouble in arranging for us to treat our Rottweil hosts and friends to a formal dinner at Hotel Baren, in Rottweil Altstadt. We had invited a good many local guests.

Very good talks were given by the Oberburgermeister of Rottweil and by Dr Gilder, who in addition brilliantly translated other people's speeches. My own personal guests were Herr and Frau Leopold Vetter. They were grateful to all of us; but it was touching to find how they remembered Aunt Patricia, who had sent them food parcels during the five years or so when food was very scarce in Germany after the war. We entertained two sisters from the convent: of these Sister Oberin Apronia, the spiritual leader at Rottenmünster, said Grace for us all. The evening ended with wonderful music by Rottweil Male Voice Choir in which Julius Kienzle was a gifted songster.

In a report about our journey back to England and home after our visit to Rottweil, Reg Haldane said,

> Tuesday saw us saying farewell. That day we travelled through the Moselle valley visiting the birthplace of Joan of Arc on our way to our overnight destination at Lignyen Barrois, where the nineteen of us enjoyed our own Reunion Dinner. After a pleasant meal, Jack Palmer got to his feet. He spoke of the tremendous influence for good the Skipper [Stanley Gilder] had had on our lives and the strength he gave us during those dark days. On behalf not only of those present but also of many absent friends he then presented the Skipper with a silver salver which was suitably engraved with the signatures of the friends he had helped. In reply, the Skipper paid tribute for all the hard work that Jack had put in over the years to establish the annual reunion and presented to Jack, on our behalf, a Steiner mug as a small token of appreciation.

I am completing the first draft of this saga near the end of January 1983 and must bring readers up to date. Less than a week ago I met Henrik Schulze at Witney Mill and as usual when we meet I greeted him with the words, 'Grüsz Gott': as usual we then slipped into English. This time Henrik philosophised — briefly: after all he was at the Mill to work! — by saying, 'You know I co-operate'. I responded with a question, 'Am I right in supposing you stayed in England after war because you fell in love with an English girl?' 'That's right', he said, 'That was part of my co-operation'.

Today, as often before, Frank Clack and I met in Witney Market Square. Frank has remembered that Heinz Koselack in East Germany is anxious to get some more Channel Island postage stamps; since Heinz became almost as fond of these Islands, where he was in the German Army of occupation, as he later became of Witney, Oxford and Bristol, where he was a prisoner.

So during the present day we wonder about the future. Every sane human being must abhor modern war. If another world war

193

were started it might well involve the wiping out of whole communities of men, women and children. A few might be left disfigured and in pain to endure until they suffered a lingering death in a devastated world. Such death and misery could be caused by one person pressing a button in a safe retreat; probably because someone else who claimed to be in authority gave the order. A nuclear attack could indeed start by accident. but human beings, all of us, would bear responsibility. There are wicked people in the world distributed amongst all nations. There are also very fine people in every country: we prisoners and ex-prisoners have got to know both sorts.

There is Frank Clack collecting used postage stamps for Heinz Koselack. There is Henrik Schulze and several others I know such as Alex Konjevic and Ernie Klein, who have fallen in love with, and married, those in lately enemy countries. Stanley Gilder cared for and saved the lives of those from many nations. I expect he still does. German·doctors dropped from aircraft into battle zones and proceeded to treat the wounded friend and foe, which ever needed help most. There is the German blanket maker Fritz Döttlinger, showing trade rivals round his Mill in Calw and Kit Tanner giving his life rescuing his fellows from a manmade shipwreck. I also have a note from Karl Stuhlinger, who was run into by a careless prisoner in the dark small hours, writing to ex-prisoners in England, 'mit freundlichen Grüszen', after the war.

The foregoing are a few mostly previously mentioned in this book, whose activities during and after the war led towards peace. There are others, whom I am proud and grateful to call friends, who by now, forty years after, have left us for another world. There is Jack Palmer of the RAMC, who organised our reunions after the war and kept us German, English, French and Serbs in touch with each·other when the hostilities had ceased. I knew equally well and for a good deal longer period Ted Winfield of the Boys' Brigade 1st Witney Company and blanket maker of Witney of forty years' standing. He, like his friend, Francis Hicks, also of the BB, spent much of his spell in the army, as he had in Witney, teaching gymnastics, swimming, life saving, first aid and games that induce fitness and good. sportsmanship. Sadly, I have also learnt that that little saint, Julius Kienzle, at his home in Rottweil-Altstadt, has recently died in his eighty-first year. I cannot help adding the name of The Queen, to whom he wrote. Whether Queen Elizabeth

194

II visits an overseas country, such as Mexico or, indeed, visits Witney Mill, as she once most graciously did, Her Majesty radiates and stimulates affection, confidence and peace. When remembering these people, their ideals and the fervent wish that a great proportion of mankind have for peace, a statement by the Prophet Elisha comes to my mind. It is, 'Fear not: for they that are with us are more than they that be with them'.

The words above come at the start of a story somewhat unusual for the Old Testament. Having, with these words, reassured the King of Israel, who was surrounded by hostile troops of the King of Syria, Elisha prayed to God that the Syrian army should be struck blind. Whether the prayer was granted literally is not exactly explained. However, the Syrian troops missed their way completely and, completely lost, wandered away from their objective, finding themselves in Samaria. The King of Israel followed and entrapped the disorganised Syrian rabble. Seeing that the enemy lay at his mercy the King of Israel said to the Prophet of God, who was still advising him, 'Shall we smite them?' Elisha replied, 'Thou shalt not smite them: wouldst thou smite those whom thou hast taken captive with the sword and with the bow?' and suggested that food and drink be given to them. There were times during our war service when we would have been glad if Elisha had come on the scene and given the same advice to Hitler! Perhaps the Reverend (Captain) Paul Guinness, our splendid chaplain when we were prisoners, would have preached one of his excellent sermons about it?

As I write there is before me a picture from the front page of the *Daily Telegraph* dated Saturday 5 February 1983. The caption underneath reads, 'The Union Jack flying yesterday from the headquarters (in the Beirut suburb of Hadach) of the newly arrived British peace-keeping contingent in Lebanon'. In the photograph one British soldier of the peace force is watching another, who is making sure the Flag is flying correctly on the flag pole in an elevated position. This seems to me to be a step in the right direction.

There are many people, who in various ways are trying to prevent another world war. There are the United Nations, the Pope and Quakers. There are others, like the farmers of southern Russia amongst the Caucasus Mountains, some of whom we knew in their extremity at Rottweil, who only want to be left in peace

195

working with their families at home. There is a common wish in the World at large to end the plague of war. Some of us, like St Paul, would add: 'Which hope we have as an anchor of the soul both sure and stedfast'.

Index

198